PRAEGER LIBRARY OF U.S. GOVERNMENT
DEPARTMENTS AND AGENCIES

The United States Navy

PRAEGER LIBRARY OF U.S. GOVERNMENT DEPARTMENTS
AND AGENCIES

Consulting Editors

ERNEST S. GRIFFITH

Former University Professor and Dean Emeritus, School of International Service, American University; former Director, Legislative Reference Service, Library of Congress; and author of *The American System of Government* and *The Modern Government in Action*

HUGH LANGDON ELSBREE

Former Chairman, Department of Political Science, Dartmouth College; former Managing Editor, *American Political Science Review;* former Director, Legislative Reference Service, Library of Congress

The United States Navy

Daniel J. Carrison

Captain, USN (*Ret.*)

FREDERICK A. PRAEGER, *Publishers*
New York · Washington · London

FREDERICK A. PRAEGER, PUBLISHERS
111 Fourth Avenue, New York, N.Y. 10003, U.S.A.
77–79 Charlotte Street, London W.1, England

Published in the United States of America in 1968
by Frederick A. Praeger, Inc., Publishers

© 1968 by Frederick A. Praeger, Inc.

Library of Congress Catalog Card Number: 68–16081

This book is No. 12 in the series
Praeger Library of U.S. Government Departments and Agencies

Printed in the United States of America

To my parents,
Henry and Phyllis Carrison,
who have always been partial to Navy blue

Acknowledgments

For their assistance in providing me with material for this book, I should like to thank F. F. Meigs and other employees of the Navy Department Library, as well as members of the Speech Bureau, the Pictorial Section of the Office of Information, and the Recruiting Aids Branch of the Bureau of Naval Personnel. Vice Admiral E. W. Grenfell, USN (Ret.), was kind enough to read the chapter on nuclear propulsion and Polaris, and to make several helpful suggestions. Finally, for his useful advice and comments, my special thanks are due to Commander R. W. Kennedy, USN, who read the entire manuscript.

DANIEL J. CARRISON
Captain, U.S. Navy (Ret.)

Washington, D.C.
May, 1968

Preface

In approximately two hundred years of existence, the United States Navy has attained a proud record of achievement. It owes its being to the fortunate geography of the country, with the land tied strongly to the sea, and to generations of seafarers who liked to "do business in great waters."

Throughout its history, the Navy's primary objective has been to use the sea in a manner advantageous to the United States. This is still its mission, but the scope has expanded to include not only the surface of the water, but also the air above it and the depths below. In many important particulars, naval tradition remains unchanged, but there is little resemblance between today's great fleets and the tiny Continental Navy that supplied George Washington's army with powder and bullets. In general, the Navy's expansion has matched the growth of the country and the advances in technology that have changed the face of the world. Time has seen many changes in ships, weapons, and equipment, as well as in naval organization and methods of operation.

Years ago, naval science was the art of the seaman, who was a rugged individualist and absolute ruler of his command. Today, the U.S. Navy tends more toward big business, requiring management and executive talent for its direction. As the span and speed of communications have increased, and weapons grown more powerful, commanders at sea have surrendered much of their traditional initiative to centralized control. And, as costs of war machines have soared, the naval leader ashore has come to look more and more to civilian economists and industrialists for advice.

In spite of these changes, the U.S. Navy is still a fascinating profession that continues to attract promising young men. For others like them yet to come, and the general reader, the pages that follow give a brief account of American naval history and describe the modern Navy, its mission today, and its prospects for the future.

Contents

List of Maps and Charts

A section of photographs follows page 118.

The United States Navy

I

The Tradition and the Record

The U.S. Navy is a mixture of the old and the new. If John Paul Jones could come aboard a nuclear-powered destroyer, he would probably feel quite at ease. He would be piped aboard by a boatswain's mate, who "tended" the side with four "side boys." His visit would be noted in the ship's log by a quartermaster, and he would be greeted by the ship's captain, who would introduce him to the "officer of the deck." If he chose, he could visit the general mess for the noon meal, inspect the liberty party before the men left the ship, and drink a cup of coffee in the officer's wardroom.

The captain would take him on a tour of the ship, starting forward to the forecastle, where he could understand instantly the operation of the sea keeping system—"ground tackle" (anchor) and the lines that secure the ship to the dock. Moving aft, he would have little difficulty in comprehending the functions of the bridge and general means for ship control. Then, instead of departing over the brow to the dock, he might accept the offer to use the captain's gig and leave via the accommodation ladder on the off side, stepping into the gig and giving the coxswain directions.

Except for different uniforms, bulkheads of steel instead of wood, and a mysterious power plant in place of sails, little on board the destroyer would seem strange. Routine and customs, the titles of ship's personnel, the age-old practices of good seamanship—all these would represent little change from those Jones knew aboard a man-of-war in the Continental Navy almost 200 years ago.

3

THIRTY-FOUR SHIPS AND 5,000 MEN

The U.S. Navy traces its origin to the navy created in 1775 by a reluctant Continental Congress at the insistent urging of General George Washington. That early navy's primary mission was to supply Washington's revolutionary troops with powder and arms, and the Continental Army survived an unequal conflict on a trickle of cannon, muskets, and powder that American ships brought from the West Indies or took from the British on the high seas.

At peak strength in 1777, the Continental Navy mustered thirty-four ships and 5,000 men. Initially, its affairs were directed by a congressional "Naval Committee," which established rules and regulations for naval administration and operation. The regulations were principally the work of John Adams, of Massachusetts, who was familiar with the practices of the British Navy. Only slightly modified through the years, his Navy Regulations withstood the test of time and were later adopted permanently. But it is more charitable to remember the Naval Committee for this work than for its cumbersome, indecisive direction of the Navy. Management became so poor that, in 1781, the Congress shifted the responsibility to one man—Robert Morris, then superintendent of finance. Under the title Agent of Marine, Morris established a reputation for skillful direction of naval affairs.

During the Revolution, the Continental Navy had ships large and strong enough to challenge British men-of-war, but the naval operation was still only a small part of the total American war effort at sea. In addition to the "regular" Navy, there were eleven state navies, as well as hundreds of small, privately owned ships that preyed upon British shipping. It has been estimated that, during the Revolutionary War, privateers captured prizes worth $18 million (in the value of the period). However, many of these prize cargoes were sold back to British agents when Americans could not produce the necessary funds. Nevertheless, the combined actions of colonial privateers and commissioned navies were a nuisance to the Royal Navy and had an acute impact on the British public. In England, "King George's War" was by no means universally supported, and some British troops mutinied when they were ordered to the American colonies. The government was forced to hire German mercenaries; during the course of the war, thirty of eighty-seven regiments sent against the colonists were Hessian troops.

On this side of the Atlantic, too, the war was unpopular. More colonists served in the king's army than joined General Washington. In such an atmosphere, it was difficult for the fledgling navy to recruit. Most of its personnel came from the merchant service; captains with distinguished records as privateers were especially sought for billets as officers. The first navy became a mélange of many nationalities, and a substantial portion of its personnel came from somewhat questionable backgrounds. Among these crews, the only officers who survived and succeeded were strict disciplinarians, inspired leaders, or both. A few truly outstanding officers either drove or led their hard-bitten crews to accomplish deeds of valor that have enriched American naval tradition and served as inspiration for almost two centuries.

One outstanding officer was John Paul Jones, a Scottish merchant shipmaster and ex-midshipman of the Royal Navy, who journeyed to Philadelphia, in 1775, to volunteer his services in the cause of American independence. He was sponsored by his friend Joseph Hewes, a well-to-do shipper and congressional delegate from North Carolina, who introduced him to the other members of the Naval Committee. These introductions served Jones well and directly influenced the Committee to offer him a commission as lieutenant. It was typical of the times that an exile from Scotland was the first to hoist the flag on an American man-of-war.

The British Navy made many strategic mistakes during its conduct of operations in the Atlantic. Debilitated by the corruption of the Earl of Sandwich's regime as First Sea Lord, it was but a shell of its former strength. However, even with the Royal Navy's weakness, the American naval effort was not enough to influence decisively the outcome of the Revolution. It was the French Navy that broke the back of the British campaign against the colonies and sealed Cornwallis' doom at Yorktown. By this time, the handful of American ships had dwindled, and time had run out for the Continental Navy. At the war's end, in 1783, the frigate *Alliance,* under Captain John Barry, was the sole Continental Navy ship at sea.

The contributions of the American naval forces during eight years of action were these: logistic supply of war goods for the Army; nuisance raids against British shipping on the high seas and off the coasts of Scotland; a brave but inadequate defense of American coastal waters; transportation of agents and envoys to foreign countries; and several significant cooperative operations with the Continental Army.

In the wave of economy that followed the Revolution, the Continental Navy was disbanded, and the remaining ships were sold. During the years 1784–94, there was no navy at all. Most of the intrepid captains returned to merchant service, and John Paul Jones departed to serve in foreign navies, where he became an admiral, but never equaled his accomplishments in the War of Independence.

PRIVATEERS AND PIRATES

In the years of peace after the Revolution, American merchant trade expanded rapidly, and by 1789 was back at pre-war prosperity. Ships carrying the American flag were forbidden by England to trade in the West Indies; their captains turned instead to the Mediterranean and the western coasts of Europe. This expanding merchant fleet, entirely unprotected, soon fell victim to barbarism, piracy, and insult on the high seas. The greatest offenders were the Barbary pirates from the north coasts of Africa, but uncontrolled French privateers were equally guilty. Thomas Jefferson, U.S. envoy to France, vainly tried to stop the French depredations with diplomacy and endeavored to buy off the Barbary pirates with tribute. Finally, he gave up in desperation and recommended to Congress that it create a strong naval force to protect the U.S. flag in international waters.

In 1794, the United States began construction of six frigates, but the work proceeded sporadically, frequently slowing to a halt whenever there was a temporary surcease from molestations at sea. By the spring of 1798, however, conditions had become impossible. The Congress took vigorous action to complete construction of the six ships in order to get the new navy into action. In addition, the legislators ordered the purchase or hire of twelve more ships and created a new agency of the executive branch of government: the Navy Department. Following passage of this act of April 30, 1798 (the date marks the official birth of the United States Navy), Benjamin Stoddert of Maryland was named as the first Secretary of the Navy and immediately plunged into a frenzy of industry. Assisted by six clerks and a messenger, he commissioned forty-nine ships within his first year in office. Many of his senior officers had seen service with the old Continental Navy. Captain Richard Dale of the USS *Ganges* was the first to get to sea, and he was soon followed by Thomas Truxton of the frigate *Constellation,* Stephen Decatur, Sr., with the *Delaware,* elderly Commodore Barry of the *United States,* and Captain Samuel Nicholson of the *Constitution.*

The new navy was first given orders to capture French privateers, but a few months later this mission was expanded to include French men-of-war, thus bringing about the most famous engagement of the undeclared war—the battle, on February 9, 1799, between the *Constellation* and the French frigate *Insurgente.* In this engagement, although the ships were almost the same size, the cleverly built American frigate outgunned its opponent with a total broadside weight advantage of 432 pounds against 282. The combination of this advantage and Truxton's superb seamanship led to a quick victory. In less than an hour, the *Insurgente* hauled down her colors, counting seventy casualties against three suffered on the *Constellation*. Lieutenant John Rodgers and Midshipman David Porter took possession of the battered ship and sailed her into harbor at the island of St. Kitts in the Caribbean. Only a few months later, Commodore Barry's foray into the eastern Caribbean with the *United States* and *Constitution* resulted in the capture of a dozen of the hated French privateers. At the close of 1799, a total of twenty-five French ships had been taken in the Atlantic and Caribbean. In 1800, the frigate *Essex* made her way around the Horn to conduct a sweep through the Pacific, where it recaptured several American prizes and drove off French naval ships that had been unopposed in that ocean.

At this juncture, just as England had been busily occupied fighting with France and Spain during the American Revolution, the French Navy now had its hands full with the revitalized British Navy under Lord Nelson. Rather than continue what was to it an annoying, trifling war at sea with the United States, France, under Napoleon, negotiated a peaceful settlement.

The new navy had effectively protected American commerce and successfully discharged its first mission. It had done something else, too. "The present Navy of the United States," President John Adams said, "called suddenly into existence by a great national emergency, has raised us in our own esteem." Moreover, during the three years' action, Navy men had gained valuable experience. It was to serve them well in the punitive wars with the Barbary States that followed.

Tired of receiving what he considered to be insufficient tribute, the Pasha of Tripoli declared war on the United States in May, 1801, and sent his navy into the eastern Mediterranean to prey on American shipping. The corsairs beat a quick retreat to home port during the summer, when an American squadron of warships entered the Mediterranean. Commodore Dale, in command of this group of frigates and schooners, set up a blockade at the entrance to the harbor of Tripoli, but he was forced to lift it several months later in order to return to the United States and muster out his crews. They had signed on for only one year's enlistment. Dale's squadron was soon replaced by another, manned with sailors on a two-year enlistment, under the command of an officer who performed so poorly that he was recalled in two years for court-martial and dismissal. The Tripolitans became even more active, forcing the United States to send another squadron to protect American interests. This time, the commander was Edward Preble, a stiff disciplinarian and quick-tempered old sea dog, who had seen service during the Revolution. Commodore Preble growled that he had been sent to war with "a group of school boys," as he called his young ship captains, who were all less than thirty years of age. But after a few months of hot campaigning, his disdain turned to affection and even admiration for the competence and cool bravery of his young officers.

The best-known incident of the campaign, and one that made Lieutenant Stephen Decatur (son of the man who had commanded the *Delaware* against the French) the idol of the Navy, was the burning of the USS *Philadelphia*. The new frigate was commanded by Captain William Bainbridge, who, in October, 1803, was the sole commander off the entrance to the harbor of Tripoli. Commodore Preble was in Tangier with the remainder of the squadron, negotiating a treaty of peace with the Sultan of Morocco. On October 31, Bainbridge chased a Tripolitan corsair too close to shore and ran aground on some uncharted reefs. Unable to clear his ship or even bring his guns to bear on the swarms of enemy ships that soon attacked him, Bainbridge surrendered the *Philadelphia* after a four-hour fight. He took the precaution to bore holes in the ship's hull, but the victorious Tripolitans quickly plugged them and, helped by an unusually high tide, succeeded in floating the warship and taking her into the harbor of Tripoli. The Pasha was delighted to have this fine prize—larger than any ship in his navy—and immediately set about readying her for action, under his own flag. Meanwhile, Commodore Preble was making plans to destroy the ship, which had changed so quickly from an asset to a liability.

Lieutenant Decatur, commander of the USS *Enterprise*, volunteered his services and won the distinction of leading a band of seventy-four men in what Lord Nelson described as "the most bold and daring act of the age." Disguising themselves as Mediterranean seamen, the Americans sailed a captured vessel, renamed USS *Intrepid*, into the harbor of Tripoli on a mission to destroy the *Philadelphia* even though she lay at anchor right under the guns of the forts that defended the harbor. With superlative luck, they sailed to within a hundred yards of the *Philadelphia* and obtained permission to moor alongside for the night. As the Tripolitans hauled away on *Intrepid*'s mooring lines, they noticed the hidden American sailors and sent up a cry of alarm. It was too late. Decatur led his men into a spirited fight, quickly finished. The frightened enemy fled, jumping over the side and swimming to safety ashore. The Americans then set fire to the frigate and returned to their vessel, where they endured a tremendous but miraculously ineffective bombardment from enemy forts and shipping during the next half-hour. The *Intrepid* escaped unharmed, and not a single American was wounded. This exploit sparked enthusiasm throughout the fleet and inspired other young officers to desperate ventures following Decatur's example.

For the next two years, the American squadron maintained a tight blockade on the harbor of Tripoli. In August, 1804, Preble launched a series of five attacks against the land and sea defenses of the harbor and inflicted severe damage on the city. His men also accounted for seven gunboats, sinking three and capturing four, with only small losses of their own. This demonstration of tenacity and determination, and especially the daring of American sailors in hand-to-hand fighting, changed the Tripolitans' attitudes. In place of the disdain they had felt for all countries who preferred to pay tribute rather than fight for their rights, the corsairs began to develop a healthy respect for the United States. Finally, a storybook land attack led by American Consul William Eaton and Lieutenant Presley O'Bannon, of the United States Marines, resulted in another victory, a treaty of peace in May, 1805, and the release of all prisoners taken from the *Philadelphia*.

The end of the fighting at Tripoli marked a sudden expansion of American merchant shipping, which had been enjoying increased prosperity during the Napoleonic Wars. However, trade with either England or France was still conducted at great risk, since both powers took measures to restrict each other. In 1806, England declared a blockade of the European coasts from the Elbe River to the French harbor of Brest. Napoleon countered with a decree that no neutral ships could trade with England. As measures became more restrictive, American merchant losses increased through violations. At length, President Thomas Jefferson issued the Embargo Act of 1807, which prohibited all foreign commerce. It remained in effect until 1809, when it was replaced by the Non-Intercourse Act, restricting trade only with England and France.

During these years, the face of the U.S. Navy changed. Although the new frigates had shown their worth against the French privateers, as well as at Tripoli, congressmen were more impressed by the need for smaller gunboats in the assaults against shore installations. Consequently, all construction of new frigates was stopped, and emphasis shifted to gunboats. By 1807, Congress had authorized construction of 278 gunboats. The same funds could have purchased eight or more frigates, but the legislators demurred, arguing that the smaller ships were less likely to incite the wrath of larger European countries. The gunboats implied coastal defense— much safer, politically, than the threat of blue-water naval activity.

The United States was to pay for this reasoning during the War of 1812, when large British frigates and sloops penetrated its coasts with impunity, and British troops, supported by a strong naval force, burned Washington, D.C.

1812–14: War at Sea and on the Lakes

During the years just preceding the outbreak of hostilities with England in 1812, the British continued to stop American ships on the high seas and to impress seamen who could not produce evidence of being native-born Americans. This practice was galling enough to a young, newly independent country when practiced against its merchant ships, but it was unbearable when U.S. men-of-war were boarded. It reached a peak in the *Chesapeake-Leopard* affair, in 1807, which took place just off the entrance to Norfolk, Virginia. The thirty-six-gun USS *Chesapeake,* under Captain James Barron, was stopped by the fifty-gun HMS *Leopard* and boarded by a small boatload of men. The boarding officer ordered Barron to give up "deserters"—Americans who had been pressed into the British Navy, but who had recently escaped and signed on with the U.S. Navy. When Captain Barron refused, the *Leopard* opened fire and severely damaged the American ship. Unable to fight, because of the condition of his ship (he had put to sea without proper preparation), Barron hauled down his flag and gave up the seamen. The country was outraged, but cautious Thomas Jefferson preferred diplomatic protest to more drastic action. Barron was court-martialed and suspended from the service for five years without pay.

The United States might have fought then, but cautious leadership delayed the declaration of war on Great Britain until June, 1812. At that time, it was estimated that the British had seized over 900 American ships during the twenty-eight years that had elapsed since the end of the Revolutionary War. Another 600 were lost to the Barbary States and to France and other European powers. When hostilities began, the United States had a navy of 14 ships to pit against the Royal Navy of Great Britain, which had over 1,000 ships. Fortunately, the majority of these were occupied elsewhere, in support of desperate measures to contain Napoleon.

Americans remember the War of 1812 for a series of brilliant ship victories, fleet actions on the northern lakes, the Battle of New Orleans, and the siege of Baltimore, in which an inspired Francis Scott Key wrote "The Star Spangled Banner." Although, in two years of conflict, the sheer numbers of the Royal Navy gradually contained the American Navy and stopped all but a trickle of trade, before the blockade became effective several single ship actions saw the American frigates victorious over the British. These hard-fought battles electrified the American public and mortified the British, who had come to believe that, ship for ship, their naval forces had no equal in the world.

The four greatest American single ship victories occurred during the first 6 months of the war. In August, 1812, Captain Isaac Hull in the USS *Constitution*, 44 guns, captured HMS *Guerriere*, 38 guns, with a display of superior gunnery. The *Guerriere* was holed so badly that she sank on the day after the battle, despite Hull's efforts to save her. Next, in October, the 18-gun USS *Wasp* soundly thrashed HMS *Frolic*, a brig of equal power. Here again the accuracy of American gunfire spelled the difference. The *Wasp* suffered only 10 casualties, while the *Frolic* had 90 casualties in her 110-man crew. The month of October saw particularly good hunting for the U.S. Navy. A week after the *Wasp-Frolic* engagement, Captain Stephen Decatur in the USS *United States* defeated HMS *Macedonian*, 38 guns, in a lusty hour-and-a-half engagement. He brought his prize to Newport, where she was repaired to sail under the American flag. Then, as the year drew to a close on December 29, the USS *Constitution*, this time under the command of Captain William Bainbridge, captured the British frigate *Java* off the coast of Brazil. In this battle, 9 Americans were killed and 25 wounded, while the British had 48 killed and 102 wounded.

Little wonder Great Britain was concerned. The one-sided defeats forced a quick reappraisal of tactics. The Royal Navy had been following Nelson's practice of closing with the enemy as quickly as possible; Nelson reasoned that there was no need for accuracy of gunfire if the range were reduced so that it was impossible to miss. Before the engagements of 1812, British naval officers were able to outmaneuver their opponents with superior seamanship, and close the range quickly to fight at close quarters, where they were unbeatable. Against the U.S. Navy, they found naval officers of equal skill and ability in handling their ships and, for the first time, met gun crews trained through incessant hours of drill to shoot accurately at long range.

Then, in June, 1813, Captain James Lawrence sailed the USS *Chesapeake* from Boston with a fresh crew that had not been trained together. He met the HMS *Shannon,* commanded by Captain B. V. Broke, who, it is said, drilled his gun crews twice every day except Saturdays and Sundays. The battle lasted only fifteen minutes. Despite Lawrence's courageous attitude and his immortal saying "Don't give up the ship," he was among the sixty-one Americans mortally wounded, and the ship was lost. The blow to U.S. Navy morale was worse than the loss of the ship. Because of their earlier victories, American sailormen had begun to think they were unbeatable. The engagement was treated as a national humiliation. Many excuses were brought forth, but none hid the fact that Broke's crew had been better trained.

But, whichever side gained the victory in these spectacular isolated ship engagements in the Atlantic, more far-reaching naval events were in the making on the northern lakes that divide Canada from the United States. United States Army operations along the inland frontier in the summer of 1812 were unsuccessful. A contributing cause, which was soon recognized as the most important element of strategy in the Northwest, was British control of the lakes and water-supply routes. All military endeavors as far west as Detroit depended upon this logistic chain. To cut the British line of communications and supply, the Secretary of the Navy sent several naval officers through the wilderness to the northern lakes. The young officers, accustomed to a swaying deck and salt spray in their faces, had to overcome new obstacles. They had to create navies out of green timber that grew down to the water's edge.

First to win acclaim was Oliver Hazard Perry. At the age of twenty-seven, he built a fleet suitable to challenge the British and, on September 10, 1813, took a conglomeration of brigs, schooners, and cutters into battle with a similar British force, led by twenty-six-year-old Robert Barclay. The British leader, who had fought in Trafalgar, regarded his task as a routine operation against a rabble and was confident he would win. The two forces met in the middle of the lake at high noon. Perry's forces maneuvered badly, leaving him to carry the brunt of the battle by himself in the USS *Lawrence* for almost two hours. When his other forces finally arrived, his flagship was badly damaged from the sustained fire of two British ships, so "Commodore" Perry transferred to the *Niagara* in the heat of the battle. With this fresh ship and reinforcements, he was able to carry the day against Barclay. The fighting was so fierce that every British leader was either killed or wounded. With considerable satisfaction, Perry reported to his senior, Brigadeer William Henry Harrison, "We have met the enemy and they are ours." This Navy victory permitted Harrison's troops to conduct a victorious campaign that won back much of the territory lost earlier.

Almost a year later to the day, another important lake battle occurred on Lake Champlain, in New York State. The American naval ships there, again made out of green timber from the Lake's edge, were commanded by Master Commandant Thomas Macdonough, who at that time had reached the ripe age of thirty. This young man's thorough preparations for battle have been held up as examples of excellence for a century and a half. He took every precaution, anchoring his fleet in a strategic spot off the town of Plattsburg where he could support the flank of U.S. Army forces, which were nervously awaiting a thrust from the north by a group of the Duke of Wellington's veterans commanded by Major General George Provost. Provost persuaded Royal Navy Captain George

Downie to attack before he was really ready; Downie's crews needed more training and practice before they could take on the Americans under Macdonough. Nevertheless, following Downie's flagship, the *Confiance,* they sailed right into the anchored line of Macdonough's ships.

At first, the battle was fairly even, but then Macdonough ordered his men to wind their ships about, using anchor cables that had been positioned before the battle. This action brought fresh American guns to bear and spelled the difference in the conflict. Downie had been killed in the first fifteen minutes of the battle, but his courageous subordinates continued to fight in traditional British fashion and tried to duplicate the American maneuver. Their attempt failed, leaving them vulnerable to murderous fire. Three of the largest ships, the *Saratoga, Finch,* and *Linnet,* surrendered, but the remainder fled. Ashore, the surprised British General who had been enjoying breakfast while he watched what he expected would be victory for the Royal Navy, gave the order to withdraw his troops, thus cutting short the threatened invasion of New York.

Had the British won at Lake Champlain, the United States would almost certainly have conceded some of its northern territory to Great Britain in the negotiations at Ghent, which were already under way. The treaty officially ending the War of 1812 was signed on Christmas Eve, 1814, but several land and sea engagements took place before the news arrived in North America—notably, the Battle of New Orleans.

At the close of the War of 1812, the U.S. Navy had perhaps the finest group of seasoned officers it has ever had. These men had fought at Tripoli, against the French, and, during the war with England, had won many victories against the world's greatest navy. Now, they were free to turn their attention once more to the Barbary pirates. Stephen Decatur took a squadron into the Mediterranean in the summer of 1815, and forced the beys of Algiers, Tunis, and Tripoli to release prisoners, pay fines, and swear never again to attack American commerce.

Until the Civil War in the United States, there was little

additional formal action for the Navy. During the 1820's, several naval expeditions cleaned out nests of pirates in the Caribbean and Gulf of Mexico. During the War with Mexico, naval forces convoyed General Winfield Scott's force of 12,000 men to Vera Cruz, and overcame opposition of shore defenses to conduct an amphibious landing. The decade of 1850 was marked by Commodore Matthew C. Perry's treaty with Japan, opening up trade.

THE NAVY IN THE CIVIL WAR

At the outset of the Civil War in 1861, there was little reason to predict the important role that the U.S. Navy would play. The Confederate states did not have a navy, nor the industrial capacity to build one. In the entire South, there was not a single plant capable of making a marine engine. However, as the war developed, the South improvised, bartered, and invented sufficient craft and coastal defenses to offer unprecedented opposition to the North's superior naval force, and the role of the U.S. Navy became vitally important. The Civil War has been termed the first "modern" war in man's history, and the art of naval warfare underwent many changes. In four tumultuous years, the United States rose to a position of world leadership in naval activity.

Blockade

The greatest achievement of the U.S. Navy during the Civil War was the blockade of the southern coastline. This monumental, although unspectacular, task required long months of attrition to prove its value, but, to a great extent, the blockade dictated almost all of the naval action of the war. The Navy was spread thinly to cover over 3,500 miles of coastline sprinkled with inlets, rivers, coves, and seaports, and it hung on doggedly through chilling winters and stifling summers to tighten its stranglehold on the South, shutting off importation of war supplies from Europe and thus hastening the collapse of the Confederacy. To extend the blockade, and to support concurrent land campaigns, the Navy captured the South's principal seaports one by one, demonstrating a surprising competence in gunnery and amphibious operations. As the ports of the South surrendered, the task of blockading became easier. The Navy was able to divert more of its forces to the support of military operations—a job it did so effectively along coastlines, in bays, and on rivers that Union generals could move with a freedom of action their opponents never had.

River Warfare

Next to the blockade in importance came the Navy's river operations. In particular, the opening of the Mississippi River split the South in two and permitted a concentration of the Union armies against Lee in Virginia. River operations of the Civil War stand to this day as the largest and most extensive of history. At the time the war began, it was accepted military doctrine that a well-defended fort could defeat a naval assault. The imaginative attacks of Admiral David Farragut, Admiral Andrew Foote, and Commander David D. Porter along the Mississippi and its major tributaries soon showed the fallacy of that line of thought. Their cooperation with the Army reached a peak with Porter and General Ulysses S. Grant at Vicksburg. In this battle, the Confederates complained that they themselves were "wretchedly weak on the water."

Many strange craft and tactics emerged from the river campaigns. U.S. Navy forces ranged from Farragut's seasoned warships to "Pook's turtles"—a cross between a river steamer and an ironclad box. There were also the "tinclads"— fast, unarmed ships with metal rams in the bow that slashed the bottoms out of their slower opponents. The Confederates responded bravely with "cottonclads"—a name derived from the practice of protecting their inadequate ships with bales of cotton as they fought unequal battles with deadly determination. Southerners also invented the mine (which they called a torpedo), and they used the new weapon extensively throughout the war. The first recorded successful use of a mine occurred in 1863, when the USS *Cairo* was sunk by mines in the Yazoo River.

The Monitor *and the* Merrimac

The most famous naval action of the Civil War was, of course, the battle between the ironclads *Monitor* and *Merrimac* in Hampton Roads.

On March 8, 1862, the Confederates sent their "impregnable" *Merrimac* against a whole fleet of wooden Union ships in Hampton Roads. Great parties of observers flocked from nearby Norfolk. It would have been certain death for a wooden ship to defy odds of almost forty to one, but the cumbersome, metal-sheathed *Merrimac* plodded along at her maximum speed of five knots right into the hottest fire the Union broadsides could deliver. Her guns were protected by a casemate of four-inch armor plate that turned aside enemy shot with ease. Commanded by Captain Franklin Buchanan, formerly an officer in the U.S. Navy, the *Merrimac* terrorized the Union fleet. The Confederate vessel sank the frigate *Cumberland* and burned her sister ship *Congress* before the day ended. On the following day, Sunday, March 9, the *Merrimac* entered the Roads again to finish off the Union fleet, only to find opposition. A strange looking craft had arrived the night before. The Union's response to the South's new naval threat, named the *Monitor* by its Swedish inventor John Ericsson, this ironclad ship looked, someone said, like "a cheese box on a raft," with its single turret that revolved 360 degrees. It was a marvel of invention and forced-draft production. Although barely seaworthy in choppy water, it was an equal match for the *Merrimac*.

The *Monitor* was commanded by Lieutenant John Worden, who had a volunteer crew of ten officers and forty-five men to pit against the *Merrimac's* greater number of guns and crew of 350. The Confederate ship poured broadside after broadside at the *Monitor* and received a slow, steady fire from the smaller ship's turret. Worden adopted the tactic of steaming in large circles about his slower opponent, reloading his guns during lulls, and closing to point-blank range when the *Merrimac* ran aground on a shoal.

At one time, he was immediately alongside the heavier Confederate ship, but he backed off when the commander (Lieutenant Catesby Jones, who had relieved the wounded Buchanan) called away boarders. The *Merrimac* pulled free, and the battle continued well into the afternoon. While at close quarters, the *Monitor* took a direct hit on the pilot house. The shot struck as Lieutenant Worden was peering through the observation slit and blinded him temporarily. His next in command, Lieutenant Dana Greene took the ship to safety in shallow water to look out for the captain. Returning later to renew the engagement, Greene found that the *Merrimac* had withdrawn, thinking the battle over. The fight ended with each side claiming victory. But the *Merrimac* never came out to challenge again.

The most significant naval developments of the Civil War were the ironclad, Ericsson's revolving turret, the mine, and the submarine. Although the submarine was not considered seriously for several decades after its fatal attacks in Charleston harbor, the perilous, flimsy, hand-driven undersea boat of the Confederates heralded the submarine fleets of later years that almost swept merchant shipping from the seas.

When the Civil War ended, the U.S. Navy was understandably cut back; many ships were auctioned off or broken up for scrap. Others, including the best ironclads, were left to rot at anchored graveyards. For reasons of economy, the Navy 'went back to sail, and for a while forbade captains of ships doubly equipped (with both sails and steam engines) to use their engines unless they could justify their reason for doing so. In this atmosphere, there was little to encourage advances in technology or adventures in new tactics. However, a small, dedicated corps of officers maintained the essentials of discipline and study to keep the entire Navy from ennui and retrogression.

THE MAHAN RENAISSANCE

The period from 1865–98 saw the Navy engaged in "gunboat diplomacy" at various ports around the world. Naval ships and personnel also figured prominently in Arctic exploration and laid the groundwork for the later discovery of the North Pole. While these events were taking place, a scholarly naval officer instructor at the Naval War College in Newport, Rhode Island, revolutionized naval thought with his penetrating studies. Captain Alfred T. Mahan traced the influence of sea power on history and pointed the way for future success by nations that exploited sea power intelligently. Mahan succeeded in changing naval strategy from one of blockade and commerce raiding to one of creating a powerful fleet to defeat the enemy's naval forces. But his books, immensely popular abroad, at first received little attention in the United States.

The renaissance in naval thought finally had effect in the Congress. In the 1880's, the United States started a building program to replace the antiquated relics of the Civil War and the poorer-class ships that the Navy had been forced to build under economic constraints. As the nineteenth century drew to a close, the U.S. Navy was revitalized with new ships of modern design, and the naval shore establishment was reorganized from top to bottom for better administration and stronger support of the forces afloat.

The rejuvenated Navy was soon put to use.

THE SPANISH-AMERICAN WAR

In 1896, the United States recognized a state of belligerency between Cuba and Spain. A year and a half later, when the American Consul General in Havana suggested that warships might be needed to protect American citizens from harm, President William McKinley sent the battleship USS *Maine*. After a stay of about three weeks, on February 15, 1898, she was blown up at her moorings with the loss of 250 men. Separate boards of inquiry convened by the navies of the United States and Spain found different reasons for the explosion, but indignation against Spain mounted as the cry "Remember the *Maine!*" swept across the United States. On April 25, the Congress declared war.

The Spanish commander, Admiral Pasquale Cervera, had sortied from Cadiz in early April and stationed his fleet at the Cape Verde Islands in readiness to move west. Residents on the East Coast of the United States shivered with fright that the Spanish fleet would bombard their cities. So great was the clamor for protection that the Navy Department in Washington was forced to divide the Atlantic fleet into two squadrons—one at Key West poised to campaign against Cuba and another, called the "Flying Squadron," at Norfolk to defend the coast. But Cervera did not appear, and so matters stood for several months of the war.

On the other side of the world, the conflict developed rapidly. Commodore George Dewey had readied the Asiatic Squadron in Hong Kong during the uncertain weeks before war was declared. When word came, he was prepared to move. He took his fleet into Manila Bay in the dead of night and attacked the Spanish fleet at anchor off Cavite at dawn. Dewey's squadron consisted of four cruisers and two gunboats; all were more modern than their Spanish counterparts. However, the seven Spanish ships were anchored behind a protective minefield and defended by well-equipped shore batteries. Their position was considered impregnable by military authorities and observers in Manila. Following basic strategy that he had learned as a young officer under Farragut, Dewey kept his ships in column and steamed continuously back and forth across the Cavite anchorage, always presenting a moving target. His fleet remained practically undamaged, but his well-trained crews poured such an accurate fire into the Spanish ships that all were either burned, sunk, or abandoned. When the day was over, Dewey had not only destroyed the enemy, but had also captured the naval base at Cavite and was in possession of the city of Manila, which lay helpless under his guns. He demanded and received the surrender of the fort at Corregidor, cut the cable from Manila to the mainland, and sent one of his ships to Hong Kong to wire home the news of his victory. The American populace went wild with joy. Congress presented Dewey a vote of thanks and a sword, and the President immediately promoted him to Rear Admiral.

Meanwhile, Cervera's position in the Atlantic continued to cause concern. The "mystery fleet" arrived off Martinique for fuel on May 11, and proceeded to Santiago, Cuba, anchoring in that harbor May 19. Some thirteen days later, a squadron under Commodore W. S. Schley located Cervera's force and established a close blockade about the entrance to Santiago. The U.S. force was soon augmented by Rear Admiral W. T. Sampson's Key West squadron, gaining, with this addition, significant superiority over the bottled-up Spanish fleet. After several weeks of blockade (and an unsuccessful attempt by the Americans to sink a ship across the entrance), Cervera took heavy losses and fought his way out of the harbor. On Sunday, July 3, the Spanish fleet sortied at high speed, catching the American ships by surprise at morning devotions. The U.S. squadrons had maintained readiness to steam during their long vigil, however, and soon were speeding after their quarry.

Cervera led the escaping ships in his armored flagship *Maria Teresa,* which bore the brunt of the American gunfire. The remainder of his force—three cruisers and two destroyers—followed behind in his smoke. The U.S. battleships *Brooklyn, Oregon, Texas, Iowa,* and *Indiana* led the chase, but the converted yacht *Gloucester* took on and destroyed the two Spanish destroyers. One by one, the out-gunned ships of Cervera's fleet dropped out of action and were beached on the Cuban coast. At day's end, the rout was complete; Spanish losses were 160 men killed and 1,800 captured. American naval losses amounted to one man killed and one wounded. Shortly after the naval battle, Santiago surrendered. When it became evident that her possessions in the Caribbean were lost and that the U.S. fleet could now attack the Spanish coast itself with little opposition, Spain sued for peace, and as part of the treaty, gave up all claims on the island of Cuba and ceded Puerto Rico, Guam, and the Philippines to the United States.

In both the Philippine and Cuban operations, American commanders had to make some arrangements for mobile supplies. Dewey purchased colliers before setting out for Manila Bay. Sampson's forces were supported by a repair ship, a hospital ship, and several cold storage supply ships. (These early mobile support vessels were the beginning of the great service force that supported the U.S. Navy all over the world during World War II, and so effectively during the Korean War.)

Several other lessons were learned during the war. First, it was obvious that the Spanish ships burned easily because they were well appointed, with wooden paneling and wooden decks; accordingly, the U.S. Navy instituted an austerity program to reduce the amount of wood and other combustible material aboard its ships. It was plain, too, that American gunnery needed improvement, and the Navy instituted a strenuous program to improve both the accuracy and rate of fire of naval guns.

During the next two decades between wars, the American populace and Congress listened to the teachings of Mahan expostulated by Theodore Roosevelt and others who saw the new and important role that the country would soon play in world affairs. The United States launched a naval building program that surprised naval-conscious powers in Europe and proceeded to establish coaling stations and bases in her newly acquired possessions.

THE NAVY IN WORLD WAR I

The entry of the United States into World War I in April, 1917, brought the Navy the new and formidable challenge of Germany's submarine warfare. British shipping losses to German submarines had gone far beyond England's capacity for replacement, and the supply situation in the British Isles was acute. Government authorities estimated that they had only enough of some essential supplies to last three weeks. Russia had collapsed. It was imperative for the United States to send supplies and armed reinforcements to bolster the staggering allies.

The Convoy System

Rear Admiral W. S. Sims, USN, who was sent to London as a liaison officer with the British admiralty when the United States entered the war, immediately cabled home for destroyers and other small ships needed for submarine suppression. He insisted on substituting the convoy system for the then current British practice of elusive routing, and he won his point. The amount of war material and the number of troops convoyed safely from America to Europe in a short time surprised the German High Command, and probably provided the margin necessary to tip the scales of war in favor of the Allies.

Rear Admiral Albert Gleaves was put in command of the Atlantic convoy system. Under his able direction, and with the energetic operation of U.S. naval escorts, about 1 million American troops were carried safely to Europe. This mammoth operation required merchant shipping, naval ships, aircraft, and a system of bases. By the end of the war, ports of embarkation and naval bases dotted the eastern coasts of Europe and the British Isles.

The convoy operation was by far the greatest contribution of the Navy to the war effort.

Minelaying

Among other important activities of the U.S. Navy in World War I, the most notable was the mining of the North Sea. The Royal Navy had considered a mine barrage, but had rejected it as impracticable because of the number of mines required. However, the U.S. Navy's Bureau of Ordnance developed an improved mine and antenna system that reduced the number to manageable proportions. The Allied navies set about minelaying in earnest in June, 1918, and between that time and the Armistice on November 11, sowed a total of over 70,000 mines in the North Sea. It has been estimated that eight German submarines were sunk in the mine fields, and many more damaged, although exact figures were never determined. The Armistice was signed before the effect of the northern mine barrage was fully felt, but later historical analysis showed that the mine barrage, the greatest in history (about 230 miles long and from 15 to 25 miles wide) was a contributing factor in the mutiny of the German Navy in the last days of the war.

Naval Aviation

American naval aviation had its beginnings in World War I. In June, 1917, a small naval aviation detachment was stationed in France. By the end of the war, it had grown to significant size, having 16,000 men and 500 aircraft that operated from twenty-six different air stations overseas. These forces were primarily employed in antisubmarine patrols during the first part of the war, but later participated in bombing attacks on submarine bases. As with the mine barrage, however, the influence of U.S. naval aviation was just beginning to be felt when the war ended.

1918–41: EXPANSION BETWEEN WARS

Postwar chores of ferrying the troops home and sweeping the North Sea clear of mines proved unexciting, but demanding and necessary work for the Navy. Some units were sent to Black Sea ports to aid in evacuating refugees from the Russian Revolution. Substantial naval forces were required in the Eastern Mediterranean and the Adriatic Sea during the unsettled period of 1918–20. Another force was needed in the far Pacific to support the U.S. Army in Siberia. Finally, these requirements dwindled, and the majority of U.S. naval forces came home.

World War I had awakened the United States once again to the importance of the sea and the need for a navy to protect commercial shipping. The shipbuilding program born in the war years was continued with the enthusiastic backing of President Woodrow Wilson, but it raised doubts and anxiety abroad. Great Britain was particularly unhappy to see a rising naval power, no matter how friendly, and during the Peace Conference in Paris, English officials approached American representatives on the matter of naval limitation. This was the beginning of talks that led to the Washington Conference on Naval Limitation in 1921, in which President Warren G. Harding and Secretary of State Charles Evans Hughes offered to scrap sufficient American naval power to establish a five-five-three ratio of capital ships for the United States, Great Britain, and Japan, respectively, to be followed by a ten-year holiday in capital ship building. When the conference ended in February, 1922, this original proposal was honored, as well as other limitations on specific size of battleships, cruisers, and aircraft carriers. At the instigation of Japan, the final treaty contained a clause that forbade fortification of island bases in the Pacific. The Washington Treaty at the time was considered a significant accomplishment in the cause of peace, but retrospect reveals that its very provisions contained the seed that led Japan to try to conquer the Pacific in 1941.

Other disarmament attempts were made later at Geneva and in London, but none served to stop the aggressions of Japan in Asia or Italy in Ethiopia, or to keep the Germans from rebuilding their navy. From 1936 on, therefore, only lip service was paid to existing naval limitations. Under President Franklin D. Roosevelt's leadership, the United States launched a shipbuilding program to strengthen and modernize the Navy. In addition to constructing battleships, Congress supported an expansion of submarines, ordered more amphibious and service ships, and approved the most important innovation of all—the construction of aircraft carriers.

It was none too soon. War clouds were gathering over Europe, and the world moved inevitably toward World War II.

WORLD WAR II

The Navy's first major assignment as the United States edged closer to active participation in World War II was again, as in World War I, occasioned by German submarine warfare. In May, 1941, President Roosevelt declared a security zone in the Western Atlantic to protect neutral shipping, thereby initiating the undeclared "shooting war" that caused increased tension as each month passed.

American Navy patrols along shipping routes to Iceland soon began to have brushes with German submarines. The USS *Greer* spotted two torpedo wakes on September 4, 1941, and immediately counterattacked with depth charges. The torpedoes and depth charges alike missed their marks, and the incident was written off. Then, on October 31, the USS *Reuben James* was torpedoed and sunk with a significant loss of lives. President Roosevelt retaliated by ordering the U.S. Coast Guard under control of the Navy for the duration of the emergency, and asked Congress to amend the Neutrality Act to allow the arming of merchant ships.

Although it was fairly evident that the situation in the Atlantic was headed for a naval showdown, the sudden Japanese attack on Pearl Harbor shifted primary attention to the Pacific —and immediately drew the United States into the war.

Pearl Harbor

While Japanese envoys were still talking peace in Washington, D.C., the Japanese Navy, operating in strictest secrecy, had prepared and launched a surprise attack on the U.S. Pacific Fleet units at anchor in Pearl Harbor. Japanese aircraft flew from the decks of carriers stationed to the northwest of the island of Oahu. They sped in undetected and struck without warning, first disabling U.S. aircraft at Army and Navy airfields, and then concentrating on the fleet. The battleship *Arizona*, target ship *Utah*, destroyers *Cassin*, *Downes*, and *Shaw*, and minelayer *Oglala* were lost. The *Oklahoma* capsized, several other battleships were seriously damaged, and others sank to the bottom to rest in the mud of Pearl Harbor until they were salvaged. The United States suffered 3,000 casualties, including 2,300 dead, but the attack served to unify the American people.

The immediate effects, of course, were extremely serious. The Japanese Navy lost only forty-one planes and three midget submarines at Pearl Harbor and, with its stunning victory, was now free to support combined offensive operations throughout the Far East. In a succession of well-planned moves, Japanese forces conquered the Philippines and pushed on into the Malay region and the Netherlands East Indies. By the spring of 1942, the Japanese had conquered New Guinea, New Britain, and the Solomon Islands, and it looked as if nothing could stop an extension of the invasion into Australia. The Allied Navy had joined units of Dutch, Australian, and U.S. navies to fight a courageous holding action to delay the advance, but by this time the stronger Japanese Navy had wiped them out.

Immediately after the attack on Pearl Harbor, a tremendous effort was launched in Hawaii and in shipyards back in the United States to get enough ships together for an offensive campaign. None of the American aircraft carriers had been in Pearl Harbor during the attack, so Admiral Chester W. Nimitz, who had taken command of the U.S. Pacific Fleet, organized strike forces built around these carriers. At first, these new units were used only in hit-and-run raids on remote island outposts, but the time soon came when they were used in major naval engagements.

Coral Sea and Midway

On May 3, 1942, in an engagement between two carrier task forces in the Coral Sea, the steadily successful Japanese aggression was checked for the first time. Planes from the USS *Yorktown* and USS *Lexington* located and damaged the Japanese aircraft carrier *Shokaku* and sank the *Shoho*. At the same time, planes from the Japanese ships attacked the American aircraft carriers and damaged the *Lexington* so badly that the U.S. commander ordered it sunk by an American destroyer. This was the first naval engagement of history in which the opposing surface ships never sighted each other. The drawn battle at Coral Sea marked the end of the U.S. Navy's defensive holding action in the Pacific, and blunted the Japanese threat toward Australia.

A short lull followed the Battle of the Coral Sea, but naval intelligence correctly pointed to a large Japanese operation in the central Pacific—probably against Midway. American units that had been in the South Pacific were hurriedly recalled to form a defending force under the command of Admiral Raymond Spruance. The U.S. fleet was composed of aircraft carriers *Yorktown, Enterprise,* and *Hornet,* eight cruisers, fourteen destroyers, and supporting submarines. The Japanese High Command made a fatal mistake in overplanning for this operation, and entangled themselves in the complicated operations that followed. Several times in the early development of the battle, slight changes in their plans might have turned the tide. As it was, however, their main forces were dispersed, and the Japanese carrier forces that attacked Midway on June 3 were struck by aircraft from Spruance's carriers with devastating effectiveness. The Japanese Navy lost the carriers *Akagi, Hiryu,* and *Kaga* by air attack, and the *Soryu* was sunk by the submarine *Nautilus* after being severely damaged by American dive bombers. Japanese Admiral Isoroku Yamamoto tried in vain to bring his superior surface fleet in contact with the U.S. carrier task force, but Admiral Spruance wisely retired eastward at night to foil this attempt. With the next dawn, American aircraft, which now had won control of the air, relentlessly pursued the remnants of the Japanese fleet for two days, inflicting additional damage. During the melee on June 3, enemy aircraft succeeded in damaging the *Yorktown,* slowing her down until she was easy prey for a Japanese submarine, which sank the *Yorktown* and her escort, the destroyer *Hamman,* on June 6. The results of the Battle of Midway were heavily against the Japanese, who lost the major portion of their veteran carrier capability, and suffered their first serious setback of the war.

Two months after the Battle of Midway, the First U.S.

Marine Division landed at Guadalcanal, giving notice to Japan of the United States' determination to take the offensive. The fighting on Guadalcanal raged at sea and ashore for six months in a bitterly fought campaign that ended in an Allied victory. The battle for Guadalcanal marked the beginning of the island-hopping campaign directed by General Douglas MacArthur, who had been evacuated from the Philippines and was placed in command of Allied forces in the Southwest Pacific. From Guadalcanal on, the trend of battle in the Pacific was Allied offense to the north and to the west in the direction of Japan.

The Battle of the Atlantic

On the other side of the world, a different kind of naval war raged. The Battle of the Atlantic was primarily an anti-submarine war, which had to be won before large-scale military operations involving the United States could be launched against Germany. During 1942, German submarines sank over 8,000 Allied ships, many just off the shores of America. The tide turned in 1943 in favor of the Allies, who were able to mount an increasing antisubmarine effort with new weapons and tactics, while U.S. shipyards turned out ships at a faster rate than the Germans could sink them. The United States bore the brunt of the effort against submarines from 1942 until the end of the war. During this period, the British Navy contained the German surface fleet in the North Atlantic and conducted the major portion of the naval war in the Mediterranean.

Amphibious Operations

As Allied military forces fought their way to the heartland of Germany, the nature of operations changed, to feature a number of amphibious landings on the coasts of Africa and Europe. The first of these began on November 8, 1942, with landings in North Africa. Six months later, the German Army had been driven from Tunisia, and the Allies moved across the Mediterranean to invade Sicily and Italy. This large, joint amphibious landing was eminently successful, and the direct cause of the Italian surrender.

Then, on June 6, 1944, the greatest landing in history took place. Combined Allied naval forces and merchant marines employed 5,000 ships in the first phase of the operation on the Normandy beaches. After the initial landings, in which naval gunfire played an important support role, the beach-head was built up at a rapid pace with a shuttle service of merchant supply vessels. Within 100 days, a total of 2 million men, 250,000 vehicles, and 4 million tons of stores were landed on the eastern coast of France. A parallel operation of lesser magnitude commenced on the French Mediterranean coast on August 15. It, too, was successful, and Allied troops from the beachhead in southern France soon joined those that had landed at Normandy. This action completed the amphibious phase of the war in Europe, and units of the U.S. Navy were hastily redeployed to the Pacific for final thrusts against Japan.

New Pacific Actions

The war in the Pacific had been following a slow movement north in a combination of amphibious landings and naval engagements. Assaults were made successfully in the Gilbert and Marshall islands by the Central Pacific Force during the fall of 1943. Simultaneously, the forces under MacArthur made several landings in New Guinea, cutting off a number of strong Japanese units who were left without any hope of relief from the retreating Japanese Navy. A large naval force under Admiral Spruance made successful landings in the Marianas in June, 1944, initiating an inspired attack by Japanese aircraft carriers in the Battle of the Philippine Sea. The results were disastrous for the Japanese pilots, 400 of whom were shot down.

The month of October, 1944, saw the greatest naval engagement of the war and the ultimate defeat of the Japanese Navy. On October 10, American forces landed on the island of Leyte. In the Philippines in a daring thrust, three Japanese naval forces immediately converged on the Philippines, only to be either completely destroyed or driven back to the homeland for the duration of the war. With the loss of three battleships, four carriers, ten cruisers, and nine destroyers, the Japanese Navy never afterward presented a serious surface challenge to the Allied Navy. U.S. troops were landed to clean out enemy forces, and the scene shifted to the islands of Iwo Jima and Okinawa, both of which were taken in 1945 against tough land opposition and desperate air attacks. U.S. fleet units suffered severe damage from Japanese suicide planes.

Once these islands were taken, plans were made for invasion of Japan itself, but this operation was never mounted. The Japanese surrendered after the atomic bomb attacks on Hiroshima and Nagasaki in August, 1945.

As they had done in World War I, navy ships "brought the boys home"—this time from two theaters—for one of the swiftest demobilizations on record.

THE NAVY AND THE COLD WAR

In 1950, U.S. and U.N. intervention in Korea after the North Korean forces crossed the 38th Parallel, brought the Navy into action once more. During the course of the Korean conflict, the U.S. Navy bore the brunt of naval tasks, with assistance from naval units of ten other nations. On July 1, 1950, sea forces established a blockade of North Korea, which lasted until the end of the war. They conducted a coastal bombardment and air strikes against Communist military targets, and, throughout the conflict, gave ground troops close air support, interdicted enemy lines of communication, and provided amphibious lift for such important landings by U.N. forces as the attack at Inchon and the evacuation of Hungnam. U.N. forces enjoyed freedom of action and support that could only have come from complete control of the sea.

An uneasy peace followed the Korean armistice in 1953. Many nations were disturbed by the tensions and occasional direct confrontations of the Free World and Communist powers, but it was in Asia that the most serious troubles were building. When Communist-supported forces defeated the French in a civil war in Indochina, the ensuing peace treaty created two Viet-Nams, Laos, and Cambodia. The dividing line in Viet-Nam was the 17th Parallel, but many small groups of Communist sympathizers dotted the territory of South Viet-Nam. A new round of difficulties originated in Laos in 1961, and unrest spread. Hostilities soon erupted in Viet-Nam.

During this time, the U.S. Seventh Fleet had maintained a large portion of its strength in the South China Sea in an attempt to stabilize the Asian situation. Prior to 1964, the Navy took no significant overt part in the hostilities between North and South Viet-Nam. Then, in August of that year, North Vietnamese torpedo boats attacked U.S. destroyers in the Gulf of Tonkin. They were beaten off with ship's gunfire that sank one torpedo boat, and President Lyndon B. Johnson ordered carrier aircraft to bomb torpedo-boat bases of North Viet-Nam in retaliation.

Early in 1965, U.S. forces, including the Navy, became involved in the conflict on a steady basis. In retaliation for terrorist raids against U.S. camp sites and military posts, President Lyndon B. Johnson ordered air strikes on military targets in North Viet-Nam—an action that established a pattern for Air Force and Navy aircraft. From March 2, 1965, similar raids became a continuous part of the U.S. undeclared war effort, involving a heavy commitment on the carriers of the Seventh Fleet. Other aspects of this unusual conflict, including riverine warfare, shore bombardment, an offshore patrol against illegal junk traffic, special forces, and combined amphibious operations, have heavily involved the U.S. Navy. (They are discussed in detail in Chapter X.)

NOT ALL IS CHANGED

Since it first set sail, the U.S. Navy has increased greatly in size and been reorganized many times. There have been many changes in ship design, propulsion, weapons, and sensors over the years. Perhaps the most significant innovations have been the shift from wooden ships to steel, from sail to steam, from coal to oil, from oil to nuclear propulsion, the introduction of the aircraft carrier, the decline of the battleship, installation of guided missiles, the tremendous development of submarines, and the introduction of the Polaris intercontinental ballistic missile into the fleet.

Yet, in Viet-Nam, the Navy returned to using, for river warfare, gunboats that look—and are—startlingly like the ironclads of the Civil War. And although there has been a significant increase in the span of U.S. naval interest, and in the Navy's specific roles and missions, the basic functions of the Navy today are much the same as they have always been. The remaining chapters of this book cover the more important changes, and the samenesses, as they are reflected in the modern service.

II

Missions: To Control the Seas and Defend the Nation

As proud as the U.S. Navy may be of its historical achievements, in this era of technological advance, it is healthy to question the need for military strength—on land, sea, and in the air. Why does the United States need a navy?

This question is not asked as often now as it was just after World War II, when air enthusiasts thought that the nuclear bomb would end armies and navies forever. Now that nuclear deterrence has become nuclear deadlock—and with the lessons of Korea and Viet-Nam—the views of early air extremists have been forgotten. The American Navy still sails the seas. In fact, with the use and tactical support of naval aircraft, it has become more effective than ever before.

The United States' need for sea power determines the Navy's various missions. The sea separates and connects nations, and determines many of their relationships. Sea power, important to the United States in peacetime, becomes critical in wartime. Naval power still controls ocean transportation in wartime. Such control enables the United States to fight and win wars overseas and to support allies abroad.

THE SEA—A CONDUIT AND A BARRIER

Naval spokesmen sometimes base the need for a navy simply on the fact that three-fourths of the earth's surface is water. They point out that over half of the people of the world live within fifty miles of the sea and depend in great measure on the oceans for communication and trade with each other. About 90 per cent of the world's major industrial complexes lie within 500 miles of the ocean's rim, and many of these inland activities are connected by water to the sea.

At present, ocean transport handles approximately 99 per cent of the export and import trade of the United States. The other 1 per cent is carried by air transport, which has made inroads in the transportation of high-priority cargoes. If bulk transportation of cargo (and passengers) is ever taken over altogether by air transport, sea power in its present definition will no longer be vital. However, a major scientific break-through, presently unforeseen, will be required for the pendu-lum to shift. Water transport has the advantage of economy of size. It is sure and cheap. Ships have about a twenty-to-one advantage in carrying capacity per unit of energy for propul-sion. Until the economics of movement of bulk cargo and large numbers of personnel change, sea transport will continue to be paramount in peaceful commerce and in wartime opera-tions.

In wartime, one task of the Navy is to guarantee continued use of the sea and to protect commercial shipping, essential to the economy and the war effort.

In recent times, no one has stated the case for control of the sea better than the late President John F. Kennedy, who said, after the Cuban crisis, "Events of October, 1962, indi-cate, as they had all through history, that control of the seas can mean security, control of the seas can mean peace, con-trol of the seas can mean victory."

Control of the sea is a basic premise of U.S. foreign policy today. None of the eight collective defense treaties that the United States and forty-three other countries have entered into since World War II would be credible without the promise of continued use of the sea. Each of the pact signatories relies on the U.S. Navy as the primary force to underwrite the alliances.

Such support runs the scale of possible circumstances and

international background conditions, which set the stage for use of military forces. The situation could require a large-scale landing in the Mediterranean, or it could call for a simple visit of a naval task force to a foreign port. Understanding all the kinds of naval action it could evoke is necessary in answering the questions "Why do we need a navy?" and "What does it do?"

IN DEFENSE OF A NATION

Essentially, the Navy defends America, and how it does this depends upon the immediate circumstances and prevailing world conditions (the "scenario," in military war-gaming terminology). Cold war, limited war, and general war are the possibilities that are generally considered today. In each of them, the U.S. Navy would have distinct missions. "Cold war" describes the general state of world affairs that has prevailed since World War II. "Limited war" covers situations of open, but limited conflict with conventional weapons, such as in Korea in the 1950's and Viet-Nam in the 1960's. "General war" is the term applied to unlimited nuclear war.

COLD WAR MISSIONS

The most natural, conventional use of a navy in peacetime is deployment for diplomatic purposes. The oldest role of a navy, and perhaps the one that naval personnel like best, "gunboat diplomacy," or a "show of force," as it is more often called, has worked many times, and it carries a bit of glamour with it. A display of armed ships often calms unsettled situations, and, in many areas of the world where other forms of military power seem remote, naval power can be the most effective means of preserving peace and order.

The appearance of a naval force is not necessarily alarming to knowledgeable people who live near the sea. When traveling in international waters, naval vessels do not threaten the sovereignty of any nation. Their removal is as simple as their arrival. However, seafaring people know the potential represented by a powerful ship or force and are reluctant to challenge it. In many cases of historic importance, the mere presence of a naval force has quelled ferment or prevented an unfortunate incident. Consider some examples since the end of the Korean War alone:

In 1955, the U.S. Navy, at the request of Nationalist China, figured prominently in the evacuation of the Tachen islands off the Chinese mainland. Units of the Seventh Fleet, under the command of Vice Admiral A. M. Pride, evacuated 29,000 people and many tons of supplies from these islands, which had been subjected to heavy Chinese Communist bombardment. Amphibious ships landed and loaded while combatant ships of the carrier task force shielded them. This determined show of force was sufficient to intimidate the Communist forces and permit a peaceful operation, which undoubtedly saved many lives.

A similar evacuation was effected on the other side of the world a year later. In October, 1956, during the Suez Crisis, French and British armed units landed at Suez to guarantee continued operation of the Canal. Late that month, units of the Sixth Fleet were ordered to the scene to give aid to Americans and others in need of assistance. Destroyers and amphibious ships were joined by Air Force transport squadrons in evacuating about 2,000 persons from Suez and the surrounding area. Heavy combatant ships stood by to provide protection.

In July, 1958, President Chamoun of Lebanon requested assistance from the United States to establish peace and to help to put down a local revolution. In response to this request, units of the Sixth Fleet converged in the Eastern Mediterranean and landed a force of 1,500 U.S. Marines at Beirut on July 15.

Later that year, in another tense situation, the Seventh Fleet concentrated forces in the vicinity of the Quemoy-Matsu islands off the mainland of China, and formed a defense perimeter near Taiwan at the request of the Nationalist Chinese Government.

The pages of history are dotted with similar incidents—involving American and many other historic naval powers.

In addition to fulfilling U.S. requirements for displays of force, the Navy frequently supplies ships for humanitarian acts. In recent years, Navy ships have provided relief to widely separated areas of the world devastated by typhoons, hurricanes, and earthquakes. This kind of mission is very different from a display of force, but nevertheless, serves as an extension of diplomacy by sea power. Similarly, friendly naval demonstrations and reviews create favorable impressions abroad. (Occasionally, it must be admitted, bad impressions are made —and promptly decried by American representatives abroad.)

The Navy also performs a number of miscellaneous support tasks. Its role in the "Man in Space" program during the 1960's is an excellent example. This mission required considerable detailed planning and involved a variety of ships, aircraft, and communications facilities. Naval officials participated in negotiations for overseas support of foreign countries, obtained commitments of their forces, and gained permission to "overfly" U.S. communication vans, paramedical units, and search aircraft across international boundaries. Other examples include the support of Arctic and Antarctic research expeditions and exploration of the ocean floor and other forms of oceanographic research. Ships at sea send in periodic meteorological observations, answer calls of distress on the high seas, and take scientific measurements of water depths on routine transits.

Watchdog Overseas

One very important mission of the Navy is the daily support of U.S. interests abroad. American armed forces are deployed around the world—primarily in Europe and in the Orient. In almost every nation, there are large numbers of Americans serving in diplomatic, information, and aid missions of the U.S. Government, as well as in international organizations. Over 2 million U.S. citizens are involved in industrial enterprises overseas. All of these people are dependent upon the sea lanes that support and link them with the United States. In particular, the military forces overseas, often positioned in forward areas where they can exert force in an emergency, would be hampered severely if they could not be supplied and supported from home by ocean transport.

The role of "protection" in a Cold War situation is implicit in the naval support of American nationals abroad. In the spring of 1965, the Navy was called on to protect the lives of U.S. citizens in Santo Domingo, when factions of the Dominican Republic's military establishment threatened civil war. Informed by Dominican military officers that the situation was getting out of control and that they no longer could guarantee the safety of American lives, U.S. Ambassador W. Tapley Bennett, Jr., appealed to Washington for help, and President Lyndon B. Johnson ordered the Navy to land a force of Marines from ships standing by in the vicinity. The first Marines landed on April 28 and were followed by other Marine units, Army paratroopers, and, eventually, 25,000 American troops. In June, 1965, the Organization of American States relieved the United States of further unilateral responsibility and formed an international police force to handle prolonged occupation of the city.

Watchdog of Home Shores

The operation in the Dominican Republic was geographically quite close to home shores for the United States, but less startling in its implications than the Cuban incident of 1962, which was precipitated by a daring Soviet power play. The Russian move in October of that year to establish an IRBM (intermediate range ballistic missile) base and airfield facilities for the Soviet IF-28 aircraft on the island of Cuba was discovered just before it became operational. Given a few more weeks, the Soviet Union would have been firmly entrenched, with a nuclear base ninety miles from the United States.

Once the nearly completed installations were discovered, President Kennedy moved quickly. Nuclear deterrent forces were alerted and conventional forces deployed to meet the threat. The U.S. leadership considered several courses of action carefully. The most provocative limited action would have been to invade the island and destroy the missile sites. Next came the choice of destroying the sites by bombing. Both of these courses were discarded, at least temporarily, in favor of a plan that offered victory without loss of life, success without demanding complete Soviet surrender—a naval quarantine.

For years, the U.S. Navy had claimed that it had the power to control or even close sea lines of communication. President Kennedy gave naval leaders their chance. The only way that the Soviets could move the necessary supplies, missiles, and aircraft into Cuba was by sea. Deeming this action "warlike" in terms of international law, the President asserted the belligerent's right of declaring a "quarantine on aggressive weapons" and ordered the U.S. Navy to visit and search suspect ships at sea for these articles of contraband.

Units of the Second Fleet moved a surface quarantine force across the sea lanes to Cuba on October 24. With the aid of long-range patrol planes and carrier-based aircraft, the Navy gathered intelligence on Soviet merchant traffic, and placed combat ships in a position to intercept. The ships were ordered to inspect and, if required, divert any Cuba-bound shipping that carried contraband material. On October 25, the USS *Gearing* intercepted the Russian tanker *Bucharest,* conducted an inspection of cargo without boarding, found no contraband, and let the *Bucharest* proceed. On the following day, two destroyers, the USS *John R. Pierce* and USS *Joseph P. Kennedy,* stopped and boarded the SS *Marukla,* a Soviet-chartered merchant ship sailing under a Lebanese flag. Again, finding no contraband, the destroyers allowed the merchant ship to proceed. During the month-long operation, naval units inspected a total of fifty-five ships and allowed them to proceed through the quarantine. Many suspect ships turned back before they reached the quarantine zone.

The Navy also verified the departure of missiles from Cuba by closing with merchant ships leaving Cuban ports to count the missiles carried topside. By November 7, the Secretary of Defense was able to announce that all known missile bases in Cuba had been dismantled. Two weeks later on November 20, President Kennedy ordered the Navy to rescind the quarantine.

The use of a naval quarantine in lieu of a blockade was one of the most important and far-reaching aspects of the Cuban crisis. A blockade implies either the sinking of nonneutral ships, or their condemnation in prize courts. It is clear that this choice in the Cuban situation could have led to greater loss of Soviet face, and might easily have raised tensions beyond measurable control. The naval quarantine, founded in international laws governing contraband and the right of visit and search on the high seas, is a much more delicate use of force. In its first use in modern times, the United States established a new concept—the joint diplomatic-naval operation, carefully controlled and timed to exert increasing pressure, but leaving the enemy an out. With the changing nature of the Cold War, now less a bipolar struggle between power blocs and more a contest for influence in underdeveloped areas, the use of a naval quarantine somewhere again becomes a possibility. Western sea power can be used as a protective shield around a new nation that is having difficulty solving national problems and needs time to build a stronger economy and viable government.

LIMITED WAR MISSIONS

In recent years, the United States has sent thousands of men to fight so-called limited wars in distant lands. The logistics requirements to keep those armed forces supplied have been

staggering. Fortunately, no country tried to cut the long
supply lines with a naval quarantine or other tactics. Had such
an attempt been made, the Navy's task would have been much
greater than it was.

Even so, as Bernard Brodie has pointed out in his book
Naval Strategy, the role of sea power in the Korean conflict
was comprehensive. "It could not be decisive in winning the
war for us so long as we lacked the means or the determination to win it in the land battle," he said. "But it was decisive
in the sense that we would surely have lost, and quickly, without it." In both the Korean and Viet-Nam conflicts, although
the inseparability of naval, ground, and air strategy was time
and again demonstrated, the importance of the Navy's role in
control of the sea was also clear. Without control of the sea, it
would not be possible in limited war for the United States to
project its power overseas, support allies, and fight far from
home.

To Guarantee Transport

The statistics of logistical supply for the Korean War alone
prove the need for sea power to guarantee transportation of
men and supplies. The war was fought 6,000 miles from the
United States across the Pacific. To meet demands for shipping
and other naval operations, the Navy took about 2,000 ships
of all types out of "mothballs." In the first month of the war,
military and commercial sea transport moved 40,000 men,
500,000 measurement tons of cargo, and 2 million barrels of
petroleum to the Far East. In the first four months of the war,
the United States shipped more men and equipment to Korea
than it did to North Africa for the invasion during World War
II.

Again, in Viet-Nam, despite the growing capabilities of air
transport—which, in 1966, was 300 times that of 1961—sea
transport still bore the brunt of logistic support to Southeast Asia, some 10,000 miles distant from West Coast ports.
Rear Admiral P. N. Charbonnet, USN, stated, in 1966, that

"of all the supplies that this nation (the United States) has sent to Viet-Nam, more than 98 per cent of the material has gone by sea . . . along with 50 per cent of the men."

Accounts of both these wars give little attention to the great "sea trains" that supported them—perhaps because there is not much excitement in the routine transport of supplies across the sea. The U.S. Navy's own account of its contribution to these conflicts always emphasizes the role of combatant ships in air strikes, shore bombardments, and amphibious landings. But these efforts are not the ones that exert the decisive influence in bringing limited war to an end. The daily arrivals of tons of supplies, thousands of gallons of aviation fuel, food, ammunition, and all other necessities of war have a more lasting effect.

It is important to remember that the Navy's ability to guarantee that sea transportation of large bodies of men and huge quantities of goods will get through depends on freedom of the seas. For the Korean and Viet-Nam operations, there was, in effect, a sea sanctuary. The sea train between the United States and the Far East ran a marvelous schedule, hampered only by weather and saturated ports of disembarkation. If these supply routes had been interdicted by submarine or air attack, as they were in World War II, the role of the Navy would have been different. For long months, the outcome of that war rested on sea lines of communication. Sir Winston Churchill said: "Regardless of all else that was happening, the Battle of the Atlantic was the dominating factor . . . and we viewed its changing fortunes from day to day with hope and apprehension."

Analysis of naval force requirements to fight another "Battle of the Atlantic" or "Battle of the Pacific" today in large measure determines the modern Navy's authorized force structure. The protection of the sea train against air or submarine attack, and the defense of the naval units involved, dictates a number of necessary capabilities and characteristics. Farragut said, during the Civil War: "The best defense is a well-directed fire from our own guns." In some aspects of conventional war, the

best way to defend forces at sea is to seek out the enemy
wherever he might be, and to destroy him. These aspects of
antisubmarine and anti-air warfare are discussed in Chapter
IV. At this point it should suffice to say that a combination
of aircraft, ships, and submarines is needed; that the effectiveness of naval force units must be continually reviewed and
decisions carefully weighed lest much of the total lifetime
costs (twenty to twenty-five years for a ship, seven to nine
years for an aircraft) be wasted; and that, however limited its
role in limited war, the Navy must always have sufficient
strength to defend its own forces and U.S. shipping, as well as
the shipping of friendly nations.

To Provide a Striking Force

Another important role of the Navy in limited war is that of
a striking force. This requires mobile air power—aircraft
carriers. Perhaps the most significant military lesson of the
Korean and Viet-Nam wars has been the recognition that air-
ground cooperation, air interdiction of enemy communications, close air support of ground forces, and air strikes on
military targets deep inland are vital in over-all operations. In
both conflicts, these capabilities were supplied by the Air
Force and the Navy jointly. In both, it was clearly demonstrated that aircraft carriers provide the most effective means of
furnishing tactical air power quickly in distant operations. In
these "unprepared theaters," it was particularly difficult for
land-based air forces to get an early start.

Thus, during the Korean War, Navy support of the Eighth
Army at the Pusan perimeter in July, 1950, was invaluable.
The late Vice Admiral C. Turner Joy, Commander Naval
Forces Far East, in commenting on the dark days around
Pusan, when it appeared that U.N. ground forces were doomed,
said:

> Without the Navy the Pusan perimeter could never have been
> held. The unspectacular role of carrying personnel and supplies
> to Korea was perhaps the Navy's greatest contribution. Next in

importance was the Navy's support of the Eighth Army by bombardment, interdiction, and close air support missions, as well as the timely landing of the 1st Cavalry Division at Pohang. The vital role played by our carriers in this connection cannot be overemphasized.

In August, 1964, President Johnson looked to naval air power for a quick "limited and fitting" response to North Vietnamese torpedo boat attacks against American forces in the Tonkin Gulf. He ordered immediate air attacks against patrolboat concentrations and their support facilities on the coast of North Viet-Nam. Aircraft from the carrier USS *Ticonderoga* flew sixty-four sorties in this disciplinary mission, destroying or severely damaging twenty-five patrol boats.

The early support of ground operations in both wars set the pattern for thousands of sorties flown later. At least four carriers supported Korean operations during most of the war. It required five carriers to meet the needs for naval tactical air support at Viet-Nam.

Although it is difficult to isolate the contribution of naval air power from the contributions made by other military forces, approximately 50 per cent of both the night and day air effort in Viet-Nam was provided by the Navy and Marine Corps. In around-the-clock sorties against military targets in North Viet-Nam, and precision attacks against selected in-country targets in South Viet-Nam, naval aircraft poured tons of bombs and rockets on the enemy. The total load is impressive, but the discrimination of targets and accuracy of naval aircraft were more important, particularly in operations close to U.S. land forces. Wars are not won by statistics alone, and it is futile to try to rate specific combat operations by order of merit. Moreover, none of these operations can be considered without the logistic support that made them possible in the first place. It is far better to view each of the primary combat operations as a part of the whole and, perhaps, to conjecture on how difficult the job would have been without any one of these major efforts.

To Provide a Landing Force

Next in importance after the role of a striking force comes the Navy's role in amphibious operations and shore bombardment. The U.S. Navy has over 100 years' experience in making amphibious landings, having first made such assaults during the Civil War. The siege of Charleston and the capture of Mobile Bay and of Fort Fisher in the 1860's are recognized as early examples of devastating amphibious thrusts. In World War II, the Navy perfected new techniques in a series of large-scale landings on enemy shores. From Africa, Italy, and the coasts of France to the Japanese strongholds in the Pacific, amphibious forces stormed ashore to make history. Each conflict reflected the steady attempts of the Navy and the Marine Corps to introduce new weapons and concepts and to utilize fully the landing craft, rocket-firing ships, underwater demolition teams, close air support, and mine sweepers of the 1940's. All of these elements were used again in Korean landings—and here, for the first time, the helicopter came into its own, making possible the new technique of "vertical envelopment," in which armed troops are flown over coastal defenses to land behind enemy lines.

Less than three months after the beginning of the Korean War, the U.N. forces under General Douglas MacArthur electrified the world with a daring and spectacularly successful landing at Inchon. Early on September 15, 1950, three cruisers, five destroyers, and a battleship led the assault with heavy shore bombardment. The enemy was so surprised by this sudden development, that the troops of the X Corps, consisting of the Marine 1st Division and the Army 7th Division, landed against only token opposition. These forces raced across the Korean Peninsula and cut the lines of communication leading south to the North Korean forces attacking Pusan. Shortly thereafter, the entire North Korean line collapsed, and in a few days the forces of the United Nations recaptured everything that they had lost below the 38th Parallel.

Later, during the Chinese Communist offensive, naval forces executed an amphibious landing in reverse, evacuating surrounded U.N. troops from the port of Hungnam in an Asian Dunkirk. Fighting against great odds in the bitter cold of December, 1950, ground troops, supported by naval guns, held a perimeter defense zone to permit embarkation operations. The amphibious forces under Vice Admiral James Doyle removed approximately 105,000 troops and 98,000 Korean civilians and salvaged 305,000 tons of equipment during the two-week operation.

At this writing, amphibious operations have not been used to such advantage or on such a large scale in the Viet-Nam War as they were in Korea or in World War II. The technique has been held as a constant threat, however.

Naval gunfire has been used extensively in wars to support land operations, to break up attacks, to harass, or to destroy land and sea lines of communications, and to bombard supply dumps. Precise naval gunfire against shore targets came into its own during World War II, when it was used with telling effectiveness in both the European and Pacific theaters. In the Italian campaign, gunfire from destroyers and cruisers broke up German tank attacks near the coast. Heavy shore bombardment such as that delivered against Japanese installations at Kwajalein leveled everything to the ground in what was nicknamed "Spruance haircut," after the naval leader, Admiral Raymond E. Spruance, who planned the operations.

During the Korean War, naval guns saved Pusan, beat off enemy attacks during the evacuation at Hungnam, and threatened everything that moved along coastal railroads or highways above the 38th Parallel. The Korean operations saw the expansion of air control of naval gunfire. The air spotter worked along with the shore fire control liaison officer in calling for gunfire missions. This technique has come into more extended use in Viet-Nam, where gunfire support has been used more heavily than in Korea. For example, during the first 10 months of 1966, gunfire support ships fired more than

250,000 rounds of 3-inch, 5-inch, 6-inch, and 8-inch ammunition into Viet Cong targets along the coasts of South Viet-Nam. In most of these incidents, American ships were firing into territory that contained friendly troops and inhabitants. Their presence called for accurate fire, precise control, and close cooperation with gunfire liaison officers ashore.

General War Missions, Presuming Nuclear Attack

In the limited wars since World War II, sea power has made it possible to transport troops to the scene of action, where naval forces have supported them all through the campaigns and provided them with a mobility and freedom of action denied to the enemy. One result has been fewer over-all force requirements. The influence of sea power is greatest in a long war of attrition like the American Civil War, but mid-twentieth-century conflicts have demonstrated that naval forces on the scene can react with greater effect than other forces that take longer to get organized and to become operational at distant locations. What do these apparently somewhat contradictory facts mean in terms of the U.S. Navy's tasks and roles in a general war—in particular, all-out nuclear war?

There are differences of opinion.

Then Secretary of the Navy Paul H. Nitze, testifying before Congress in the middle 1960's, stated:

> The keystone of U.S. strategy is a nuclear superiority which provides unconditional assurance of a capability to inflict unacceptable damage upon the enemy, his homeland, and his society in a central (nuclear) war . . . the Navy's primary contribution to the strategic damage assurance capabilities is the fleet ballistic missile submarine force. . . . If a nuclear attack against the United States were to occur today, the deployed SSBN's (Polaris Submarines) alone would be capable of striking back within minutes and inflicting damage on the Soviet Union and Communist China at a level which they would probably consider completely unacceptable.

At the same hearings, Chief of Naval Operations Admiral David McDonald spoke of the "incredibility of all-out nuclear war" and said that its very improbability had removed some of the past uncertainties in international affairs, but that the apparent restraint in this area had led to irresponsibility in other areas. He used this development as a point of departure to justify naval forces for limited war and made the revealing admission that aircraft carriers no longer were considered as a vital part of the nuclear-deterrent forces. "Although our attack carriers will always have a residual strategic capability," he said, "they are basically mobile tactical airfields."

There have been many discussions of other sea-based systems for the nuclear-deterrent role, such as the MLF (multilateral force, manned by personnel of several nations) but, to date, none of these has come into being. Instead, the Polaris missile, fired from nuclear submarines below the water's surface, constitutes the Navy's nuclear deterrent.

The Polaris Missile

The Polaris is the Navy's answer to President Kennedy's requirement for "an invulnerable missile force powerful enough to deter any aggressor." In 1962, after witnessing a firing test, President Kennedy said, "Once one has seen a Polaris firing, the efficacy of this weapons system as a deterrent is not debatable."

The Navy's Polaris force is part of the nation's strategic offensive force, which, in combination with missile defense forces and civil defense, has, according to Secretary of Defense McNamara, two strategic operations. These, he told Congress, are:

1. To deter a deliberate nuclear attack upon the United States and its allies by maintaining a clear and convincing capability to inflict unacceptable damage on the attacker, even were that attacker to strike first; and
2. In the event that such a war should nevertheless occur, to limit damage to our populations and industrial capacities.

These two objectives have acquired generally accepted short titles; the first is "assured destruction," the second, "damage limitation." The national policy of the United States, which President Kennedy expressed in the words, "Our arms will never be used to strike the first blow," requires a capability for a so-called second strike. That is, the deterrent forces must have the ability to absorb a nuclear attack and survive with sufficient strength to attack enemy cities and industrial complexes, thus assuring that punishment for an attack on the United States, no matter how devastating, will inevitably be visited on the attacker's homeland.

The survivability of the Navy's fleet ballistic missile (FBM) submarine force is generally concluded to be very high; for that reason, it figures prominently in the assured-destruction role. Even though these submarines may cruise off the Soviet heartland well below the water's surface, they are responsive to instant control from Washington. Admiral McDonald told the Congress that the command, control, and communications system of the FBM force has proven in tests that it is "virtually 100 per cent dependable." The missile system itself is also highly reliable, as indicated in 1966 by forty-six out of forty-eight successful firings of the Polaris A3 missile from submerged submarines at Cape Kennedy. The combination of high survivability, dependability, and reliability make the FBM force extremely effective in competition with other methods of achieving assured destruction, including fixed missile sites and bomber forces.

The second objective, damage limitation, is generally considered to pose a counterforce role for ballistic missile forces. This role presumes that an enemy has delivered the first strike, but that he has remaining reload, defective but easily repaired, or withheld missiles, which could be destroyed in an immediate counterattack. Obviously, destruction of these missiles at their source would reduce any further damage to the United States. The Navy's FBM forces would of course figure in the damage limitation role—as would any other naval forces, operating, for example, against Soviet missile-firing submarines off the coasts of the United States.

After 1967, the present U.S. fleet of forty-one FBM submarines will, according to Admiral McDonald, average twenty-two on station, seven being overhauled, and twelve in various stages of refitting. The refitting figure is important. It implies that the FBM force is scheduled to install the Poseidon missile to replace the Polaris missile. Experts have stated publicly that the new Poseidon missile will have about twice the "payload" (deliverable kilopounds of explosive material on target), and that it will also have other desirable characteristics. Assuming a minimum twenty-year life for the FBM submarine, it appears that the Navy's contribution to the strategic offensive forces of the United States will be invaluable through the 1980's, after which the submarines may come up for replacement. At that time, depending on the intervening technological and political developments, a judgment for the appropriate course of action can be made. (For a full discussion of the development of nuclear power and the FBM force to date, see Chapter VI.)

Speculation over various aspects of general nuclear war continues—with arguments for and against the recent decision of the U.S. Government to deploy a "Chinese-oriented" light anti-ballistic-missile defense system. It is possible that a "MIRV" (multiple individually-targeted re-entry vehicle) missile can counter the antimissile missile. A MIRV would have a large warhead, which, on approaching enemy territory, would separate into several smaller warheads, each maneuvering under its own power to strike a different target in the same general area. This is but one possible future development.*

Other Possible Naval Responses

Perhaps the best way to begin an assessment of the Navy's additional roles in general war is to imagine the condition of the world after a nuclear exchange. If the enemy should make a simultaneous first strike against American cities, industrial

* Interested readers may wish to consult a research paper, "Factors Affecting the U.S. Choice of the Mix of Land-Based and Sea-Based Missiles in the 1970's," by Captain Dominic A. Paolucci, U.S. Navy, that appeared in the 1966 edition of *The National War College Forum* (The National War College, Washington, D.C.).

complexes, and military targets, the United States would lose a great portion of its industrial capacity, and fatalities could run as high as 150 million, depending on the nature of the attack —and U.S. anti-ballistic-missile (ABM) defense and the number of available fallout shelters. Most U.S. seaports and naval bases would be destroyed, along with naval units in port. Ships at sea—particularly submarines—should survive almost intact.

If sufficient leadership and purpose should exist among the population still living in the United States to carry on a follow-up or "broken back" war, and if the enemy—presumably also hit by a nuclear counterattack—should have the strength to follow through and wage war from the ashes of his own country, it would fall to the U.S. Navy to project overseas such military forces and supplies as it could. In any military action that might develop, naval units would be able to employ tactical nuclear weapons with great effect, particularly in anti-submarine and anti-air warfare. Carrier strike forces, which could augment strategic nuclear forces in a second strike, would also have a residual nuclear attack capability for later phases of the war.

Some authorities believe that control of the sea would be the deciding element in a war following a nuclear stalemate; others believe it absurd even to think about it. For example, Sir Peter Gretton, Vice Admiral, Royal Navy (Ret.), wrote in 1966,

> After a full-scale nuclear exchange, the problem would not be one of deciding who had "won" or even what was to be done to complete the victory, but of how the survivors could stay alive and rebuild some form of civilized life.

He went on to point out that he did not believe that surface forces could continue to operate usefully at sea, and added;

> With these firmly held beliefs, it seems to me to be unrealistic to talk of preparing to fight a long general war at sea, and absurd to put forward claims for the exercise of maritime strategies in such a war.

Bernard Brodie, an American scholar and authority on naval strategy, supports Gretton in this regard, saying:

> . . . it is difficult to imagine such intensive continuing support from the home front as would enable "conventional military operations to be conducted on a large scale and over a long enough time to effect any such large and positive purpose as "imposing the national will on the enemy." . . . it does seem unrealistic to suppose that in such a war there would also be a need for the Navy to retain command of the seas in the traditional sense, or that it would long remain able to do so.

However, in the final analysis, whether or not a nuclear attack were followed by "broken back" warfare, it seems feasible to believe that there would remain the need for some kind of naval response. Since it appears that naval forces would have the highest survivability in nuclear war, it also seems likely that the United States would look to the Navy to bring succor to the survivors, to help maintain discipline in an unsettled world, and, if necessary, to continue to provide whatever defense or offense might still be required.

III

Organization: Ship to Pentagon

Today's modern navy is a flexible, complicated structure of seagoing forces, shore bases, and command echelons. It operates and maintains almost 1,000 ships and 7,000 aircraft with some 750,000 highly trained people. The seagoing, or operating, forces are backed by bases, stations, depots, navy yards, and miscellaneous commands that form the "shore establishment." The whole is directed by higher naval echelons in Washington, where the Department of the Navy, headed by the civilian Secretary of the Navy, is one of three military departments in the executive Department of Defense.

Usually a description of a large organization starts at the top, or highest level of command, and works down. Since there is little room at the top and more of general interest nearer the bottom, this description will begin with a hypothetical seaman aboard a destroyer and will trace the organizational chain from his living compartment to the E-Ring of the Pentagon, where the Secretary of the Navy and his boss, the Secretary of Defense, have their offices.

THE OPERATING FORCES

Joe Smith, seaman apprentice aboard the destroyer USS *Eversail,* is eighteen years old, a high school graduate with above average intelligence, who has had basic Navy training before joining the *Eversail.* Upon reporting aboard, he is assigned to the Weapons Department and is told that he must spend his first days in learning all about the ship and his own responsibilities as a member of the crew. A senior petty officer takes Joe and other new arrivals in tow and conducts a "school of the ship." The men learn that the *Eversail* follows the standard ship's organization, being set up in four departments: operations, engineering, weapons, and supply.

The *Operations Department* handles communications and operates the combat information center, where intelligence gathered from radars, lookouts, sonar equipment, and radio receivers is synthesized, displayed, and passed along to those who are responsible for maneuvering and fighting the ship. Its electronic technicians maintain the electronic equipment, while the radarmen operate the air and surface search radars. Quartermasters and signalmen take care of the bridge, navigation, and visual communications. Radiomen run the "radio shack" and communications office. The ship's office is run by yeomen and personnelmen, who take care of all personnel records and miscellaneous administrative tasks required by a modern ship.

The *Engineering Department* operates "the plant" that provides power to drive the *Eversail's* propellers, makes fresh water, and furnishes electricity for guns, radars, radios, air conditioning, and other auxiliary machinery. Boiler tenders make steam to drive the main engines, the pumps, and associated equipment that is operated and maintained by machinist mates. The boiler tenders and machinist mates form "M Division." Another group of miscellaneous ratings make up "R Division," which runs the machine shop, the auxiliary machinery, and electrical equipment. They are responsible for the upkeep and repair of the ship's structure and for maintenance of internal communications, the electrical switchboards, and the engines of the ship's boats.

The *Weapons Department* takes care of the guns, torpedoes, and fire control systems, operates the sonar (sound) gear, and keeps the ship's sides and other exterior surfaces clean. The deck gang is expert in the art of block and tackle, transferring at sea, anchoring and mooring, running the boats, and taking charge of all other seamanship evolutions. Gunner's mates and fire control technicians line up the ship's batteries for accurate firing and handle the challenging tasks of tracking and killing elusive submarines. These men maintain all of the ship's armament and ordnance, the fire control, and sonar equipment.

Feeding, clothing, and paying the crew is the primary task of the *Supply Department*. The galley, the mess hall, and general store rooms are operated by cooks, bakers, commissarymen, and storekeepers. Disbursing clerks maintain pay records and the disbursing officer holds payday every other Friday. The supply officer operates the laundry, ship's store, fountain, and barber shop. His stewards take care of the officers' living spaces and serve the officers' mess in the wardroom. On small ships, the medical branch and sick bay are also assigned to the supply department.

The departments are divided into divisions, each with "leading" petty officers and a division officer. Each department is headed by a more senior officer whose activities are generally directed by the executive officer, the second senior officer aboard ship. The *Eversail* is commanded by a line officer with the rank of commander. Like all officers in command of a ship, regardless of rank, he is called "Captain." His responsibility for the ship is complete, and his power and authority, within the bounds of navy regulations, absolute. He is responsible for the leadership, training, morale, discipline, and general well-being of his crew and is held accountable for the smartness of operation, safety, and appearance of his ship. His ultimate responsibility is to mold ship and crew into an effective fighting unit of the operating forces.

This basic organization holds for most ships of the U.S. Navy, with a few changes depending on the type of ship and its size. In general, naval vessels are divided into three classes: combatants, auxiliaries, and service craft. The bulk of combatants are warships, including aircraft carriers, cruisers, destroyers, submarines, amphibious warfare ships, mine warfare, and patrol ships. The auxiliaries include underway replenishment ships (oilers, ammunition ships, store ships) and other auxiliaries such as tenders, transports, cargo ships, repair ships, tugs, and salvage ships. There is a wide variety of service craft, ranging from harbor tugs, lighters, barges, crane ships, and barracks ships to floating derricks and dry docks. (The functions and operational use of the more important ships listed above will be described in a later chapter.)

When Joe Smith, aboard the USS *Eversail*, has completed the "school of the ship," he will have learned the general organization, been given rather complete instructions on living and working safely amid the machinery and high-voltage electrical equipment, and been cautioned about the dangers of the sea. (No matter how careful navy personnel are, some men are lost overboard each year, and some are the victims of tragic accidents with machinery and electrical equipment.) Now, Joe is transferred to the *Eversail*'s First Division and is turned over to the division's leading petty officer, who assigns him a bunk and locker. Joe's name is entered into the division Watch, Quarter, and Station Bill, which lists his duties for a "cleaning station," battle station, watch assignment, fire drill, and other miscellaneous drills and ship's evolutions. He is assigned to a section—determining when he has the "duty" in port or can have liberty to go ashore. When the ship is under way, his section assignment determines when he is to go on watch, when he can work at his cleaning station, and when he can turn in and sleep. He finds that his time is spent primarily at standing watch, drilling, studying, and working at his cleaning station. As a member of the First Division, his battle station is in a five-inch mount, his sea detail is on the forecastle, and he stands watch as helmsman in the pilot house with the second section. His fellow recruits are also given specific assignments to other departments. In a very short time, Joe and the other "boots" from the training station become men-of-warsmen and settle down to the routine as if they had been doing it all of their lives.

THE CHAIN OF COMMAND

The gap between Joe and the Secretary of Defense is a big one, and the chain of command is complex. The Navy has a flexible "task" system, which is superimposed on the more stable administrative organization. For example, the *Eversail* might be a permanent part of the First Division (four ships) of Destroyer Squadron Five (eight ships). The entire squadron reports to the Commander of Cruiser-Destroyer Flotilla Seven, which, in an administrative sense, is a part of the Cruiser Destroyer Force, Pacific. This is the organization chain for operating funds, repairs, personnel control, standards of training, inspections, and other administrative chores.

During the *Eversail*'s "cycle" of about thirty months between yard overhauls, she moves in and out of the administrative chain of command, depending on the cycle. While the ship is in the yard or in refresher training, her operations are controlled by a "type" commander—in this case, Commander Cruiser Destroyer Force, Pacific. During the intermediate period of training, the ships, the division, the squadron, and the flotilla "chop" (change operational command) to a fleet commander—for Joe's ship, Commander of the First Fleet, and are designated a task group for operational purposes. As the ships gradually increase the tempo of training, they are shifted to a "ready group" and soon sail to the Western Pacific for a tour with the Seventh Fleet, where they change to another task organization. At the end of about six or seven months, Flotilla Seven is relieved by another flotilla and returns to its home port, reporting back to the First Fleet.

Throughout the entire cycle, all of the ships are a part of U.S. Pacific Fleet, the world's largest naval command. The Commander U.S. Pacific Fleet is under the operational control of a "unified" commander, Commander U.S. Pacific Command, who controls all fighting forces in the Pacific and reports to the Joint Chiefs of Staff in Washington, who, in turn, are responsible to the Secretary of Defense.

The streamlined description above relates only to the operational and administrative cycle of a typical destroyer; it does not include some important area and type commanders, such as Commander Hawaiian Sea Frontier or Commander Submarine Force Pacific. These, as well as special commands like

THE U.S. FLEETS

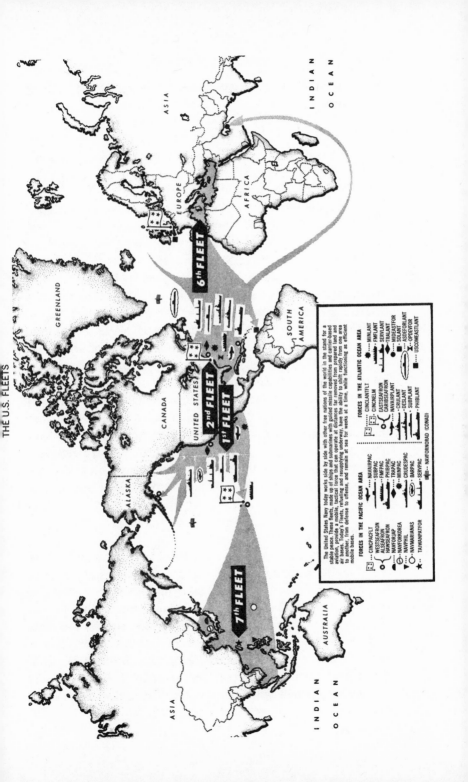

The United States Navy today works side by side with other free nations of the world in the stand for a stable peace. These fleets, made up of ships and submarines with guided missile capabilities and carrier-based aviation, provide a mobile, tactical force that can operate at distances far removed from pre-positioned air bases. Today's Fleets, refueling and resupplying underway, have the ability to shift rapidly from one area to another, from defense to offense, and remain at sea for weeks at a time, while functioning as efficient mobile bases.

FORCES IN THE PACIFIC OCEAN AREA

- CINCPACFLT
- WESTSEAFRON
- ALSEAFRON
- HAWSEAFRON
- NAVFORJAP
- NAVFORKOREA
- NAVPHIL
- NAVMARIANAS
- TAIWANPATFOR
- NAVAIRPAC
- SUBPAC
- FMFPAC
- PHIBPAC
- TRAPAC
- MINPAC
- CRUDESPAC
- BARPAC
- SERVPAC

FORCES IN THE ATLANTIC OCEAN AREA

- CINCLANTFLT
- CINCNELM
- EASTSEAFRON
- CARIBSEAFRON
- NAVAIRPLANT
- CRULANT
- DESLANT
- SUBPLANT
- PHIBLANT
- MINLANT
- FMFLANT
- SERVLANT
- TRALANT
- MIDEASTFOR
- SOLANT
- ASDEFORLANT
- OPDEVFOR
- USCOMEASTLANT

NAVFORNORAD (CONAD)

6th FLEET · 2nd FLEET · 1st FLEET · 7th FLEET

Commander Antisubmarine Warfare Forces Pacific, will be discussed later.

Atlantic and Pacific Fleets

Since the *Eversail* is in the Pacific, the discussion thus far omits the fleets of the Atlantic. Actually, the naval organization in the Atlantic parallels that of the Pacific to a great degree. Whereas the fleets and squadrons are even numbered in the Atlantic, they are odd numbered in the Pacific. Thus, the Second Fleet in the Atlantic is very similar to the First Fleet, and the Sixth Fleet in the Mediterranean covers the underside of Europe just as the Seventh Fleet protects U.S. interests in the far Pacific. Individual ships in the Atlantic have an administrative and operational cycle like the one described for the *Eversail*. In times of crisis, such as the war in Viet-Nam, some units of the Atlantic Fleet are temporarily assigned to the Pacific Fleet. The reverse was true during the Cuban crisis of 1962, when many Pacific units were transferred to the Atlantic for the duration of the crisis. Through all these changes of operational command, the individual ships remain with their permanent administrative chain of command and keep their home port assignment. In this way, each ship has a permanent base, or home, where the families of the ship's crew live and wait out the long absences while the ship is deployed to distant duties.

Command Echelons

In order to complete the description of the organization that connects the *Eversail* to the Pentagon, it is necessary to leave the confines of the ship and take up the major command echelons beyond. The destroyer squadron usually has two divisions of four ships each. The division commander—in rank a junior captain or senior commander—supervises the administration and exercises immediate operational control of his division. In turn, he reports to the squadron commander, who is a senior captain with many years of destroyer experience.

The squadron commander's duties are similar to those of the division commander, but on a larger scale. He is the "Big Commodore," and the division commander is a "Little Commodore." (The venerable title of Commodore, resurrected from the old Continental Navy, is an honorary one used to differentiate between the unit commander and the ship's captain.) In the U.S. Navy, the division and squadron commanders do not command an individual ship concurrently with their unit command. They are carried as supercargo and have small personal staffs. In the British Navy, as well as in many others, the unit commander is also in command of one of the ships of the squadron. He is the senior skipper of the outfit, and is called "Captain D" to distinguish him from the other captains. The U.S. Navy has found that the operational demands and the tempo of operations of its deployed ships require a full-time supervisor, or unit commander, for best performance. The wisdom of this arrangement has been demonstrated many times in joint operations with ships of other countries. Two weeks or more of round-the-clock, intensive operations at sea will tire the Commodore—but will completely exhaust Captain D, who has the duties of a unit commander imposed on those of commanding officer.

The *Eversail*'s administrative chain of command described up to this point covers Destroyer Division Fifty-One and Destroyer Squadron Five. These are part of Cruiser Destroyer Flotilla Seven, which is commanded by a rear admiral. The Navy adopted the flotilla organization in 1961, when the influx of ships of new construction, and with advanced weapons systems, changed the nature of the force. A growing proportion of the force became equipped with guided missiles or markedly superior antisubmarine warfare and equipment, and the homogeneity of the force disappeared. Moreover, operational experience in the numbered fleets indicated the advantage of group training and group deployment wherever possible. To meet these changes and new requirements, the separate cruiser divisions were dissolved and individual cruisers were assigned as flotilla flagships. Each flotilla had at least two destroyer squadrons, each ideally composed of a mix of old and new destroyers. Insofar as the overhaul cycle permitted, the flotilla trained together, deployed together, and took periods of leave and upkeep at the same time. Shortly after the flotilla organization became effective in the Pacific Fleet, it was adopted, with slight modifications, in the Atlantic Fleet.

The Cruiser Destroyer Force in the Pacific consists of about 160 ships manned by 40,000 men. Its commander, a senior rear admiral, has a staff of about seventy officers and 200 enlisted personnel. Mainly involved with administrative duties and the material condition of his ships, he is called a "type commander," and, as such, does not actively operate his forces at sea. There are type commands for different classes of ships: Naval Air Force (aircraft carriers), Submarine Force, Amphibious Force, Service Force (auxiliary ships), and Mine Force.

Fleet Organization

The bulk of the operating forces of the Pacific Fleet are controlled and directed by the commanders of the numbered fleets. In general, the First Fleet operates between the West Coast of the United States and Hawaii. It is organized to deploy to the Western Pacific if required, but its primary duty is to conduct training exercises for ships in the Eastern Pacific, and, as such, is composed of transient ships, which report to the commander for work up to the training level at which they can move into the higher-tempo operations of the Seventh Fleet without difficulty. The First Fleet commander is in an ideal position to develop new tactics and to evaluate new concepts, and some of his major exercises are massive ones, involving all classes of ships and a variety of weapons.

After a stint with the First Fleet, Cruiser Destroyer Flotilla Seven is ready for a tour with the Seventh Fleet. The destroyers join up with an aircraft carrier off the West Coast for a joint sail west via Hawaii. At a designated line of longitude west of Hawaii, the entire group reports to the Seventh Fleet for assignment. The operating requirements of the Seventh Fleet, as well as the large area it must patrol, make it difficult to maintain a flotilla intact. Therefore, depending on the nature of operations and the crisis of the period, the Seventh Fleet Commander distributes the ships of a reporting flotilla to one of several task forces or task groups of the fleet.

The size of the Seventh Fleet varies directly with the nature of its task. During the Korean and the Viet-Nam wars, it was augmented by additional ships from the First Fleet and the Atlantic Fleet. Usually, however, it consists of approximately 125 ships, 650 aircraft, and 64,000 men, including Marine forces in the Western Pacific. The major task forces of the Seventh Fleet are: Task Force 70 (flagship, etc.), which is commanded by COMSEVENTH FLEET himself; Task Force 72 (Patrol Force); Task Force 73 (Logistic Support Force); Task Force 76 (Amphibious Force); Task Force 77 (Attack Carrier Strike Force); and Task Force 79 (Fleet Marine Force).

Task Force 70 is a conglomeration of many kinds of tactical forces. The first unit is the flagship of the fleet commander. Home port for this cruiser is the Western Pacific, and it does not rotate every six months with other ships of the fleet. Task Group 70.4, the Hunter-Killer Group, is built around an anti-submarine carrier (CVS) and two divisions of destroyers. The CVS carries specially equipped antisubmarine aircraft and helicopters with sonar gear that can be dipped into the water by the hovering craft. The ships and aircraft are a well-developed team; they begin by working up as a unit back in the Eastern Pacific and remain together throughout the deployment with the Seventh Fleet. Minesweepers, submarines, and reconnaissance aircraft round out the remainder of Task Force 70.

The Patrol Force (Task Force 72) is primarily concerned with submarine surveillance and the patrol of the Formosa

Straits. The force normally consists of a division of destroyers and several squadrons of patrol aircraft. The Amphibious Force (Task Force 76) is organized for quick response; it can lift a regiment of 6,000 marines at a time and land them with full ground support equipment for their aircraft. Its Amphibious Ready Group maintains a marine battalion landing team constantly at sea, ready for emergency landing at all times. Ships of Task Force 76 include attack transports, attack cargo ships, landing ships, beach landing craft, and an amphibious assault ship.

The Attack Carrier Striking Force (Task Force 77) is the heart of the Seventh Fleet. It is divided into three or more attack carrier striking groups, each centered around an attack carrier (CVA) with escorting destroyers. Each carrier has from sixty to ninety aircraft, including fighters, heavy and light attack aircraft, reconnaissance and photographic planes. Ships of the Seventh Fleet are maintained and supported at sea by the Mobile Logistic Support Force (Task Force 73). Varied logistic duties are performed by fleet oilers, refrigerated stores ships, ammunition ships, repair ships, salvage ships, fleet tugs, and other miscellaneous craft. The Fleet Marine Force (Task Force 79) is a quick-reacting spearhead force that can deploy to a trouble spot on short notice. The Marine Corps calls this force an "air ground team." It consists of a division of marines and a marine air wing with fighter and attack aircraft and a force of transport helicopters for lifting assault troops over the beaches for a "vertical" landing.

The *Eversail* could be assigned to any one, or to several, of these task forces during her six-month deployment with the Seventh Fleet. But that is not the end of the organizational chain. The commanders of the First and Seventh fleets (vice admirals with three-star rank) report to a higher commander.

Over-all direction of the two numbered fleets in the Pacific is centered at Hawaii, where the Commander in Chief of the Pacific Fleet not only watches fleet operations closely, but also directs the activities of Frontier, Force, Type, and Specialized

UNITED STATES

COMWESTERNSEAFRONTIER

LONG BEACH
SAN DIEGO

COMFIRSTFLT

CINCPAC
(UNIFIED COMMAND)

CINCPACFLT
(TOP NAVY COMMAND)

PEARL HARBOR

COMTRAPAC

COMCRUDESPAC

COMNAVAIRPAC

COMPHIBPAC

COMINPAC

FLEET MARINE FORCE

COMSERVPAC

COMSUBPAC

COMASWFORPAC

COMSEVENTHFLT

COMHAWAIIANSEAFRONTIER

COMNAVFORKOREA

COMNAVFORJAPAN

TAIWANPATFOR.
COMTAIWANDEFCOM
(UNIFIED COMMAND)

COMNAVMARIANAS

COMNAVPHILIPPINES

AUSTRALIA

NEW ZEALAND

INDIAN OCEAN

SEATO NATIONS

Southeast Asia Treaty Organization is an alliance created
for common defense against armed attack or a threat to peace and security.

AUSTRALIA	NEW ZEALAND	PHILIPPINES	UNITED KINGDOM
FRANCE	PAKISTAN	THAILAND	UNITED STATES

ANZUS NATIONS

Multilateral treaty, which went into effect in April 1952, provides for the
common defense by its members against armed attack or threat to peace and security.

AUSTRALIA   NEW ZEALAND   UNITED STATES

commands as well. At his headquarters in Makalapa near Pearl Harbor, Hawaii, the Commander in Chief of the Pacific Fleet monitors the movement of every Navy ship and man in the Pacific. A computer installation, safely underground, plots the position, course, and speed of every unit, assimilates the collection of intelligence, keeps tab on the amount of ammunition and fuel aboard, and the readiness condition of personnel and machinery. If Joe Smith's parents became alarmed because they had not received any mail from their son, the CINCPACFLT personnel officer could reassure them in a moment with facts about Joe's welfare. If necessary, the intricate CINCPACFLT communications network could beam a radio message to the *Eversail* to get an emergency message through to Joe. The operations center of the headquarters maintains a watch around the clock, in close communication with the Pentagon via teletype, direct telephone lines, and radio. Every ship at sea and every aircraft on patrol is pin-pointed, and a member of the operations division briefs the commander and other senior staff officers of the over-all situation daily. The span of interest at PACFLT headquarters extends to 400 ships, 1,800 aircraft, about 400,000 men, and a supporting network of bases and depots.

In addition to the fleet and type commands already described, CINCPACFLT exercises command through a variety of other organizations. There are Frontier commands at Hawaii, Alaska, and on the West Coast of the United States, responsible for control of local shipping, antisubmarine warfare, search and rescue, and harbor defense. Similar responsibilities (as well as other duties depending on the physical location) are shouldered by the Pacific Force commands, located in Korea, Japan, the Philippines, and in the Marianas islands. Frontier and Force commanders have the authority to take operational control of any Navy ship in their domain for short periods of emergency operations.

Over-all coordination of antisubmarine warfare and control of shipping throughout the Pacific is handled by Commander

Antisubmarine Warfare Force, Pacific—a special organization that concentrates on this important task. Coordination of training is the responsibility of Commander Training Force, Pacific; Marine affairs of the Pacific are directed by a three-star general who commands the Fleet Marine Force, Pacific. The busy SeaBees, whose construction projects range from the South Pole to Alaska, are directed by a construction staff officer, Commander Naval Construction Battalions, Pacific.

With minor modifications, the organizational pattern in the Atlantic is very similar to that in the Pacific. The Commander in Chief, Atlantic Fleet, has the distinction of "wearing two hats," because he commands the unified Atlantic Command, under the Joint Chiefs of Staff, as well as the Atlantic Fleet. He is responsible for over-all defense and general military operations in the Atlantic approaches to the United States and western Europe and has the Second Fleet under his command. The Sixth Fleet is under the command of the Commander in Chief, U.S. Naval Forces Europe.

With the exception of the nuclear missile submarines, and some aspects of naval air forces and the Military Sea Transportation Service (MSTS), the above description of the Navy's operating forces is complete. More details on the Polaris submarines and on naval aviation and MSTS will be given in subsequent chapters.

THE SHORE ESTABLISHMENT

In the days of the Continental Navy, naval ships were supported primarily by merchant ships' chandlers and commercial building yards; there was no "shore establishment" of any size. The forerunner of today's large network of shore bases and depots was the old Norfolk Navy Yard, which was founded by the British in the late 1600's and located on the Elizabeth River near the city of Portsmouth, Virginia. It was confiscated by Virginians during the American Revolution and later purchased from England by the U.S. Government in 1801. As the Navy matured, increased in size, and grew more technical, the government acquired more tidal property to meet demands for technical support. At first, these shore activities provided a place for ship maintenance and repairs, and served as depots for sea stores and munitions. Later, the shore establishment's responsibilities were expanded to include training, coordination of supply, personnel, medical, and public works matters, operation of utilities and transportation, collection of intelligence, printing, legal matters, operation of communication facilities, and the establishment of standards of discipline, uniforms, and appearance of naval personnel ashore.

The present shore establishment of the Navy is a vast system of activitie. representing a physical plant and real estate worth approximately 20 billion dollars and employing over 500,000 civilian and military personnel. Present shore activities include experimental and test stations, laboratories, large automatic data processing units, and ordnance plants and storage depots modernized to handle guided missiles and other sophisticated weapons of the fleets and naval aircraft. Specially equipped stations support and train personnel required for ballistic missile submarines and other units having nuclear power plants. Laboratories and experimental stations probe secrets beneath the sea, study the upper atmosphere and the effects of radiation, develop new propulsion plants, and seek constantly to design better ships, aircraft, and weapons. While these activities are quietly pursued, the more conventional units of the shore establishment support ships and personnel of the fleet through the operation of shipyards, naval stations, repair facilities, supply depots, air stations, training centers, hospitals, recruiting stations, colleges, and community services.

Today, there are 1,800 Navy shore activities located in the continental United States and at overseas bases. Their ultimate purpose is to support the operating forces under the general direction of the chief of Naval Operations. The command line from Washington is exercised through the commanders of the major fleets, naval districts, fleet shore activities, and naval air training, naval reserve training, and sea frontier commands.

Overlapping Sea Frontier Commands

The Sea Frontier commands (Eastern, Western, Caribbean, Hawaiian, and Alaskan) are considered to be part of the operating forces, but they embrace certain duties with the shore establishment. Naval sea frontiers include outlying land, island, and sea areas, as well as coastal areas. The responsibility of a sea frontier commander extends to the land areas of the coastal naval districts within the boundaries of the sea frontier. The command responsibility of the sea frontier commander includes the exercise of military command and area coordination over the naval districts assigned to him.

Naval Districts

Naval districts are geographically defined areas established by the Secretary of the Navy. The district commandant is the direct representative of the Secretary of the Navy and other higher command echelons in such matters as area coordination, defense, security, and standardization of naval performance and discipline.

The basic organization of the shore establishment centers on the naval district. There are eleven numbered districts, and a special one at Washington, D.C. (The general geographic limits of each, as well as the headquarters, are listed in Appendix I.) They cover the continental United States; territories, possessions, and naval reservations in the Caribbean; Hawaii; the Panama Canal Zone; and Alaska, including the Aleutians.

Bases

Where a large number of shore activities are concentrated, they are grouped together under a single command, and the entire complex is called a naval base. The three largest naval bases are located at Norfolk, Virginia; Long Beach, California; and Pearl Harbor, Hawaii. Operating under the general direction of the naval district commandant, the commander of a naval base integrates the defense plans of component activities and collaborates with local Army and Air Force representatives on matters of defense and security. He also coordinates the relationship between local components and visiting ships, aircraft, or troop units. The base commander enforces regulations that deal with security, fire protection, intelligence, communications, discipline, and general administration of the entire base complex. Commanding officers of visiting ships, aircraft, or troop units conform to these regulations while in the area of the naval base.

The largest component of a naval base is usually the local U.S. Navy shipyard. It is commanded by an officer who has had technical training in the building and repair of ships. He is responsible for providing repairs, alterations, overhaul, docking, converting, and outfitting ships, and, in some cases, supervises the actual ship construction from the keel up.

Paralleling the naval base organization, naval air base commands comprise those activities of the shore establishment that furnish the operating forces aviation logistic support, including the overhaul and repair of aircraft, fleet aviation support, materials inspection, and such research, development, and testing as support aviation. The head of a Naval Air Bases Command has military jurisdiction over the individual air bases in his area, but he in turn is under the military command of the local district.

Fleet Shore Activities

Fleet shore activities include headquarters and command facilities located on shore, and other training and logistic activities that directly support the fleets. For example, in Yokosuka and Sasebo in Japan, and in the Ryukyus (Okinawa), they furnish local ship repair and logistic support, and operate schools and recreational facilities for forces afloat in their areas. Of some 160 shore activities assigned to the operating forces, the majority are outside the geographical boundaries of naval districts.

Naval Air Training

There is another naval aviation organization within the shore establishment that is separate and distinct from all others listed so far. This is the Naval Air Training Command, which directs all air training activities, including air reserve, located in the United States. The chief of Naval Air Training has four subordinates who are in charge of air basic training, air advanced training, air technical training, and air reserve training.

Naval Reserve Training

Also within the shore establishment is the Naval Reserve Training Command, for naval reserve activities other than air and for ships assigned to reserve training. The commander is responsible for the training of naval reservists, and maintains close liaison with the active fleet and the naval districts in training matters.

THE NAVY IN WASHINGTON

By the statutes of both 1947 and 1958, the Department of the Navy is separately organized under the Secretary of the Navy, but it operates under the control of the Secretary of Defense. Only its central executive offices and bureaus at the seat of government remain to be covered to round out the picture of the whole Navy to which Joe Smith of the *Eversail* belongs.

The Navy Department includes all offices of members of the executive administration of the Department of the Navy. They are: the Office of the Secretary of the Navy; the Office of the Chief of Naval Operations; Headquarters, United States Marine Corps; the Naval Material Command; the Bureau of Naval Personnel; the Bureau of Medicine and Surgery; the Office of the Comptroller of the Navy; the Office of the Judge Advocate General; the Office of Naval Research; the offices of the staff assistants to the Secretary; and the United States

REALIGNMENT OF BUREAUS INTO FUNCTIONAL COMMANDS

Here's how the functions of the former bureaus concerned with naval material have been absorbed by the six new functional commands.

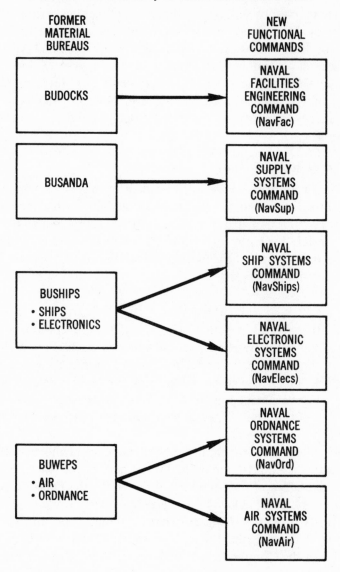

Coast Guard, when it is operating as a service in the Navy. (General peacetime activities of the Coast Guard are under the direction of the recently established Department of Transportation.)

This highest management level of the Navy, where civilian and military authority are blended for direction and control of naval forces, rests on delicate and complex relationships resulting from an evolutionary process that can be traced back to the Constitution. The authors of that document carefully spelled out the dominance of civilian authority in all military matters—they had seen enough of tyrants, dictators, and adventurers who had risen to power through the misuse of military forces—and accordingly, the Continental Navy and the original Department of the Navy, established in 1798, were administered entirely by civilian appointees. For the first hundred years of naval history, the Secretary of the Navy personally controlled and directed the naval forces. Military direction and professional advice gradually found a niche in top naval management through advisory committees created by the Secretary, but progress was slow.

During the War of 1812, the expanded size of the Navy led the Secretary to create a board of Navy commissioners to render professional advice in matters relating to the "building, repairing, and equipping of ships and superintending of Navy Yards." It is interesting to note that a dispute soon developed between the Secretary and his commissioners when the latter asked to be informed about the movement of Navy ships. President James Madison was called upon to settle the matter, and he upheld the Secretary of the Navy. This reaffirmation of civilian authority went unchallenged, generally, until the 1880's. By 1842, when the Navy had acquired two steam-propelled men of war, launched new frigates, and introduced innovations such as steel plate, rifled guns, and explosive shells, the civilian head of the department needed more technical assistance. At this time, the Navy had begun the most significant change in its history, shifting character from a predominantly personnel service to a predominantly material service. In response to the demands created by this shift, the Congress enacted legislation enabling the department to establish a system of bureaus with specific duties to discharge as the Secretary of the Navy judged "to be expedient and proper." Under slightly different names, these bureaus are still active, and still occupied with the chores their original designations—Construction Equipment and Repairs, Ordnance and Hydrography, Provisions and Clothing, Yards and Docks, and Medicine and Surgery—suggest. Later, during the Civil War, Secretary Gideon Welles increased the number of bureaus to eight, obtained authority to have an assistant secretary, and established a number of naval officer advisory boards (Strategy Board, Ironclad Board, etc.).

In 1921, the rapid growth of aviation was given recognition by the establishment of the Bureau of Aeronautics. Thereafter, the organization of the Navy Department continued essentially unchanged until the beginning of World War II. In 1942, President Franklin D. Roosevelt used an executive order to create a commander in chief of the U.S. Fleet and combined this title with that of the chief of Naval Operations, whose position had been established years before in the tenure of Secretary of the Navy Josephus Daniels. Roosevelt's order gave a new description of the chief of Naval Operations as the "principal naval advisor to the president, and the principal naval advisor and naval executive to the Secretary of the Navy."

Not until the National Security Act of 1947 (as subsequently amended) set the foundation for unification of the armed forces under the direction of a single civilian Secretary of Defense, did more change come. Even there, the thorny issues and problems arising from unification did not result in any changes in the internal organization of the Navy. The law actually redefined the Department of the Navy and gave it full responsibility for provision of forces for conducting naval warfare. Later, however, legislative reorganization of the Defense Department enacted in 1958 strengthened the authority of the

Secretary of Defense and established a command organization external to the military departments, and directly responsible to the Joint Chiefs of Staff, the President, and the Secretary of Defense. The net effect of this legislation was to remove the operational control of most combatant forces from the departmental organization to the unified or specified combatant commanders.

Today, the Navy has two firmly established principal lines of authority in the management of its affairs: military direction and business direction. In military affairs, the Secretary of the Navy delegates authority to the chief of Naval Operations and the commandant of the Marine Corps to exercise their responsibility for the task of naval command, and for their portion of command support. However, since the exercise of command by service chiefs has been severely restricted since the 1958 revision of the National Security Act, what command responsibilities they have are derived from their position as collective members of the Joint Chiefs of Staff. The forces not controlled through this line of authority are very small. In business affairs, as the military services have grown more technical, the importance of material support has had a parallel growth. For example, in 1966, the Navy Material Command—established that year, with responsibility for the majority of logistic support in the Navy—estimated that it controlled 66 per cent of the Navy budget. Its chief, Admiral I. J. Galantin, announced that his command controlled 80 per cent of Navy shore-based manpower, spent $20,000 a minute, and had under its cognizance three-fourths of the Navy shore facilities. This situation reflected the May, 1966, reorganization of the Navy Department.

Office of the Secretary

The civilian head of the Navy is appointed by the President, and his appointment is approved by the Senate. The Secretary usually has had a background in business or experience as a public servant. Some have been woefully ignorant of naval and military affairs; others have been dynamic, intelligent, and forceful leaders who have not only understood the basic strengths of the Navy, but also contributed much to naval advancement. Regardless of the individual competence of the Secretary, the career Navy officers who support and advise (and usually survive) him are the ones in whom the rank and file of the Navy place their trust for the long-range future of the service.

The Secretary of the Navy is responsible to the Secretary of Defense for the over-all operations and efficiency of the Department of the Navy. He is assisted in this responsibility by the civilian executive assistants, who are the under secretary, and the assistant secretaries, of the Navy, the special assistant, and deputy undersecretary of the Navy for manpower. Also at his call are the Navy professional assistants, career officers who hold the following positions: the chief of Naval Operations; the commandant of the Marine Corps; the commandant of the Coast Guard (when the Coast Guard is operating as a service in the Navy); and the Navy technical assistants who head the offices, commands, and bureaus described on the preceding pages. The civilian executive assistants have department-wide responsibilities for manpower, financial management, material, facilities, and research and development. The technical assistants act as technical advisers to the Secretary primarily in matters of material, technical, fiscal, personnel, and administrative support, and handle the business of their own respective offices, bureaus, or commands.

Chief of Naval Operations

The most important Navy post that a naval officer can hold is the position of chief of Naval Operations (CNO). A select few may serve as chairman of the Joint Chiefs of Staff, but that office is external to the Navy establishment. The chief of Naval Operations is the senior military officer of the Department of the Navy, and takes precedence over all other offices of the naval service (except a naval chairman of the JCS). Since the creation of his office in 1915, the CNO has seen responsibilities alternately given to him and taken away. In recent years, much of his control over naval operating forces has been rescinded, but at the same time he has acquired more control over material and logistic matters, and over naval personnel.

The CNO has both internal duties and responsibilities and others that are external to the naval command structure. As a member of the Joint Chiefs of Staff, he is responsible to the President, under the Secretary of Defense, for direction of the country's armed forces external to individual service organization. He is also charged with keeping the Secretary of the Navy fully informed on the actions of the JCS. Since the decisions of the Joint Chiefs are implemented through the Secretary of Defense, who issues orders to the respective services through the service Secretary, the command loop is closed, and both the military and civilian leaders are included in the actions of command. The CNO, then, is often in the position of having reached a decision in the office of the Joint Chiefs, then receiving an order for the decision's implementation from the Secretary of the Navy.

With regard to the internal organization of the Navy, the chief of Naval Operations (under the Secretary of the Navy) commands the operating forces of the Navy, certain shore activities, sea frontier forces, district forces, Fleet Marine Forces, the Military Sea Transportation Service, the Naval Material Command, the Bureau of Naval Personnel, and the Bureau of Medicine and Surgery. It has been indicated earlier that the majority of the Navy's seagoing forces are assigned to the unified and specified commanders of the Joint Chiefs of Staff. Accordingly, the command function of the CNO over these forces is restricted to the responsibility for their organization, training, preparation, and readiness. (The unified or specified commander retains full operational control over these forces while they are assigned to his command.) The CNO has the additional responsibility of determining the material support needs for the operating forces, including equipment, weapons and weapons systems, materials, supplies, facilities, maintenance, and supporting services. This responsibility means that he determines the military performance requirements, establishes the priority, and fixes the order of acquiring, construction, repairing, and maintaining the ships, aircraft, weapons systems, and facilities.

Apart from material needs, the CNO determines the number and kind of personnel needed for the Navy, and provides for their training, education, motivation, and advancement. He is also responsible for providing the means for the care of the health of Navy personnel and their dependents. In an administrative capacity, he exercises over-all authority throughout the service in matters relating to discipline, customs and traditions of the naval service, communications, security, and the collection of intelligence.

Commandant of the Marine Corps

The duties of the commandant of the Marine Corps are quite similar to those of the CNO, but are, naturally, limited in the size and scope of a smaller service. Within the structure of the Department of the Navy, the commandant of the Marine Corps exercises military control over Marine Corps supporting activities and those operating forces that are not assigned to the operating forces of the Navy. (Combat elements of the Corps assigned to the Fleet Marine Forces, and any subordinate units undergoing training or reequipment prior to such assignment, are considered to be part of the Navy operating forces.)*

---

* Marine Corps matters are not treated here in depth, because they are covered separately in another volume of the Praeger Library of U.S. Government Departments and Agencies, *The United States Marine Corps*, by James A. Donovan, Jr. (Colonel, USMC, Ret.)

Chief of Naval Material

By far the greatest managerial challenge in the armed service is vested in the Navy's chief of naval material.* This, the largest logistic command, was created to ensure that the tools of seapower responded to the rapid acceleration of science and technology. No other military service has the complexity of the Navy's composite warfare systems, which cover a wide span of ships, aircraft, submarines, missiles, and Marine Corps combat elements. These mobile, self-sustaining units are scattered all over the world, and require a support organization that is responsive to naval operating characteristics, the unique requirements of mobility, and the wide diversity of the seagoing weapon inventory. The chief of this command is a single, authoritative manager who can allocate material resources and define responsibilities for its development and acquisition. His primary organization is composed of project managers and six separate functional commands—Air Systems, Ship Systems, Ordnance Systems, Electronic Systems, Supply Systems, and Facilities Engineering. The project-manager method, which proved so successful with the Polaris missile, now embraces twelve different projects. The leaders of these efforts, who are managerial "czars" with across-the-board authority in their areas of responsibility, consider their jobs temporary ones that will be discontinued when the project problems have been solved.

Secretary of the Navy Nitze, who was more responsible for this new organization than anyone else, said, on its establishment May 1, 1966, that "the purpose of the reorganization is to enable the Navy more effectively to carry out its functions of preparing naval forces for assignment to unified and specified commanders and developing and providing the manpower and material sources to support naval forces." The changed organization took four autonomous bureaus, each

* It is interesting to note that the Navy uses the word "material" to denote its tools and weapons systems. In the other services, the spelling "matériel" is used.

DEPARTMENT OF THE NAVY

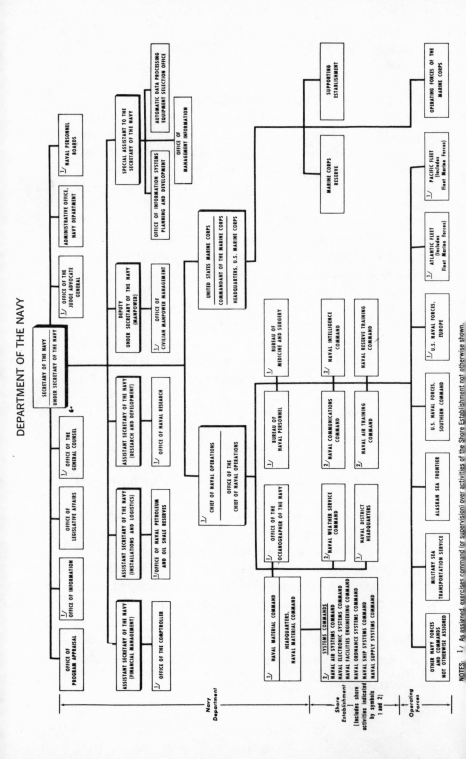

NOTES: 1 / As assigned, exercises command (or supervision) over activities of the Shore Establishment not otherwise shown.

established by an old statute to have direct access to the Secretary of the Navy, and placed them under the chief of Naval Operations. The chief of the Naval Material Command reports directly to the CNO, thus providing coordinating authority in the material field where none formerly existed.

Other Bureaus, Boards, and Offices

In the 1966 reorganization of the Navy Department, which established the Material Command, two venerable bureaus were left untouched. The Bureau of Naval Personnel and the Bureau of Medicine and Surgery were placed under the chief of Naval Operations, but were otherwise left intact. The chiefs of these bureaus, respectively, have the following responsibilities: to meet the personnel and medical needs of the operating forces, and to be directly responsible to the commandant of the Marine Corps for needs peculiar to the Marine Corps.

The chief of Naval Research, the judge advocate general, and the deputy comptroller of the Navy each commands his respective office and assigned field activities and is responsible to the Secretary of the Navy directly, or to one of the civilian executive assistants to whom the Secretary has delegated authority for specialized logistic support and aid in administration. Briefly stated, the Office of Naval Research directs the Navy's basic research program; the judge advocate general is the senior legal officer of the service; and the deputy comptroller assists the civilian comptroller of the Navy in financial matters and preparation of the budget.

Operating under directives signed by the Secretary of the Navy, there is a group of offices and boards whose primary function is to assist in the administration with their specialized talents. The administrative officer handles management services; the chief of industrial relations administers civilian personnel; the chief of information gathers and distributes naval information to the public; the chief of legislative affairs is the navy expert on legislative affairs and congressional relations; the Office of Management Information monitors the progress of important programs and reports their progress to the Secretariat; the director, Office of Naval Petroleum and Oil Shale Reserves, conserves, develops, and operates navy petroleum reserves; and the director of the Office of Program Appraisal analyzes and reviews program performance and special studies of importance to the Secretary. All of the special assistants listed above are authorized direct communication and access to the Secretary of the Navy, and to one another, in their respective areas of responsibility. This free exchange of information and integration of actions contribute to the general efficiency of the department.

Fashioning and employing the tools of sea power is both a technical art and big business. Naval personnel now have to specialize to an extent never before realized. The old adage that a naval officer was a "jack of all trades and master of none" may have been true in the days of sail. But in today's Navy, with its nuclear power, jets, guided missiles, and complex systems, both sailormen and officers need education in depth, and constant brushing up to keep pace with the advances of new technology. Similarly, the organizational structure for the Navy's operations and administration cannot remain static, but must be flexible to accommodate new ideas and new developments.

IV

The Navy's Functional Forces

The primary instruments of naval warfare are ships, submarines, and aircraft. Every navy in the world has had distinctive ways of building and organizing these basic tools to help meet its country's national objectives.

The oldest instrument is, of course, the ship, and its development through the years is an interesting record of invention and battle experience. With each advance in technology that produced a new weapon, a different kind of protection, or a new means of propulsion, the design and capabilities of the warship changed to meet combat requirements, and the professional naval officer, given improved tools, developed new tactics to exploit this advantage. Through the age of Nelson, naval battles culminated in close action that frequently ended in hand-to-hand fighting, but improved guns (and their modern extension, the aircraft) have gradually increased the distance between fighting units at sea. As noted earlier, this trend reached a peak in some important battles of World War II, in which the ships of opposing fleets never sighted each other.

Gradually, warships have evolved into specialized types, each with its own primary mission. However, they have seldom been used alone because of the potential advantages of a mix of different types of ships. The development and use of a combination of naval forces moves slowly in peacetime when innovations are expensive and there is no sense of urgency. In the U.S. Navy, the greatest eras of naval progress occurred during the Civil War, already discussed in some detail, and

World War II, which saw the development of functional forces that exploited the individual capabilities of different classes of ships, but blended them with the inherent advantages of the team concept. It was this experience that led to the growth of functional forces for several kinds of warfare—strike, antisubmarine, submarine, amphibious—and air defense. The great distances over which these forces operated led to the growth of the mobile logistics service, which kept the combatant units at sea for unusually long periods of offensive operations. The functional forces that took shape in World War II naval operations and their supply train constitute the greater part of the U.S. Navy today, and, although they have been improved through technological advances, their basic tasks remain generally unchanged.

A description of the Navy by its major functional forces necessarily omits some classes of ships. Mine sweepers, tenders, repair ships, tugs, rescue vessels, hydrofoil ships, and other craft all perform important functions. But there is only one U.S. Navy, and personnel assigned to a ship in the above miscellaneous group can expect eventual rotation to duty in one of the larger functional groups. Each is important in its own way, and each has its loyal supporters.

Strike Forces

The Navy's strike forces are intended primarily for swift and heavy attack on enemy air and naval units—including their bases and control facilities—that threaten the fleet. Recently, in limited war experience, strike forces have also been used in tactical air support of ground units and in interdiction of enemy lines of communication. The aircraft carrier is the heart of the strike force and provides its greatest punch.

Carriers were developed originally to integrate the airplane with naval forces and offset the limitations of land-based aircraft, which are effective in coastal waters or land-locked seas, but have little capability at extreme ranges on the high seas. Theoretically, a string of island bases at strategic locations around the world might overcome this range limitation and provide the fleets with adequate air support, but for geographical, political, and practical military reasons this solution is not practicable. To be effective, such island bases, even if they existed in necessary numbers at exactly the right locations, would include airfields, hangars, parking aprons, fuel storage, repair shops, communication facilities, barracks, and other supporting logistics.

The essentials of these "ideal islands" are incorporated into the aircraft carrier, which is, at once, a formidable fortress and a mobile air base that does not rely on external support and can operate for weeks at a time with only an occasional replenishment from support ships. Attack carrier forces, intimately integrated with other surface ships for mutual support, can be moved quickly from one area to another. They can be split into groups or units for dispersal or deployment, or concentrated to provide overwhelming superiority at remote locations. As evidenced in Viet-Nam, attack carriers can mount air operations immediately on arrival. Before air bases can be established ashore, a logistic infrastructure—ports, roads, fuel dumps, etc.—must be built. Even then, these bases are subject to guerrilla attack and require security forces for protection.

Neither the example of the Korean War nor the Viet-Nam War fully demonstrates the capability of naval strike forces. Because of the apparent desire on both sides in both conflicts to keep the fighting from escalating beyond "conventional" levels, the aircraft carrier became a kind of sanctuary, with no serious opposition mounted against it. The opposite was true during World War II when the aircraft carrier was the prime target of submarines and aircraft alike.

Thus, in spite of the dangers of thinking in the past, the best way to explain the role and capability of modern navy strike forces is to cast the carrier in terms of its accomplishments of World War II, and then to show the probable influence that advances in weapons and aircraft since that time might impose.

During World War II, the United States lost a total of 11 aircraft carriers—10 in the Pacific and 1 in the Atlantic. The Japanese lost 21 carriers, and the British 10. Although aircraft carriers were used in the Atlantic and in the Mediterranean, their primary role in those areas was either for antisubmarine warfare or in support of amphibious operations. To see the carrier in its best use as a strike unit, it is necessary to look to the Pacific operations of the war, and the record that the American strike forces compiled against the Japanese Navy. U.S. carrier aircraft destroyed 12,000 enemy aircraft, 168 enemy warships (including 11 carriers, 5 battleships, 19 cruisers, and 31 destroyers), and 359 merchant vessels totaling 1.39 million tons, and carried out thousands of sorties against military installations on land.

As used by both the Japanese and American navies, the attack aircraft carrier played the dominant role in naval warfare in the Pacific. In early 1942, the Japanese clearly demonstrated—in areas ranging from Hawaii to Ceylon—the advantages of concentration of air power. Their swift successes resulted from bringing overwhelming air power to the point of contact and maintaining air superiority over the objective area. With the majority of its battleships ineffective after Pearl Harbor, the United States was hampered in devising plans to carry the war to the Japanese in the Pacific. But, taking a lesson from the enemy, the U.S. Navy created fast carrier task forces composed of aircraft carriers supported by cruisers, those battleships that were still available, and destroyers. The task force punch was delivered by carrier aircraft, with the supporting ships providing antisubmarine, anti-air, and surface protection.

The wisdom of planning these strike forces was soon demonstrated in the battles of Coral Sea and Midway. In the first, each side lost a carrier; at Midway, the Japanese lost 4 carriers, the United States, 1. Other surface units played only a minor, defensive role in each of these engagements. By the end of 1942, the Japanese had lost 6 of its original 10 carriers and the United States had lost 5 of its 9. Each side then withdrew its carriers from active fighting for a period to allow new construction to plug the gaps in its forces—and in the unequal production race that followed, the United States won hands down.

In late 1943, the U.S. Navy started its drive across the central Pacific, with aircraft carriers forming the spearhead of the thrust. On only two occasions did the Japanese try to check this offensive drive. In June, 1944, during the Battle of the Philippine Sea, the Japanese lost 400 aircraft and 2 aircraft carriers. Later in October, the opposing fleets met in the battle of Leyte Gulf. This battle consisted of a series of air and surface engagements: Surigao Strait; the Battle off Samar; and the Battle of Cape Engano. At the end of four days' fighting, the Japanese fleet was all but annihilated; they lost 3 battleships, 4 carriers, 10 cruisers, and 9 destroyers. The United States lost only 3 small carriers and 3 destroyers.

From that time until the end of the war, the fast American carrier task forces dominated the Pacific. They overwhelmed the Japanese wherever they met, establishing local air and surface superiority at Luzon, Iwo Jima, and Okinawa. By the summer of 1945, the carrier task force was large and strong enough to permit U.S. war strategists to plan an invasion of the Japanese mainland. Already the carrier forces had demonstrated their ability to conduct air strikes into the heart of Japan. By then, the U.S. Pacific Fleet was the largest and most powerful naval force ever assembled. During the February, 1945, attack off Tokyo, the fleet consisted of 19 aircraft carriers carrying 1,200 aircraft. The carriers were protected by a screen of surface ships, consisting of 8 battleships, 17 cruisers, and 81 destroyers. Operating under cover of bad weather, or executing rapid overnight dashes to dawn launch points, the carrier forces often achieved complete surprise. They would remain on an operating station only long enough to mount their planned strikes and recover their aircraft, and then would move quickly to another location, often for another surprise air strike.

What bearing do the accomplishments of World War II

strike forces have on today's naval thinking? To answer this, it is necessary to translate the tactics employed into terms of modern ships, sensors, and weapons—the arsenal available to friend and foe. Air-to-surface, surface-to-air, and air-to-air guided missiles add to the complexity already introduced by jet aircraft capable of greater speeds than the flyers of World War II would have believed possible. Orbiting observation satellites will dispel the element of surprise, and high speed nuclear submarines, some carrying surface-to-surface cruise missiles, will present formidable opposition. In addition, any future conflict involving carrier strike forces would differ not only in weapons and aircraft, but also in purpose. The fundamental mission of the aircraft carrier is different today.

Intercontinental ballistic missiles (the Air Force's Minuteman and the Navy's Polaris) have drastically altered the possible value of carrier strike forces for strategic bombing of an enemy's homeland in any but limited war. In nuclear conflict, carrier strike forces would play a secondary role. They would represent the "second strike" capability (discussed more fully in Chapter II) after the great exchange of missiles had taken place. In this role, the strike forces would have accomplished their mission once they reached a launch point and had their aircraft in the air. After that phase, survival of the carriers would be problematical.

However, in limited war, carrier strike forces are still supreme. As noted earlier, they have the advantages of mobility, discrete target selection, and quick response demonstrated in Korea and Viet-Nam. The retention of carrier strike forces in the nation's defense arsenal is no longer questioned. Under current plans, the attack carrier strength in the 1970's will be kept at fifteen. Four of these will be nuclear powered, eight of the Forrestal class, and three Midway class. The introduction of new weapons and equipment has speeded up the action and increased the distances from which carrier aircraft have to operate, but technological advances in strike warfare, both offensive and defensive, are about equal. In a war of conventional weapons, U.S. naval strike forces can operate now as effectively as they did in World War II against shipping, troop concentrations, and coastal targets alike.

ANTISUBMARINE FORCES

The tasks of antisubmarine forces have changed little since the famous Battle of the Atlantic of World War II. The many kinds of ships and aircraft used are faster, the weapons and sensors better, but the problem remains the same: to seek and destroy enemy submarines.

The most sinister threat to the U.S. Navy today is the Soviet submarine force. Statements of Soviet military authorities indicate that they have done their historical homework, and have paid particular attention to the German U-boat near-successes in two world wars.

There can be little doubt that the Russians have been building up their submarine force as the most effective way to challenge the western world at sea. Today, the Soviet submarine fleet is nine times as large as the one that Germany had at the beginning of World War II, and its boats are more advanced. U.S. and British intelligence sources estimate that the Soviet Union has 400 submarines, about 300 of which are ocean-going. According to figures in the 1967–68 edition of *Jane's Fighting Ships*, the authoritative reference book on the world's navies, fifty of these submarines are nuclear-powered, some carrying six or eight missile launchers. This Soviet force is a threat at all possible levels of conflict—from the Cold War to a thermonuclear exchange. In any conflict, Soviet torpedoes can threaten every naval task force and each merchant ship on the high seas, and Soviet missile-launching subs can strike important targets inland. Most U.S. military installations, centers of government, industrial complexes, and large cities are within range of the surface launched ballistic missiles.

It is apparent that the Soviet Union intends to use this force in time of war. In 1963, Russian Fleet Admiral Sergei Gorshkov stated in *Pravda*, "The Soviet Navy is an ocean fleet capable of successfully combating the enemy at great distances from its base, destroying ships and submarines in the ocean, and delivering strikes against any target on enemy territory." Today, the Soviet Navy is operating more and more outside of the Bering Sea, the Baltic, and the Black Sea, which were formerly their only exercise areas. Their submarines have been sighted off the coasts of the United States and on the high seas, far from their parent bases. In 1962, U.S. naval forces pinpointed six Russian submarines and forced them to surface in waters near Cuba. During the Arab-Israeli War of 1967, Soviet naval units followed the Sixth Fleet's every move in the Mediterranean.

Vice Admiral Charles B. Martell, then director of Antisubmarine Warfare, summarized the threat in 1967 as follows:

> The Russians are building modern submarines at an impressive rate and these include nuclear powered submarines. In addition, they are building modern support tenders capable of transferring missiles and torpedoes on the high seas. We observe them constantly in the Mediterranean and Philippine Seas and elsewhere outside their normal local operating areas. As they gain more and more operational experience in operating their submarines at great distances from home, they will develop the ability to support these forces throughout the world. The threat posed by the submarine is on the increase, and will be for the foreseeable future.

A look at submarine campaigns in World War II will help to put modern antisubmarine warfare into proper perspective. The pendulum of technological advance has moved back and forth between the submarine and the antisubmarine force since the dark days of 1942; today, the box score is about even. Neither force has won a major breakthrough that would give it unquestioned superiority over the other.

In 1949, Sir Winston Churchill wrote, "The only thing that ever really frightened me during the war was the U-boat peril." British merchant shipping losses nearly brought England to its knees in the early part of the war. From June, 1940, to

June, 1941, the U-boat toll was three to four British ships a day—representing a staggering loss of 5.7 million tons of merchant shipping and countless quantities of valuable cargo. In those years, antisubmarine warfare was mainly defensive, and centered on the protection of merchant shipping. The success or failure of this "dirty, dull war" (in Churchill's words) was measured in terms of submarines and merchant ships sunk, as well as in merchant ships constructed. From 1939 to 1942, the Allies suffered a net loss in merchant tonnage, but thereafter the successes of antisubmarine forces and increased ship production produced a more favorable ratio. The story is told graphically in the table below, which was included in Admiral Ernest J. King's third report to the Secretary of the Navy.

Year	German Subs Sunk	Allied Ships Sunk	New Construction (Thousands of Tons)			Net Gains or Losses
			U.S.	British	Total	
1939	9	810	101	231	332	−748
1940	22	4,407	439	780	1,219	−3,188
1941	35	4,398	1,169	815	1,984	−2,414
1942	85	8,245	5,339	1,843	7,182	−1,063
1943	237	3,611	12,384	2,201	14,585	10,974
1944	241	1,422	11,639	1,710	13,349	11,927
1945	153	458	3,551	283	3,834	3,376
Totals	782	23,351	34,622	7,863	42,485	19,134

The Battle of the Atlantic against German submarines in World War II was the greatest antisubmarine campaign of history. Prior to the entry of the United States into the war, Great Britain fought a losing battle and suffered an acute shortage of escort ships to protect her merchant convoys. German Admiral Doenitz initiated "wolf pack" tactics, which made the U-boat even more deadly. He would station from ten to twenty submarines at intervals along Allied shipping lanes. The first submarine to sight a convoy would not attack, but would radio his sighting to Doenitz's headquarters. Using broadcast communications that would not reveal the locations of his other subs, the German admiral would issue instructions sufficient to gather a number of his wolf pack ahead of the unsuspecting merchant ships. Then, he would turn over local command to the senior submarine commander, who would coordinate successive attacks on the hapless convoy.

When the United States declared war, German U-boats began operating off the Atlantic coast. Through the use of supply ships called "milch cows," they could remain on station for long periods. During the first four months of 1942, these submarines sank eighty-two merchant ships, many of them within sight of spectators on shore. As the war dragged on, the German submarine performance grew even better with the introduction of the snorkel underwater breather and the acoustic torpedo that "homed" on a ship's propellers.

Allied efforts to counter the submarine threat began with production of a smaller, diesel-powered escort vessel, which could be turned out in quantity. This "destroyer escort," as it came to be called, was equipped with a weapon system known as the "hedgehog," which reduced considerably the amount of error in surface attacks and was much more effective than the standard stern attack with depth charges. The use of land-based patrol aircraft was increased, and, with improved airborne radar, these patient scouts trapped many a U-boat on the surface. Effective air patrols and increased escorts for convoying soon turned the tide of battle. The Combined Chiefs of Staff instituted a massive air-bombing campaign against German industrial facilities that built submarines or U-boat parts, and submarine bases, assembly plants, and repair yards.

The outstanding Allied innovation into the antisubmarine arsenal was the escort carrier, which was teamed with a number of surface escorts in what became known as the "hunter-killer" group. When this group appeared in the mid-Atlantic, where German submarines had been used to operating without fear of aircraft, the results were rewarding. Carrier aircraft would either destroy the surprised U-boat on the surface, or would drive him beneath the sea where the surface escort ships would take over. As these tactics became highly coordinated, the "hunter-killer" teams achieved more and more successes. By war's end, the U.S. Navy had developed and refined this phase of antisubmarine warfare into the pattern used today.

Modern antisubmarine forces are designed to win a war of survival. The U.S. Navy is well aware that the Germans lost 87 per cent of their U-boats and 70 per cent of their trained submarine personnel during World War II, and the Japanese lost 91 per cent of their submarines in enemy action. Today, the aim of U.S. antisubmarine forces is to inflict similar heavy casualties on the enemy as rapidly as possible. This strategy of offense promises quicker results permitting the United States to utilize the seas to greater advantage and to support overseas operations.

Admiral Martell, who was known before his retirement as the Navy's "antisubmarine czar," described antisubmarine warfare as follows:

> The Navy basically views ASW, in the positive and total sense, as being the measures taken by the aggressive, offensively oriented team of our aircraft, destroyers, and submarines, operating with an offensive spirit and intent in all areas of actual or potential submarine concentrations. . . . (This includes) all naval formations and convoys; in ocean areas from which submarine missiles can reach our coasts; in the vicinity of potential enemy bases and support forces; and along transit paths between the submarines' bases and their objective areas.

The "offensively oriented team" consists of land-based aircraft (primarily long-range patrol planes equipped with excellent sensors and acoustic torpedoes), carrier-based antisubmarine aircraft, similarly equipped, destroyers with improved sonars and weapons (including "bottom-bounce" sonar and rocket-thrown torpedoes), helicopters with dipping sonar and homing torpedoes, and quiet, nuclear-attack submarines. This team, in conjunction with fixed listening arrays, can play the antisubmarine game with deadly effectiveness.

No one part of the team can do the job alone, but each has its primary domain, in which it is superior to the others. For example, the nuclear submarine can operate on long covert patrols under the nose of the enemy home-land defenses. Land-based aircraft operating from bases scattered around the broad oceans, can cover a great area, picking up submarine locations by use of passive sonobuoy detection fields, and following with deliberate search and attack. Within several hundred miles of their base, these patrol aircraft can operate more effectively than carrier-based aircraft. At greater distances, the odds favor the sea-based aircraft. (Analysis of cost effectiveness, which will be treated in a later chapter, shows that life cycle costs of the two separate systems indicate that a combination of land- and sea-based aircraft is the best way to do the job in antisubmarine warfare.) Destroyers are still, and seem likely to remain, indispensable for close-in defense of merchant shipping and naval task forces on the high seas.

Antisubmarine warfare is usually conducted under difficult conditions. To date, the only important means for probing underwater depths is with sound waves, and more often than not, these are distorted, bent, or delayed by unstable temperature layers beneath the surface. This kind of search involves the use of "active" sound systems that send out pulses of high-energy sound waves to strike a distant object and produce an echo. These waves will detect a submarine even if it is lying quiet, but it takes a skilled operator to discriminate between the echoes generated by a submarine from those of a whale or other marine life. A submarine in transit can be detected with "passive" systems using sonobuoys or stationary hydrophones that simply listen to the noises made by an underwater object, but a submarine that is motionless and quiet can avoid discovery. Submarine hunters find this fact frustrating. However, they get some satisfaction in knowing that a motionless submarine cannot make successful attacks on surface shipping unless the unwary ships run right over him.

Submarine hunting has been likened to guerrilla warfare beneath the ocean's surface. The submarine's greatest advantage is in concealment, and, just as the guerrilla soldier does, the submarine commander uses every means available to capitalize on it. A successful submarine hunt is divided into four separate operations: detection, classification, localization, and kill. Detection is accomplished with either active or passive sonar systems, but all they tell the hunter is that he has an underwater target that might be a submarine. It could be a sunken bulk on the bottom, or it could be a large fish, or school of fish. The direction, motion, and stability or instability of movement of an underwater target aids in classification by creating a Doppler effect—a predictable cadence—on the returning sound waves. In some cases, at this point, an airborne magnetic detection device can be brought into play, to determine, from variations in the earth's magnetic field, whether the target has the metallic properties of a submarine. Localization results from a series of progressive detections, which more closely establish range and bearing on the target. When the submarine is fairly well pinpointed, the kill can follow—with homing torpedoes or depth charges having a large lethal radius.

Antisubmarine warfare takes patience and persistence. The ocean is big and a submarine is a small speck. The opportunity for engagement with the enemy is only a fleeting one. The Navy has joined with industry in a scientific approach to produce incremental advances in all equipment used in antisubmarine warfare. No real breakthrough is expected, but this program of small steps has seen tremendous improvements made. It is hoped that the research and development effort of the late 1960's and the early 1970's will produce new advances for each important system in the Navy's antisubmarine warfare team.

SUBMARINE FORCES

The last combat action in which U.S. submarines took part was in World War II, when the primary mission of the submarine force was to sink enemy merchant and naval shipping, and to act as scouts near enemy lines. In the mission against surface shipping, the American submarines did a magnificent job, even though they were handicapped during the first years of action by faulty torpedoes. At the end of the war, in August, 1945, it was conservatively estimated that U.S. submarines had taken the toll of 4.8 million tons of Japanese shipping and had sunk 39 destroyers, 9 light cruisers, 4 heavy cruisers, 1 battleship, and 9 aircraft carriers. When targets became scarce, the submarines conducted special raiding expeditions and served as lifeguards for American pilots who had to ditch their aircraft in the sea near enemy shores. "Lifeguard" submarines recovered over 600 downed aviators in this mission during the course of the war. Although enemy submarines were never considered prime targets, U.S. submarines accounted for 25 of them in the Pacific—23 Japanese and 2 German U-boats that strayed away from their Indian Ocean station.

The lessons of combat operations in World War II brought about many changes in submarine construction. Newer submarine hulls were strengthened for deeper depths, the torpedo firing system was changed from compressed air (which left telltale bubbles) to a hydraulic system using water. Engines, electrical motors, generators—in fact, all machinery was made more compact and quiet. The torpedoes themselves were equipped with homing devices to offset errors in the fire control solution. Sensors, particularly of the passive kind, were greatly improved. Last, and perhaps most important, nuclear power was harnessed for propulsion, and the Navy finally had the first true submersible—a submarine that did not have to come to the surface or to snorkeling position to recharge its batteries.

With these improved boats, active-minded submarine officers sought a new role in antisubmarine warfare. Their effort began shortly after World War II, with the formation of the Submarine Development Group to solve the problem of attacking the snorkeling enemy submarine. These investigations led to the construction and conversion program that produced what is known as the "killer" submarine (SSK) and other types of submarines that could stalk another boat under the surface. As better torpedoes and improved sonar arrays became available, these sub hunters became even more effective. When the submarine and patrol aircraft joined in the same mission, they soon developed combined tactics to improve detection, localization, and kill.

Since 1955, when the *Nautilus* got under way on nuclear power (see also Chapter VI), there has been a revolution in submarine offensive tactics, and a drastic change in many of the concepts of antisubmarine warfare. The *Nautilus,* and her sister ships were able to confuse surface operating forces with unusual tactics. For example, in practice exercises these swift submersibles would approach the formation from astern undetected and take a "cruising station" in the formation where they would, at leisure, "sink" every ship around them. When their accounts of their exploits were doubted, the submarine skippers would produce color photographs of each target (taken through the periscope), including the side number, range, and bearing at the time of the simulated torpedo launch. This convinced even the most stubborn skeptics, and planners went back to the drawing board to study ways to deal with this new phenomenon.

As the Navy turned to missiles to augment gun batteries, the submarine force began adapting missiles to their boats. Before the breakthrough with the Polaris missile (see Chapter VI), several boats were equipped with the Regulus missile, which looked like an advanced design aircraft and was fired from the surface. In a carefully supervised test off the coast of California in 1959, a submarine surfaced one morning and fired a Regulus missile over the California mountains to hit a target in the Mohave desert 500 miles away. The demonstration showed that, in the hands of an enemy, such a missile posed a grave threat to the continental United States. Although the Soviet Union has developed a similar missile and has installed it on a number of submarines, the United States has phased out the Regulus in favor of the more effective Polaris.

Within the concept of a limited war with conventional weapons, the possibility that there will be a war at sea always exists. (See Chapter XII.) Should this occur, the mission of the modern submarine force will be to conduct a war of attrition against enemy merchant ships as before. In addition, it will join surface and air forces in the war against enemy submarines.

The primary role of the submarine force in the antisubmarine mission is in the forward area just outside the enemy's harbors, where there will be ample targets in a small geographic area, and the hunting submarine will not have the complications of identifying friend from foe. Any other submarine making a noisy transit in that area will be hostile.

Aside from the forward area patrol, the submarine can work very effectively in an air-submarine barrier. In this role, the submarine capitalizes on her long-range passive detection capability, combined with the aircraft's speed in making an attack. The two work together in an area of known strategic importance where enemy submarines have to pass in order to reach their own operating areas. A basic assumption to this tactic is that the United States has control of the air, or that its aircraft are protected from air attack. The air-submarine team works on a simple principle: the submarine makes initial detection of a transiting enemy sub, calls its air partner on high frequency radio, and vectors the plane on the bearing of the target. Frequent exercises at this tactic show that it is practical and effective.

There is a third role for the submarine in antisubmarine warfare. This is in perimeter defense of a naval task force or high priority convoy. Here, the submarine joins the air-surface team in submarine defense, by taking its station submerged and ahead of the surface units for passive detection of the enemy, or within the surface ships' convoy, where it will use its active sonar—a tactic involving problems of communications and identification, but one that fleet exercises show is feasible.

In addition to the antisubmarine roles of forward area operations, air-submarine barriers and close-in surface ship defense, the modern submarine can carry out any of the other tasks that were required of submarines in World War II. This includes such jobs as scouting, trailing, life guard station, mining, transporting, underwater demolition operations and radar picket duties. Undoubtedly, if war should come, the versatile submarine force will think of still more tasks that submarines can do better than any other unit.

AMPHIBIOUS FORCES

The first amphibious war operation occurred eons past when primitive men landed primitive boats on a hostile beach, and stormed ashore after their enemies. The amphibious assault is officially defined by the Navy as a "form of military combat which the attacker commences on water and carries ashore against a defender lodged close to the shoreline." This concise definition includes all of the elements originally used in amphibious warfare, but omits the modern innovation provided by military aircraft. Despite this advance, amphibious assault is still primarily an operation of ships, men, and equipment, and it is one of the most complicated of all military evolutions. It is also one of the most devastating blows that a country can strike against another in armed conflict. Even if it is only used infrequently, amphibious attack is a viable threat that can pin down great numbers of troops for defense.

When Napoleon was conducting his brilliant campaign in Austria, British raids on the Flemish coast caused him to say, "With 30,000 men in transports at the Downs, the English can paralyze 300,000 of my army, and that will reduce us to the rank of a second class Power." In the early years of the American Civil War, General Robert E. Lee was put in command of the entire South Atlantic coast to bolster Confederate defenses against the amphibious thrust of the Union forces. Noting sadly that the Confederacy had no guns that could resist the Union fleet, Lee pointed out to the War Department in Richmond that the North's amphibious threat could be "thrown with great celerity against any point, and far out-numbers any force we can bring against it in the field." At the same time, General Grant was learning how to use mobile water support for his armies at Vicksburg. He found that the river forces under Commander David Porter gave him an advantage he described at the close of the siege in these words: "The Navy under Porter was all it could be during the entire campaign. Without its assistance the campaign could not have been successfully made with twice the number of men engaged."

It was in World War II that the amphibious landing really came into its own. A succession of great sea invasions studded that conflict, led by the German invasion of Norway and the Japanese landings, first in the Philippines and then throughout Southeast Asia, and soon followed by even larger Allied operations. One of the most concise records of these landings can be found at the football stadium of the U.S. Naval Academy at Annapolis. Emblazoned in large letters across the face of the grandstands are the names of the more famous naval engagements of the war: North Africa, Sicily, Salerno, Normandy, Guadalcanal, Tarawa, Kwajalein, Saipan, Leyte, Iwo Jima, Okinawa. To a student of history, that list of landings is enough to make the case for amphibious warfare.

Although technological advances have brought about numerous changes in amphibious assault concepts since World War II, the requirement to land and support troops in over-the-beach operations still holds. The advantages of surprise and concentration of forces on a pivotal point—the lack of which plagued Napoleon, Lee, and Hitler alike—can still be realized by a sea power. Amphibious strike forces of today are faster, better designed, and employ a wider variety of vessels and weapons than before, but they have to accomplish the same goal. The final battle is still won by the infantryman ashore with a rifle in his hand. Every nation hopes that that final battle will be on someone else's territory. For this to come about, that infantryman will, no doubt, have been landed over the beach in an amphibious operation of some kind.

There is a significant difference between an assault and a nonassault landing. If ground forces are to be landed at a friendly allied port, the problem is simply one of forward logistics to prevent overcrowding and to move men and equipment ashore efficiently. The majority of Army unit movements overseas now envisioned are of the nonassault type (but the Army's record in World War II, from North Africa to Okinawa, is one of proud achievement in the assault phase). The current concept calls for an amphibious assault landing by a Navy-Marine Corps team, followed by rapid assembly of heavy Army forces to carry out a sustained land campaign. One kind of force, combat-loaded is needed for assault landings; another kind of force, administratively loaded, for nonassault landings.

There are many prerequisites for a successful amphibious assault. First is the wherewithal—a naval amphibious force of specially designed ships and landing craft; next is the hard-hitting landing force; and last the follow-on echelon (or "sea tail") that brings in the supplies and equipment to give the landing force staying power. Aside from having the right equipment to support an assault landing and maintain logistic supply to the troops ashore, there are other operational considerations. The operational commanders need adequate reconnaissance to select a suitable beachhead and landing site. With reconnaissance and intelligence estimates, the commanders can make fairly accurate estimates of the enemy's capability to oppose the landing, and can alter their plans for the most effective combat force to neutralize this defense. Detailed planning includes: loading arrangements for embarking troops, vehicles, and equipment; the formation for landing; specific choices of beaches and helicopter landing areas; the maneuvers necessary to seize beachhead objectives; and plans for operations ashore. Finally, a port of embarkation must be selected and the ship-to-shore movement plan prepared.

Proper utilization of ships not only to lift the troops to the objective, but also to maintain the tactical integrity of the landing force, requires professional knowledge. During the past few decades, members of the Navy-Marine Corps amphibious team have attended special schools and have participated in numerous realistic exercises to develop and maintain the required "know how." They know, first of all, the characteristics and capabilities of the many different assault ships and loading craft—both the older models and those added to the naval inventory since World War II—and how to use them to best advantage.

One comparative newcomer is the amphibious command ship (AGC), which supplies a floating headquarters for both the Navy amphibious task force commander and the Marine landing force commander. Landing operations are supervised from the command ship until the landing force is firmly established ashore. Then the scene of command is shifted as the headquarters staff moves to the beachhead. The more recently developed helicopter troop carrier (LPH) also has command facilities, but is primarily intended to transport the vertical assault elements of a landing force. Carrying from twenty to thirty helicopters and up to 1,800 troops, the LPH incorporates many of the features of the older attack cargo ship, the escort carrier, the attack transport, and the command ship. Another recent addition is the amphibious transport, dock (LPD). This utility ship can lift a balanced load of troops, vehicles, and supplies; up to 840 men can be landed from either the well deck (which opens on the water's surface) or the flight deck.

Still on the drawing board (or, to use the lingo of the trade, in "concept formulation") are two more important additions to the amphibious craft inventory. The first is a new fire-support ship, which will provide the gun support that worked so well in softening up beachheads during World War II. The second is a larger and faster multipurpose amphibious ship, featuring a "roll-on, roll-off" capability for loading and unloading and a sustained speed of over twenty knots, and incorporating the features of several different specialized types.

The remainder of the ships of the amphibious force are essentially the same as those used during World War II. This includes the landing ship (dock) (LSD) and the familiar old landing ship (tank) (LST, fondly nicknamed "Large Slow Target"), attack transports, cargo ships, and many miscellaneous landing craft for tanks, mechanized equipment, personnel, and even a troop-carrying submarine, the APSS.

The Navy's amphibious assault force is designed to lift and land the assault echelons of a Marine expeditionary force (MEF), as the Marine strength considered to be most appropriate for situations involving sustained combat against significant opposition is designated. Totaling about 43,500 men, the MEF consists of a Marine division, a Marine aircraft wing, a logistic support group, and a command element. Smaller units of this large force include a Marine expeditionary brigade (MEB) of about 10,200, which consists of a regimental landing team and an aircraft group, and a Marine expeditionary unit (MEU) of about 2,700, which has a battalion landing team and a smaller air group.

The ships of the amphibious force are organized administratively for routine deployment and relief in both the Atlantic and the Pacific. Consequently, they are seldom brought together as a task organization with a single design. Experience has shown that this arrangement is adequate to meet requirements for transporting smaller forces in routine Cold War deployments. Should the international situation require a totally designed, larger lift, the versatile task force organization would permit administrative regrouping of the ships to handle a maximum load.

During the late 1960's, one of the most pressing problems throughout the Navy was that of block obsolescence of ships. The majority of ships in the amphibious inventory were built during World War II. They are slow, do not have adequate troop spaces or sufficient air-conditioning equipment, and are subject to frequent breakdowns. In recognition of the need for orderly replacement, the Navy shipbuilding program for the past several years has had among its objectives an increase of total lift capacity, expansion of helicopter vertical assault capabilities and the capability of deployed ready units, and the addition of more fast ships to the amphibious force. This program has had the support of the Secretary of Defense, who authorized construction of a total of fifteen new amphibious ships in fiscal year 1966 (total cost $494 million) and twelve new ships in fiscal year 1967 ($306 million). As a temporary measure to meet demands in Southeast Asia, he also directed the Navy to reactivate three medium landing ships, rocket (LSMR), and to retain two heavy gunned cruisers that had been scheduled for inactivation. Both steps were taken to provide increased ship-to-shore fire power to cover landing forces during any assault operations that might be required in Viet-Nam.

The discussion thus far has been limited to the amphibious force units per se. But a large, well-planned amphibious operation requires the use of almost every type of ship in the fleet. For example, the attack carrier force would make preliminary strikes to knock out enemy air facilities. The enemy beach defenses would be subjected to intense, sustained naval gunfire. Antisubmarine forces would be needed for protection of the amphibious task force. Before the first assault wave could land, the waters would be swept by mine sweepers or helicopters, and frogmen would reconnoiter the beaches, blowing up such off-shore defenses as survived the minesweeping. More likely than not, the frogmen would be transported in close to the beach by submarine. When all was in readiness, the amphibious ships would come to their anchorages and disgorge their loads. This climactic ship-to-shore movement has been described aptly as "organized chaos." The landing movement could be entirely over the beach, or it could be augmented by helicopter vertical envelopment in which significant forces would be airlifted beyond the beach behind enemy lines. When all men and equipment were ashore, including the Marine Corps portable computer that kept track of the entire operation, and the matted aluminum airfield, the ships of the amphibious force could retire to the safety of deep water. Then the problem of logistic supply to support the troops ashore would require new naval ships and planning.

MOBILE LOGISTIC SUPPORT

With a strategy that requires the projection of power away from its homeland, the United States has to rely on mobile logistics. War has been called a matter of fire and movement, and both of these elements imply logistical support. In the days of sail, men-of-war were almost self-sufficient. Captain Cook demonstrated this in the eighteenth century when he took small sailing ships on voyages of discovery that lasted as long as three years. Admittedly, he was an excellent ocean shopper, and he stopped frequently for fresh water, green vegetables, and meat when he could find it, but he remained long from home without basic replenishment.

Today's ships normally carry a supply of provisions that is "thirty days fresh, ninety days dry." This phrase means that the crew can subsist for a month on a well-balanced diet of fresh or frozen foods and for three months on dry staples and canned provisions. But ships that burn oil for propulsion are inevitably tied to some source of supply for refueling. The naval men-of-war with, as sailors say, the "shortest legs," are the sleek destroyers. Their exceptional power and speed are achieved at the sacrifice of fuel stowage. When operations permit, these ships are refueled at sea about every other day. All conventionally powered forces have a need for oil that is measured in days, not weeks, and arrangements have to be made for their resupply on long voyages. Cruisers, amphibious ships, and even aircraft carriers, all of which have large fuel capacity, are often called upon to "top off" destroyers at sea or in an advanced base. But the majority of resupply at sea is provided by the underway replenishment groups that the U.S. Navy developed in World War II.

The Service Force

Although the basic requirement that instigated the formation of these groups was oil, the Navy found that normal wartime expenditures of ammunition and aviation gas also necessitated regular replenishment of these items. Fresh and frozen food supplies dwindled rapidly, too. Therefore, the well-rounded underway replenishment group soon came to include oilers, ammunition ships, and provision ships (or "beef boats"). More recently, the unusually high usage rate of spare parts for the advanced weapon systems and electronics gear on modern ships has led to the construction of a new class of stores ships. Today, all of these underway replenishment vessels belong to the Navy's Service Force, whose ships are not actually a part of combatant task forces, but who plod along not far behind.

The art of replenishing at sea began before World War II, but the Navy only played at it. When that global war made it a matter of necessity, naval officers developed the state of the art quite rapidly. As late as 1940, the replenishing ship passed a towing hawser from a forward chock to a position on the bow of the ship alongside, and the two cruised slowly while supplies were transferred. However, it soon became apparent that, at a speed of about twelve knots, good seamen could maintain position alongside twenty to thirty yards apart, without the towing hawser. At first, this was considered a dangerous operation, but the familiarity of frequent experience soon reduced it to a routine. Today, ships replenish at sea frequently, remaining alongside each other for hours, changing course while together, and conducting the operation day or night. The latest wrinkle is called a "vertrep," which means "vertical replenishment." In this method, the supply ship transfers most of its cargo by helicopter. The technique is especially suited to the transfer of guided missiles at sea.

A typical underway replenishment begins when a task force commander arranges a rendezvous at sea with the group. He requires each of his ships to signal its requirements, thus allowing the individual supply ships to prepare their cargoes for efficient transfer. The commander then publishes the order of ships alongside, and everyone makes preparations. The two groups of ships meet at the rendezvous point—usually at dawn, occasionally at night. The group of faster combatant ships overtakes and merges with the replenishment group, on a signaled course and speed. At the signal to commence replenishment, the well-kept formation becomes a mass movement as individual ships jockey for approach or waiting stations. Since the two groups are more vulnerable to attack during this operation than they are steaming singly, the task force commander maintains a destroyer screen against submarines and keeps fighter aircraft overhead for air defense. On occasion, aircraft carriers launch and recover aircraft while alongside an oiler. In 1967, the cruiser *Canberra* set a record for nonchalance by continuing shore bombardment off Viet-Nam during a replenishment operation.

MSTS

Underway replenishment groups are only a part of the Navy's total sealift. Although the underway replenishment of naval combatant ships at sea is important, the supply line to the air and ground forces ashore in distant combat is equally important. This kind of supply is met by support ships of Military Sea Transportation Service (MSTS), augmented when necessary by merchant ship charters. The governing criterion is gross shipping requirement—the tons of military cargo and numbers of personnel, and the time schedule for their movement.

When the shipping requirement exceeds the capacity of the MSTS nucleus fleet, the Navy uses operational merchant ships, activates older cargo ships from the National Defense Reserve Fleet, or, as a last resort, turns to foreign flag vessels. The use of merchant ships involves the government in the payment of war bonuses and purchase of war risk insurance, as well as in charges for demurrage incurred by lengthy turn-arounds. For example, during the eight months' period from July, 1965, to February, 1966, the government incurred costs of $14.5 million for seamen's war bonuses, $7 million for risk insurance, and $1.5 million for demurrage—all from delivery of cargoes in support of war operations in Viet-Nam. Regardless of cost, the supplies have to get through.

FORCES FOR AIR DEFENSE

There is no separate anti-aircraft force in the Navy in the sense that it has carrier strike forces, antisubmarine and submarine forces, and amphibious forces. Any armed soldier, ship, vehicle, or fixed installation capable of firing a weapon into the air can be used in anti-air warfare. Planes have been shot down by gunfire from tanks, by the rifle fire of a lone Marine, by submarines, land anti-aircraft batteries, other aircraft, and surface ships. Many of these incidents were accidental, but the majority of aircraft shot down at sea have been victims of a studiously organized anti-aircraft defense.

In this kind of battle, first fought in World War I, the pendulum of advantage for naval forces has swung back and forth several times. The Navy has come a long way since General "Billy" Mitchell proved in the 1920's that undefended battleships could be sunk by bombs. Unlike many aspects of modern combat, the efficiency of anti-aircraft defense can be tested in live firing exercises, and these, plus experience in World War II, have been responsible for many changes.

Early in its history, the anti-aircraft gun was fired against a sleeve towed by a "target" aircraft within firing range of the ship. The tips of machine gun bullets were dyed to leave telltale markings on the sleeve, and to identify the gunners responsible for hits. As the air-defense weapons increased in size and range, it soon became a routine matter for an anti-aircraft battery to shoot down the sleeve by cutting the towing wire; on some occasions, the projectile exploded on target and shattered the sleeve into small shreds. With the invention of the radio-controlled "drone" aircraft, anti-aircraft practice became more realistic. The drone plane would take off from a coastal airfield in company with its mother planes, who could shepherd it over a naval force for live firing practice. This permitted much more realism, greater altitudes, and ranges. With the invention of jet-powered drones, the fire control problem became almost too great for conventional guns, and the Navy turned to supersonic surface-to-air missiles. The number and different types of these missiles available today results from a steady program of improvement by exploratory development and tests.

In World War II, the battle between the airplane and surface warship was fought many times. Even the stanchest advocate of anti-air ship batteries will admit that the queen of air defense in that war was a friendly fighter aircraft. By far the greater number of enemy aircraft downed at sea were the losers in aerial dogfights with other planes. Navy task forces (and convoys wherever possible) were given fighter cover as the first defense against hostile air attack, but some attackers inevitably got past the fighters and pressed home their attacks on surface ships. In isolated engagements where large numbers of aircraft attacked a single ship, the result was disastrous. For example, the British battleship *Prince of Wales* and the battle cruiser *Repulse,* caught at sea by over sixty Japanese aircraft, were quickly sunk before land-based air cover could reach the scene. Similarly, in the last months of the war, U.S. carrier aircraft sank the Japanese superbattleship *Yamato.* However, it was a different story when surface ships teamed together for mutual support and were equipped with improved weapons.

The American carrier task forces in the Pacific soon demonstrated that they could go just about where they pleased and fought off determined Japanese air attacks with a system of organized firepower that was the forerunner of modern anti-aircraft defense. At the first sign of an approaching enemy air attack, the protective fighters circling aloft on "combat air patrol" were vectored out to meet the attackers. Additional fighters were launched immediately. When the surviving attackers came within the ship's gun range the carrier fighters broke off their attacks in order to leave a clear field for anti-aircraft gunfire. Usually the surface ships were drawn up into a circular formation with a ring of destroyers and cruisers about the carrier in the center. After some months of trial and error, it was found that results were better if the ships in the outer ring fired away from the formation. In some confused situations, the gunfire could get extremely wild, particularly if ships fired across the ring, or if an enemy plane itself flew into the center. In such melees, many ships were struck by fire from others in the formation. To avoid these tragic errors, the local commanders established radio communication nets especially to control the batteries. When strict discipline was exerted, the defending ships worked like a well-organized team, passing targets from one sector to another with aplomb in the midst of erratic evasive maneuvers, day or night.

The concentric ring of anti-aircraft batteries became the basic defense, but changes and additions to it were required. During the latter part of the war, when carrier task forces ventured closer and closer to Japanese-held land bases, the enterprising Japanese pilots adopted the tactic of following returning carrier aircraft back to the aircraft carrier. In many cases, these trailers were not discovered until it was too late, and they were able to make a successful attack. This development led to the use of a picket destroyer at some distance from the main force. The picket ship would be assigned a group of fighters who patrolled overhead, under his control. Returning carrier strikes would pass over the picket to be "deloused"—or inspected by the combat air patrol to make certain that they were not being trailed. The picket ship provided another advantage; if stationed in the most likely direction of attack, it would invariably have radar warning of attacking enemy aircraft before the ships of the task force could. This additional time was critical, because it allowed the carrier to launch additional fighters for protection. The importance of the radar picket soon dawned on the Japanese attackers, of course, and, especially at Okinawa, the role of a radar picket became hazardous indeed. One destroyer skipper made a joke of the situation, fashioning a large sign that read "I am a radar picket

—the nearest carrier is 60 miles south," and displaying it with an arrow pointing out the direction.

Today's modern arsenal of airborne weapons includes air-to-surface missiles that can be launched with great accuracy and effectiveness at some distance from the surface targets, and surface ships have been equipped with guided missiles for defense. Therefore, the anti-aircraft defense problem has taken on new dimensions, with slightly different formations. Picket ships are still used, but there is now a "picket" aircraft, as well. This early warning aircraft is equipped with adequate radars and communication gear to control fighter aircraft while it is on station. It is particularly effective against low fliers who attempt to bore in under the surface ships' radar umbrella. Picket ships, usually equipped with guided missiles as well as height-finding radar, can add to the defense with either their own missiles or by vectoring fighters to intercept the attackers. With the additional capabilities of certain kinds of deception, the problem is highly complicated. In general, the Navy today relies on defense in depth, the use of every applicable weapon, and a computerized tactical data system to keep the senior commanders on top of the rapidly shifting pattern of conflict.

Among the newer weapons disclosed in the testimony of the Secretary of Defense before the Congress in recent years have been the "Three T's" of surface-to-air missiles—Tartar, Terrier, and Talos. Actually the Terrier missile has been in the fleet since 1955, when it was first installed on the USS *Boston*. The earlier version was fitted with a guidance system based on the beam-riding principle, but newer Terriers have a homing system that is much superior. Talos, the largest of the lot, is carried only on cruisers; it has a range of over sixty-five miles and can reach aircraft at extremely high altitudes. The smaller Tartar missile is primarily for destroyer installations, for use on the outer perimeter of air defense formations. Naval aircraft today have two tried and true air-to-air missiles—the Sparrow and the Sidewinder, which travel at supersonic speeds and "home" on their targets. Needless to say, newer and more sophisticated missiles of both types are scheduled for later production.

The function of air defense is bred into all ships that can carry gun or missile batteries. The classes of ships better designed and equipped for this kind of action than any others, however, are the cruisers and multipurpose destroyers. They are fast enough to keep pace with the aircraft carriers and can provide badly needed air defense in the event of an air attack. When their services are not needed for this purpose, they can, with equal effectiveness, give gunfire support for amphibious landings. Destroyers can be assigned to join antisubmarine forces, to convoy high-priority cargo ships, or to repulse surface attacks. When the Navy is on the offense with carrier striking forces, the general-purpose destroyer and the cruiser with guided-missile batteries accompany the carrier to round out the capabilities of the task group.

In the near future, a close-in point defense surface missile system, using the air-to-air Sparrow missile, may be installed on combat ships. But this would not change the team concept of air defense in which aircraft and surface ships combine to strengthen their defense.

The next chapter moves to the subject of carrier aircraft available to Navy flyers, whether for defensive or offensive operations—and to the larger story of naval aviation.

V

Naval Aviation

Undoubtedly, the airplane was one of the greatest developments of naval warfare. It introduced the third dimension of air space to what had heretofore been a simple problem of using the world's waters, both at and beneath the surface. A second cousin in the inventory of naval weapons in its infancy, the airplane rose to ascendancy during World War II and has enjoyed pre-eminence in the Navy for almost thirty years now. It made the battleship obsolete and revolutionized naval tactics.

Although other military systems compete with naval aviation today, and have supplanted it in some missions, the airplane still has capabilities in naval warfare that are irreplaceable, and its future seems assured for some years to come. Pound for pound, a naval aircraft is the most expensive weapon in the nation's arsenal, so the aircraft system remains under constant scrutiny by cost analysts of the Defense Department. To survive this surveillance, naval aviation has to be able to perform some military missions better than any other force.

Throughout the history of naval aviation, the flying profession has attracted many inquisitive and intelligent naval officers. Their imaginative thinking has left no avenue of aircraft employment unexplored. In developing this new military system, the Navy has also been ably assisted by the aircraft industry, whose engineers early demonstrated the drive, tenacity, and creativeness that made the United States one of the leaders

115

in world aviation. At the beginning, naval planners foresaw needs for fighters, dive bombers, torpedo planes, and scouting aircraft. All but the last had to be relatively small and maneuverable. Consequently, they were only able to fly short distances without refueling. Since these aircraft operated from land bases, they had limited value for the wide ocean reaches where the Navy wanted to roam, as well as for the faraway locations where conflicts might occur. It was soon obvious to air pioneers that naval aviation could realize its full potential only if mated to a ship of some kind.

Despite its tremendous advantages, a sea-based system presented formidable obstacles. The solution of these problems brought forth the combination land-based, sea-based system that the U.S. Navy has today. With great dedication, a small band of aviators barely tolerated by their brother officers during the early years, stuck to their task of working out the techniques of naval aviation. In retrospect, it is clear that their determination and imaginative theories saved the Navy during World War II.

TEDDY ROOSEVELT'S LEAD

Although the Navy did not receive its first aircraft until 1911, it can trace the awakening of interest in naval aviation to a letter written by Theodore Roosevelt in 1898. At that time, "Teddy" Roosevelt was assistant secretary of the Navy, and he sent a memorandum to Secretary John Davis Long to inform him of the potential of Professor Langley's "flying machine." "The machine has worked," he wrote. "It seems to me worth while for this government to try whether it will not work on a large enough scale to be of use in the event of war." Roosevelt went on to recommend the formation of a board of Navy and Army officers "of scientific attainments" to "examine in to" the flying machine and make recommendations for its use. Almost seventy years later, naval officers of scientific attainments are still "examining in to" flying machines, continuing the tradition of methodical exploration that has proven so successful in the past.

The controversial Secretary of the Navy Josephus Daniels was the first to sponsor naval aviation. He accelerated its development as a tool of sea power. In 1914, he announced that "aircraft must form a large part of our naval force for offensive and defensive operations," and backed his statement by establishing the first naval air station at the site of the old Pensacola Navy Yard in Florida. Daniels was persuaded to take this action by several of the achievements of pioneer aviators.

FIRST FLIGHT OFF THE DECK

In 1911, civilian pilot Eugene Ely had landed a biplane on a makeshift wooden deck built on the armored cruiser *Pennsylvania*. At intervals across this platform were stretched twenty-two manila lines, each anchored to a fifty-pound sandbag, to serve as the first naval "arresting gear." Ely's plane had been fitted with hooks to snag these lines and bring him to rest before he crashed into a protective screen at the end of the "flight deck." The contraption worked, and the triumphant Ely turned his plane around and took off from the same deck to fly safely back to land. This event officially marked the beginning of naval aviation. However, the Navy did not pursue the idea of adapting land planes to ships for the time being, but concentrated on the flying boat and smaller seaplanes.

During maneuvers in 1912 and 1913, Navy pilots had used their aircraft for scouting, locating submarines, and collecting intelligence. The first naval air photography, though hazardous and clumsy, had pointed the way toward the heights that it would achieve later. At Annapolis, aviation engineers had developed a compressed-air catapult for launching seaplanes from a wall along the Chesapeake Bay. Designers already had drawn up plans to install similar launching devices aboard larger ships. The band of young navy pilots was full of new ideas and anxious to try them out. Some of their enthusiasm rubbed off on Secretary Daniels.

The air station at Pensacola began with the arrival in 1913

of the Navy's nine planes and the flying detachment consisting of six commissioned pilots and twenty-three enlisted men. The seaplanes operated from a hastily constructed ramp and were housed in tent hangars. Most of the flying detachment was quartered on a station ship that was away more often than it was in its home port. Supplies were hard to get, payday was sometimes delayed, but flying went on with scheduled regularity. The seasoned pilots studied every development that Navy Intelligence could glean from the war in Europe, and some wild reports filtered through, creating consternation until they were found to be wrong. For example, there was a report that the German Zeppelins "could see through the clouds." What new device was this? Further investigation showed that the imaginative Germans simply lowered a man in a basket from the airship to a position below the cloud cover, while he communicated his observations via a field telephone.

WORLD WAR I AND AFTER

The Navy remained interested primarily in seaplanes and flying boats throughout World War I, but after the war began to show an interest in specially constructed aircraft carriers and followed closely the early developments of the use of air power by the British Navy. The small U.S. Navy had acquitted itself well during the war, and had grown in size to a force of 39,000 officers and enlisted men by the end of the conflict. This Navy had over 2,000 planes, and made valuable surveillance flights from bases in England and Europe. Its airmen conducted attacks on twenty-five German submarines before the Armistice and claimed to have sunk or damaged twelve of them.

First Trans-Atlantic Flight

Shortly after the war, the Navy took delivery of several large flying boats of the NC class and decided to test their stamina in a flight across the Atlantic. To aid in navigation over water, which was still a difficult feat, the fleet commander

John Paul Jones, captain in the Continental Navy during the American Revolution, whose ship, the *Bon Homme Richard,* captured the heavier-gunned British *Seraphis* in one of the classic engagements of naval history.

The venerable USS *Constitution,* also known as "Old Ironsides," was part of the fleet that destroyed the power of the Barbary pirates. Now rebuilt, she is a tourist attraction at her permanent berth in Boston Harbor.

U.S. Bureau of Ships

Civil War Admiral David Glasgow Farragut.

Admiral Farragut's Mississippi River gunboats helped to win the Battle of Vicksburg.

This modern U.S. Navy PACV, similar in design and function to the earlier gunboat, is here shown patrolling the coast of Viet-Nam. Crew members board a junk suspected of carrying contraband to the enemy.

The Battle of Santiago, 1898.

Admiral George Dewey, Spanish-American War hero.

Destroyers rush fr[om]
Boston to Queensto[wn,]
Ireland, shortly after [the]
United States ent[ered]
World War I, to help [the]
British halt German [U-]
boat raids on Atla[ntic]
shipping.

Today, the destro[yer]
USS *Cony* stea[ms]
through heavy seas.

odern techniques for fueling at sea: the aircraft carrier *Kitty Hawk* and the destroyer USS *almann* are serviced by the oiler USS *Kawiwa.*

e USS *Tecumseh*, a clear submarine, with crew topside, arrives Apra Harbor, Guam.

Crew members check out control consoles aboard the USS *George Washington,* in preparation for the firing of a Polaris missile.

A Polaris missile, fired from a submarine, breaks through the ocean's surface.

An F4 Phantom jet is catapulted off the deck of the USS *Enterprise*.

On the flight deck of the nuclear-powered *Enterprise*, during a Mediterranean cruise, the crew spells out Einstein's theory of relativity.

The **USS** *Seadragon* at the North Pole after the historic rendezvous under the ice with the **USS** *Skate*.

strung out sixty-eight destroyers between the east Atlantic Coast and the Azores as markers. In addition, five battleships were stationed about four hundred miles apart to serve as weather relay stations. When all was ready, three NC aircraft started their hazardous flight hampered by heavy fog. Two of them had to land in order to check their position and never managed to get airborne again. But after early difficulties, one —the NC-4—, with Lieutenant Commander A. C. Read, USN, as chief pilot, flew all the way to the Azores without mishap. There he and his crew rested a few days and continued on to Lisbon, where they arrived on May 27, 1919, completing the first successful trans-Atlantic crossing.

First Aircraft Carriers

Afterward, in the 1920's, the achievements of naval aviation were partially eclipsed by the more sensational exploits of the Army Air Service pilots, but aviation made continuous progress in the Navy. In 1922, a Navy coal ship was converted to an aircraft carrier and renamed the USS *Langley*. Nicknamed "The Covered Wagon" in the fleet because of her strange silhouette, the *Langley* had a flight deck 534 by 64 feet (about the size of the "jeep" carriers of World War II). The first aircraft to operate from her deck were conventional land planes with reinforced landing gear and arresting hooks. The most troublesome problem was to arrive at an acceptable design in the arresting wires; the first on the *Langley* were similar to those used on the *Pennsylvania* in 1911—simply bags of sand at the end of each wire. By trial and experiment, Navy aviators and aircraft engineers finally settled on a design that used hydraulic cylinders in place of the weights. This system, periodically refined and improved, was essentially the one that saw the large carrier force through thousands of landings during World War II.

Carrier aviation received an unexpected benefit from the Washington Disarmament treaties of 1922, which limited the number of capital ships for the major naval powers, and set the displacement of future aircraft carriers at no more than 27,000 tons. The treaty also stipulated that hulls already under construction, and now due to be scrapped, could be converted into carriers if they did not exceed 36,000 tons' displacement. At that time the United States had on the building ways two partially completed battle cruisers. Finishing construction was out of the question because they would bring the total number in their class above treaty limits. Led by Rear Admiral W. A. Moffett, a small group of officers proposed that the battle cruisers under construction be converted to aircraft carriers. Thus the USS *Lexington* and *Saratoga* became the first large, fast carriers in the fleet. They had flight decks 800 feet long and over 100 feet wide. The island structure and smoke stacks were offset in such a way as to give aircraft unhampered use of most of the flight deck. This innovation soon became a standard characteristic for all aircraft carriers, although the divided smoke stacks (three on each side) of the *Lexington* class soon changed, with one large stack structure on the starboard side in later designs.

The *Lexington* and *Saratoga* were commissioned in 1927 during a period of reduced military appropriations, but their arrival in the fleet set off a program of naval air advancement that has been unrivaled in any period of naval peacetime development. With large patrol planes operating from established land bases and supported by seaplane tenders (especially designed air support ships), and with smaller seaplanes attached to battle ships and cruisers, the Navy already had a sizable air arm. The fleet now had the air complement of three aircraft carriers to add to its air potential.

At first, aircraft carriers joined fleet maneuvers to scout and to provide overhead protection for the battleline, and to lay smoke screens or spot the fall of shot in surface gunfire exercises. Soon, they were required to undertake more mundane duties such as towing aerial targets for gunnery practice and dropping mail. Gradually the aircraft found a greater role in the offensive and defensive operations of fleet war games, and by the 1940's had come into its own as a major offensive unit.

This tactical advance was accompanied by a significant progression in technical development. Naval pilots and engineers pioneered in the refinement of aerial torpedoes, air-cooled radial engines, the all-metal airplane and catapults. They helped in the development of better instruments and radios, in perfecting folding wings and landing gear that could take the abuse of carrier landings, and in the installation of a bomb sight suitable for dive bombing. The Navy investigated all aspects of the problem of taking aviation to sea, including repairs and maintenance, urgent delivery of critical spares, operating from advanced bases, and the installation of support photographical, electronic, and weapons work shops either aboard their carriers or as an integral part of the advanced base. Aviators knew the advantage of mobility and fashioned their squadron organization into highly mobile subunits. Equipment, records, essential spares, fuel, and munitions were adapted to the mobility concept. To attract more persons to share the hazards of aviation, early in its history naval aviators persuaded Congress to authorize additional pay for flying personnel. The inducement of flight pay, plus the popularity of aviation, kept the rolls of aviation personnel filled with little difficulty during the 1920's and 1930's.

Navy Dirigibles

The newly created Bureau of Aeronautics (July 12, 1921) next looked at gas-filled airships to see if they could contribute to the growing naval air arm. Airships (or dirigibles) had made an impact during World War I, but their history of accidents created as many airship skeptics as enthusiasts. The tragic loss of the ZR-2 in England added to the suspicion with which many of the military regarded these craft. However, Admiral Moffett, an ardent dirigible fan, persisted in his campaign to add airships to American naval aviation. The early successes with the USS *Shenandoah* in 1923 appeared to justify his faith in the program. The *Shenandoah* was 680 feet long, with a diameter of 79 feet, and was powered by five 3,000-horsepower engines. She was designed to cruise at 50 knots at altitudes of 6,000 feet or more. The Navy delighted in using the *Shenandoah* to improve its public image and to promote naval aviation. Admiral Moffett installed temporary mooring masts at Fort Worth, Guantanamo, San Diego, and Tacoma, and sent his pride and joy off on spectacularly long trips. Nevertheless, when it crashed in a storm during 1925, breaking apart and falling in two sections, the *Shenandoah* lost as much prestige for the Navy as it had earlier garnered. Fourteen of her crew were killed in this mishap.

Unfortunately for the airship program, the larger ships were all more or less accident prone, and a series of disasters with the USS *Akron,* USS *Macon,* and others soon spelled the death knell of the huge dirigible. Smaller, nonrigid craft were used with some success in antisubmarine warfare during World War II, but this part of naval aviation has never lived up to expectations.

The Expanding Air Arm

In 1926, President Coolidge appointed a group of distinguished men to study the problems of naval aviation. As a result of the recommendations of this group, the Morrow Board, the Navy established a five-year plan to expand its air arm. Construction began on the first aircraft carrier designed "from the keel up" to serve as a sea-based platform for naval aircraft. This new ship, the USS *Ranger,* was commissioned in 1934. Two others of more modern design, USS *Yorktown* and USS *Enterprise,* were added to the fleet in 1937 and 1938. Growing unrest in Europe spurred the growth of naval aviation, production of aircraft was speeded up, and larger classes of students were enrolled for flight training. In 1938, the number of students at Pensacola was 605, as compared to 30 in 1933. In that same year, President Roosevelt asked Congress to authorize a 20 per cent increase in the naval building program, and was surprised when congressional leaders added a clause in the authorization bill that provided for additional naval aircraft up to a total "not less than 3,000 useful airplanes." The Bureau of Aeronautics immediately recommended enlargement of naval air stations and the construction of new ones. The flight training program was increased again, and construction of the next carrier, USS *Wasp,* was pushed ahead. The Naval Aviation Reserve Act of 1939 was passed to alleviate a shortage of pilots and to solve the problem of having to keep naval aviation cadets on active duty rather than return them to the Reserve as originally planned.

The important role of naval aviation in World War II, the Korean War, and the Viet-Nam War has already been discussed. These achievements could never have been attained had it not been for the long uphill struggle of men who pioneered in the early developments of aviation. Many of them were killed accidentally. Others went on to become the leaders of the Navy in wartime operations. It is difficult to select individuals from such a group, but the names of Bellinger, Saufley, Towers, Chambers, Moffett, and Mustin stand out among the earlier leaders, while Halsey, Mitscher, and McCain serve to represent those of World War II.

The Modern Carrier

Of the many elements required to provide a well-rounded naval air arm, the aircraft carrier is the most interesting, versatile, and glamorous. No description of naval aviation is complete without an account of air operations and the organization of one of these complex ships. At this time, the new USS *Enterprise,* a nuclear-powered giant of a ship with four and one-half acres of flight deck, is typical of the modern aircraft carrier of the late 1960's. Because of the expense of such nuclear-powered ships, the Navy plans to have only four out of fifteen attack carriers (CVA) equipped with nuclear propulsion in the 1970's. However, the means of propulsion is just one aspect of the ship, whose primary function is to serve as a mobile airfield to project naval power across the seas. The hull provides the space for living quarters and houses the equipment needed; the propulsion plant moves this great weapons system through the water. From there on, the intricate operations to fly and recover aircraft and to defend the ship are almost universal with all vessels belonging to the attack carrier class.

The major elements of any warship fall logically into two parts: the ship and the crew. With an aircraft carrier, there is a third dimension in the air group. This description will cover the crew, the ship itself, and her air group, in that order.

Her Men

The total crew of the *Enterprise,* including her air group, is a little over 4,500 men, who manage to consume about 14,000 meals a day, or 10 to 12 tons of food. They live in air-conditioned comfort in berthing spaces that would turn an old salt green with envy. Canned music, 90 TV sets, foam-rubber mattresses, individual climate control for each bunk, and a reading lamp are noteworthy luxuries. With all this, plus 100 modern aircraft and the ability to steam at high speed for almost unlimited operations, the crew of the *Enterprise* are justifiably proud of their unique ship and her capabilities.

Some of the most highly trained and carefully selected men in the Navy are assigned to operate and maintain the nuclear power plant and to command the ship. Each officer in the nuclear ship program is personally interviewed by Vice Admiral H. G. Rickover, Head of the Naval Reactors Division, Naval Ships Systems Command, and pioneer in the development of nuclear propulsion for the Navy. His assistants consult frequently with the Navy's Bureau of Naval Personnel to ensure that the same high standards apply to the enlisted men selected for such training. In 1959, Admiral Rickover testified to a congressional committee regarding these officers and men:

> I am more proud of what these young men have done than I am of what we have done with nuclear power. . . . When people of their caliber are exposed to the challenge and opportunity of our nuclear power program, the results go beyond

all expectations. Not only do we get these outstanding operating crews, but individual officers and sailors go on to do an outstanding job in other parts of the Navy as well . . . one out of six sailors who has been in the nuclear power program has already been selected for officer programs.

In support of his opinion, it is interesting to note that most of the commanding officers of nuclear surface ships have also been selected for promotion to flag rank.

The *Enterprise* has three officers of the rank of captain in her complement: the Captain (Commanding Officer); the Executive Officer; and the Flight Surgeon. This is an unusual departure from the normal Navy system, which provides only one officer of the rank of captain for each ship's complement. But in this case it is justified. The period of training before being assigned to the ship is long, and the tour of duty aboard is about twice the normal Navy tour for senior officers. In effect, the officers are "frozen" in the nuclear program, and sacrifice some other career-enhancing assignment during that period. The results so far show that this is to their advantage in the long run.

The other key officers aboard an aircraft carrier are the Operations Officer, the Air Officer, and the Chief Engineer. The duties of all but the "air boss" have been discussed in Chapter III. The Air Officer and his assisting officers and men are responsible for launching, landing, and handling aircraft. One group handles the movement and spotting of aircraft on the flight deck, another takes care of launching and recovery, a third cares for the huge hangar deck and the movement of planes up and down the elevators. Another division is responsible for receiving, stowing, and issuing aircraft fuel, and the repair gang (whose work never ends) rounds out the organization of the Air Department.

Her Capabilities

The ship itself is a mixture of superlatives and "firsts." The *Enterprise* is the largest ship in the world—1,125 feet long, about 90,000 tons' displacement fully loaded. The widest part of her flight deck is over 250 feet. Her 8 nuclear reactors furnish power to drive the ship at over 30 knots, and she can continue at high speed for 20 or more complete voyages around the world. Her flight deck is angled and equipped with 4 high-speed steam catapults, 4 elevators, and a mirror landing system. (Both the angled deck and the mirror landing system are British inventions.) But, in spite of all the superlatives, the *Enterprise* is only slightly larger than other carriers of the *Forrestal* class, and these ships can do almost anything that the *Enterprise* can. However, the conventionally powered carriers require refueling, which at times can be a most disagreeable operational necessity. For the last six decades, the naval commander at sea has been a virtual prisoner of his oil-burning power plants. In fact, several World War II battles, particularly that of Leyte Gulf, were decided by fuel shortages. In response to this customary problem, the nuclear-powered *Enterprise* demonstrated in December, 1965, that she could make the 16,000 mile passage from Norfolk, Virginia, to the South China Sea and go into action on the day of her arrival. On that day, she flew 100 missions and on the next day set a record for the number of combat sorties launched in one 24-hour period from a single carrier in any war.

These records are important and impressive, but the "Big E" still has limitations in combat operations. A fact of life for the *Enterprise,* as for any other carrier, is that she must have resupply of aviation gas and ammunition. However, since the *Enterprise* does not require large fuel oil tanks, as other ships do, these spaces can be devoted to stowage of aviation gas and ordnance, enabling her to carry much more than the normal load of these expendable commodities. She can, therefore, operate for longer periods independent of her supply train.

The engineering plant of the *Enterprise* consists of eight nuclear reactors, steam generators, and steam turbines. Her four shafts are spun by over 200,000 horsepower produced by the turbines. The reactors are located well toward the center line to avoid penetration in the event of collision. They are also heavily shielded to protect the crew from radiation, but the ship's medical staff is staffed with radiological specialists— just in case. The Radiological Control Officer and his retinue of technicians are responsible for monitoring all living and working spaces to maintain radiation control.

Her Aircraft

The "business end" of any ship is her offensive weapons. Aboard the conventional combat ship, the main battery, or largest guns, determine her classification and potential in battle. Aboard a carrier, the "main battery" is her complement of aircraft, and the efficient operation and arming of these weapon systems determines the aircraft carrier's worth. In the Battle of Midway, the confusion on the decks of the Japanese carriers that resulted from changing the ordnance loading from bombs to torpedoes left them helpless to launch fighter cover when they were attacked by U.S. Navy dive bombers.

Unless the flight and hangar decks are run smoothly, the whole pattern of launch and recovery can go to pieces quickly. A well-trained air group and ship's plane handlers can put on a demonstration of skill and split-second timing that is amazing. Following techniques developed by naval aviation through thousands of similar operations and by modern electronic control devices (including TV cameras), these crews can conduct efficient flight operations day or night.

The air group on the *Enterprise* is slightly larger than the groups on other attack aircraft carriers. Its complement of aircraft consists primarily of seven squadrons of high-performance jet aircraft. The aircraft load can be varied according to the expected mission, but normally the ship carries two fighter squadrons, light and heavy attack aircraft, and some reconnaissance and AEF (airborne-early-warning) airplanes.

The supersonic interceptors, equipped with Sidewinder or Sparrow air-to-air missiles, are tactical fighter aircraft that can intercept enemy air raids in any weather, day or night. At present, the *Enterprise* carries the McDonnell F-4 Phantom, the Douglas A-4 Skyhawk, the Grumman A-6 Intruder, the North American RA-5c Vigilante, as well as a tanker detachment, helicopters for rescue, a COD (carrier on-board delivery) aircraft for high-priority logistic flights, and a detachment of Grumman E-2A Hawkeyes for early warning. (Plane designations beginning with "A" are attack aircraft, those beginning with "F" are fighters, and those beginning with "R" are reconnaissance planes. The "E," as in E-2A, stands for "special electronics installation.")

The steam-driven catapults can launch aircraft at a speed of 160 miles per hour, in a carefully controlled acceleration that keeps the "G" forces of gravity below the damage threshold for either the pilot or the plane. It accomplishes this launch over a distance of 250 feet and does a job that would normally require from 3,000 to 6,000 feet of concrete air strip. With 4 of these "cats," the *Enterprise* can launch aircraft at the rate of 1 every 15 seconds. Her angled flight deck permits simultaneous landing and launching operations, and it is not uncommon to recover aircraft at the rate of 1 every 40 seconds.

No statistic about the *Enterprise* is more cherished by her flight deck crew than her low accident rate. It is about two-thirds that of the average attack carrier and results from efficient operations, professional skill, and a unique feature of the *Enterprise*—she does not have the usual smokestack. Rear Admiral Thomas J. Walker, commander of a carrier task force in the South China Sea, pointed this out in a speech given on September 2, 1966, saying, "We're not bothered by smoke or stack gasses—which save thousands of man hours scrubbing up the planes." He was speaking of the corrosive effect of the combination of sea air and stack gas, which often cover the plane's metal surfaces with soot and sulphur, and require frequent washings to prevent damage.

Both Admiral Walker and his predecessor, Admiral H. L. Miller, were most impressed by the mobility of the *Enterprise* and her freedom from fuel restrictions. Both officers reiterated, however, that the "flexibility and mobility" of the entire carrier task force gave the United States an unequaled advantage on the high seas. This advantage is inherent in naval aviation, and permits the American Navy to move tactical air power all around the world on the free highways of international waters.

AVIATION SUPPORT

The glamour and fascination of the huge attack carriers and their jet aircraft often obscure the important support element of fleet aviation. A highly professional organization ashore is responsible for training pilots, procuring new aircraft, developing new operational air doctrine, and operating the overhaul and repair facilities. This is not a special group that lives out its navy life ashore; on the contrary, it is composed mainly of fleet aviators, who move in a steady career pattern from sea duty to shore duty. With this rotation, the Navy ensures fresh inputs from the operating forces, and even the hottest pilots take their turn at the planning or training job. Apart from the Navy Department, in which major aviation responsibilities rest with the deputy chief of naval operations (air), and the commander, Naval Air Systems Command, there are two other major posts that direct naval aviation. These are the chief of naval air training, and the Naval Air Force commanders—one each in the Atlantic and the Pacific.

Naval Air Training

The chief of naval air training is responsible for basic and advanced flight training, technical training of men in aviation ratings, and Naval Aviation Reserve training. He accomplishes these tasks through four functional commands: chief of naval air basic training, at Pensacola, Florida; chief of naval air advanced training, at Corpus Christi, Texas; chief of naval air technical training, at Memphis, Tennessee; and chief of Naval Air Reserve training, at Glenview, Illinois.

The Navy regards a naval aviator as an all-around naval officer as well as a pilot and conscientiously keeps this in mind in training him throughout his career. The program begins at

Pensacola, where annually over 1,700 young men enter a training system that produces both pilots and aviation observers (who are not pilots but are well trained for other flying billets, such as navigator or engineer). The pilots are among the best-trained aviators in the world, skilled in precision operations that require split-second reactions. The "observers," who prefer the title "rear-seat pilot," operate the "black boxes" and other advanced equipment that are now integral parts of many of the Navy's modern aircraft.

The major portion of pilot training at Pensacola is devoted first to preflight (ground training) and next to basic flight training. At the completion of primary training, pilots choose either jets, propeller-driven aircraft, or helicopters as an area of specialization, and move on to more advanced phases of the aviation program. Although the chief of naval air advanced training is located at Corpus Christi, the home of advanced jet training, he operates other advanced programs at different Navy air fields according to specialty. The advanced course varies in length and lasts up to twenty weeks for jet training. After this phase of their education, pilots destined for carrier operations return to Pensacola to become "carrier qualified." Following another period with faster combat planes, during which they learn to operate guided missiles and other intricate electronics systems, the jet carrier pilots are ready for assignment to a Replacement Air Group. They are now replacement pilots (RP) instead of student naval aviators (SNA), and they train in the aircraft that they will fly in their fleet squadron—with the tactics, ordnance, and special electronic equipment used in fleet operations. The training details and schedule for the other pilots differ in degree, but all last about eighteen months—the length of time normally devoted to turning out a qualified naval aviator.

It requires from fifteen to twenty technicians to keep each Navy plane flying. The majority of these skilled specialists are trained at the Naval Air Technical Training centers at either Jacksonville, Florida, or Memphis, Tennessee, in one of over thirty aviation technical schools. The chief of naval air technical training operates one of the finest technical training establishments in the world and concentrates on the operation, maintenance, and utilization of the aviation equipment peculiar to the Navy. His training course features the most modern curriculums, audio-visual training aids, and advanced teaching techniques. Many civilian schools have adopted for their own use the Navy "tech training" tested on over three-quarters of a million naval aviation mechanics and technicians, whose performance in the field has more than justified their education.

About half of the Navy pilots and enlisted technicians leave the service upon completion of their military obligation. This pool of talent would quickly disappear if it were not for the Naval Air Reserve, whose program to preserve flight proficiency through weekend flying is very popular. Reserve Navy personnel can pursue their civilian careers and keep up their aviation training without hardship at a naval air station or reserve training unit. The "weekend warrior" program has been well received, and it has proved its worth over the years. Units called up for the Korean War and other emergencies have demonstrated the value of these Air Reserve squadrons. The reserve crews fly about 100 hours a year and take a two-week period of active duty training either aboard an aircraft carrier or at a naval air station. In this businesslike professional flying organization, the reservists follow a training syllabus that not only keeps up flying proficiency, but also keeps the individual informed of the latest developments and advances in naval aviation.

Fleet Aviation Commands

The air forces of Fleet Aviation are divided into Atlantic and Pacific commands, whose chiefs direct the activities of the aircraft groups, squadrons, wings. The force commanders are responsible for the organization, maintenance, and employment of fleet aviation units, the overhaul and repair of aircraft, squadron training, the support and training of aircraft carriers, and the establishment of operational doctrine for fleet aviation. They maintain close liaison with fleet operational commanders, trouble-shoot mechanical difficulties, supervise the installation of field changes to aircraft and to weapons systems, and ensure that the best thought of fleet aviation goes into new aircraft procurement and design. Their experienced staff officers develop operating schedules, rotation plans, and training exercises, monitor the overhaul and repair of aircraft carriers and tenders, and supervise flight safety programs and the distribution of the naval air forces under their cognizance.

Aircraft Procurement

The procurement of new naval aircraft is a long drawn-out process, and it represents a compromise in flight performance, weight, maneuverability, and rugged construction. The key elements of carrier based aircraft are weight and landing speed. In view of the constant trend toward larger and heavier fighters and attack aircraft, carriers had to undergo certain modifications to accommodate them. With strengthened flight decks, angled decks, and improved steam catapults, the carrier today can handle aircraft up to 75,000 pounds, fully loaded. High performance aircraft now *land* at twice the speed that old-timers routinely *flew* their aircraft. The top landing speed is around 145 knots; this requires much heavier arresting gear, particularly when some planes are landed at full throttle. For example, in the F-4 Phantom, the pilot has to go to full thrust —or throttle the moment his wheels touch the deck. The reason for this is that he might miss the arresting gear and have to take off again. If his tail hook fails to engage the arresting cable, the heavy F-4 will not get airborne again unless the pilot applies full power immediately. A second's hesitation can be fatal, with the aircraft on full burners plowing into the water just off the side of the ship.

During the late 1960's, the Navy carrier fighter aircraft will consist of the F-4 Phantom, the F-8 Crusader, and either a version of the new F-111B or some other new-generation fighter. Because some of the older aircraft carriers (Essex Class) cannot operate the newer and larger aircraft, the F-8's will have to be retained. The anticipated introduction of the F-111B, which will be substituted on less than a one-for-one basis with the F-4 that it replaces, will reduce the number of total aircraft required. The attack aircraft during this period will consist of the A-4 Skyhawk, the Grumman A-6 Intruder, and the new A-7 Corsair II, which will have twice the range of the A-4 and will be able to carry a greater payload.

The strike weapons carried by these aircraft include the Snakeye, a retarded bomb that permits low-altitude, high-speed delivery; Bullpup, an air-to-surface missile; Zuni, a high-performance aircraft rocket; and a new 20mm gun pod that fires 4,000 rounds per minute. Newer weapons are in various stages of development. This group includes new fire bombs, better retarded bombs, more effective air-to-air missile systems, and advanced aircraft rockets. Meanwhile, since the Viet-Nam War has reduced the inventory of "iron bombs," production has been recommended to replace these tried and proven conventional weapons.

The antisubmarine warfare carriers (CVS) and their air groups represent a different tactical requirement. The backbone of the CVS air group is the "old" Grumman S-2F Tracker, a high wing twin-engined propeller aircraft that carries in a single package the latest in combined search-and-attack equipment against submarines. It has a four-man crew and a complex avionics system for monitoring sonobuoys dropped into the water for submarine detection. The S-2F and the antisubmarine aircraft carrier combine to form a mobile sea-based system that competes with its land-based counterpart —the P-3 Lockheed Orion, a four-engine long-range patrol aircraft developed from the commercial Lockheed Electra. The Orion carries a ten-man crew, a complete set of avionics for submarine detection and localization, and a significant load of antisubmarine ordnance. During the late 1960's and early 1970's an advanced version of the Orion, the P-3C will constitute all of the air antisubmarine patrol forces. The sea-plane squadrons of SP-5's will be phased out of the active forces and turned over for reserve training.

In 1967, it became evident that the antisubmarine carrier was regarded by Department of Defense analysts as an expensive system and that it needed an improved aircraft to combat the enemy submarine threat. The Secretary of Defense stated, in a January, 1967, appearance before Congress, that funds had been included in the 1968 budget for contract definition of a new antisubmarine warfare carrier-based plane, called the VSX—if Navy studies indicated that it would be of sufficient value to produce it.

The "secondary battery" of the antisubmarine warfare carrier is the helicopter, which has demonstrated proven ability against submarines. The SH-3A/D Sikorsky helicopter, configured for antisubmarine warfare, is a four-man, all-weather search-and-attack craft that can dip its sonar gear into the water and hover quietly over an unsuspecting submarine. It carries a full supply of ordnance, including the latest homing antisubmarine torpedoes. This effective, close-in protective system is also carried by attack carriers, in order to provide these ships with a degree of self-protection from the submarine threat.

Today, there are about as many different designs of naval aircraft and helicopters as there are different designs of surface ships. Each is designed for some special mission requirement, such as precision bombing, interception, photographic reconnaissance, or transport. The mainstays of naval aviation, the fighter and attack aircraft, patrol aircraft, antisubmarine planes and helicopters, and troop-carrying helicopters for Marine Corps operations have been discussed.

Plans for the future Navy include aircraft of many types, in order for the United States to continue as a sea power with unquestioned ability to control the seas and the skies above them.

VI

Nuclear Propulsion and the Polaris Missile

Many naval technological achievements (such as the aircraft carrier) have been results of team effort or a gradual evolution of progress. However, some of the major, and the most spectacular, advances in ship design, propulsion, and armament have been directed by one inspired individual. The Navy will long remember John A. Dahlgren and the naval gun, John Ericsson and the ironclad, Hyman G. Rickover and nuclear propulsion, and W. F. Raborn and the Polaris submarine. Vice Admiral Rickover and Vice Admiral Raborn, the first an aloof intellectual and the other a hard-driving management specialist, combined to give the United States an unprecedented advantage in sea power, and a stunning technical lead in underwater expertise.

RICKOVER'S LEAD

Rickover's work with nuclear reactors preceded the development of the Polaris missile, and his nuclear-powered submarine suggested the ideal platform for the Navy's sea-launched missile. The marriage of the two systems into the SSBN (nuclear-powered ballistic-missile submarine) gave the United States an added strategic offensive capability that is almost invulnerable.

Even in the absence of the Polaris missile, the adaptation of nuclear power for propulsion of submarines and surface ships was a magnificent achievement in its own right. The advantages of the swift nuclear submarine over its diesel-powered counterpart are many, and for them, the U.S. Navy owes a debt of gratitude to perfectionist Rickover, who stubbornly overcame political and technical obstacles in a long struggle to bring his ideas from the drawing board to the sea.

At the beginning of 1967, the United States had in operation seventy nuclear-powered submarines and four nuclear surface ships (the aircraft carrier USS *Enterprise,* cruiser USS *Long Beach,* and destroyers USS *Bainbridge* and USS *Truxton*). Forty-one of the seventy submarines were equipped with Polaris missiles, bringing that class of vessel to its intended goal. The end of the eight-and-a-half year construction program for the FBM (fleet ballistic missile) submarine force occurred on June 21, 1966, when the USS *Will Rogers* was launched at Groton, Connecticut. The building program for the SSN (nuclear-powered submarine) attack class submarine is still continuing at the rate of four per year. However, the surface nuclear building program was halted recently by Defense authorities in a disputed action based on cost-effectiveness studies. At the time of writing, it is apparent that the Department of Defense has reconsidered to the point of planning for three more nuclear-powered aircraft carriers in the construction programs of the future. The number of other surface ships that might be included in the nuclear construction program is problematical, and depends in great part on the Navy's analytical efforts to prove their worth and effectiveness to the Department of Defense.

The primary drawback to a complete switch from oil to nuclear propulsion is the construction cost. The *Enterprise* cost $474 million dollars; a new conventional aircraft carrier can be built for $300 million. A nuclear attack submarine costs $50 million, a Polaris submarine about $150 million. The *Bainbridge,* the United States' first nuclear-powered destroyer, cost $160 million—almost three times the cost of a conventional destroyer. Although the development of longer-lived cores and more powerful nuclear propulsion plants is reducing costs, the initial expense of nuclear-powered ships is expected to remain higher than their conventional counterparts for years to come. Nevertheless, a comparison of "life-cycle costs" (the total costs of construction and operating a ship through its lifetime) between nuclear and conventional ships is another matter. This and other kinds of effectiveness comparison, which are considered important in weapon systems evaluation, will be discussed in a later chapter.

Beginnings at Oak Ridge

The U.S. Navy's nuclear force saw its beginning twenty-one years ago when Secretary of the Navy James Forrestal obtained permission to assign a group of Navy technical personnel to work at the nuclear laboratories at Oak Ridge, Tennessee. This group was led by Rickover, then a captain and a relatively unknown engineering officer specialist in the Navy's Bureau of Ships. The Navy team began work on the development of a small stationary power plant for the generation of electrical power. Although far removed from the Navy's goal of nuclear propulsion, this effort was at least a beginning. However, the Navy could not elicit much encouragement for the engineering development of a reactor suitable for submarine propulsion, which Captain Rickover recommended. (At that time, the production at Oak Ridge was almost entirely devoted to making fissionable material for nuclear bombs.)

Backed by Dr. Vannevar Bush, head of the Department of Defense Research and Development Board, the Navy's Vice Admiral Earle Mills urged the Atomic Energy Commission to establish a program for the submarine reactor. In the summer of 1948, the AEC contracted with the Westinghouse Electrical Company to develop a submarine nuclear propulsion plant and to construct a prototype ashore. This resulted in the establishment of the Bettis Laboratory outside of Pittsburgh and the construction of the National Reactor Test Station at Arco,

Idaho. These were the locations of much of the conceptual design and research that was necessary to perfect a nuclear reactor.

Opposition from Cost Analysts

Early in the program, Rickover met many technical obstacles. These he and his group solved in time, but opposition from within the Navy itself developed, and was even more frustrating and difficult. Among Navy leaders, a group of cost-conscious planners objected to the expense of a nuclear submarine and presented studies that showed that a nuclear submarine would be only 1.41 times as effective as a conventional one. Since the nuclear submarine would cost twice as much as a conventional one, they recommended against its construction. The outraged Rickover pointed out that they were really comparing two different weapons systems, not two versions of the same system. In recalling this incident before the Joint Committee on Atomic Energy in 1966, he said,

> There was a failure of imagination and judgment—a failure to comprehend that we were talking about a significantly different weapon. It should have been easier for the analysts to see this for a submarine, because at that time the maximum speed the submarine could make submerged was about 18 knots for a half hour. Most of the submarines could make only 12 knots for one hour. The nuclear submarine gave unlimited high submerged speed.

Persisting in spite of opposition, Rickover saw his efforts rewarded when the keel for the *Nautilus* was laid on June 14, 1952, in the shipyard of the Electric Boat Division of the General Dynamics Corporation at Groton, Connecticut.

The Nautilus *and Its Power Plant*

The reactor plant of the *Nautilus* required a wholly new departure from traditional engineering processes. It is similar to other steam driven ships in that the *Nautilus* is driven by steam, but the steam is made without fire and air—the prerequisites of the conventional engineering plant. On the nuclear submarine, the steam is made from heat generated by the nuclear reactor. The major part of the reactor plant consists of the reactor core itself, the pressure vessel and pressure vessel head, the heat exchangers, pumps, and turbine generators. The heat is transferred by a pressurized water system and is carried to a steam generator, where the heat of the pressurized water is exchanged to a secondary water system under less pressure. This water flashes into steam, which is then led through a steam drum to remove moisture, and the "dry" steam is fed into the blades of the turbine generators and the steam turbines, producing power to drive the ship, generate electricity, and operate auxiliary equipment. As with conventional steam-powered plants, there is a loss of water in this process, but the loss is compensated for by the production of more fresh water in the ship's evaporators.

A number of engineering and design breakthroughs were necessary to make nuclear propulsion a reality. Special metals were needed to withstand pressure; valves and fittings had to be ground to new tolerances; welds had to be unusually strong. To prevent a transfer of radioactivity, extreme precaution had to be taken to prevent leaks. Heavy lead shielding, backed by other insulating material, surrounds the reactor. This is covered by a steel shell to give an added measure of safety to the nuclear core, or power source.

One of the reasons for the great success of nuclear-powered ships is the close supervision that the Naval Reactor Branch exerts during their construction. Quality control systems are required. For example, the Navy requires the shipbuilder to install a record-keeping system of every weld that goes into a submarine, and the name of the man who made it. The shipyards have found that by using this procedure, by tracing, examining, and checking on the welders, they have been able to identify the workers who cause the most rejections. Over the years, this careful attention to detail has saved time and money, but best of all, it has instilled a kind of individual moral responsibility among shipyard workers.

The actual inspection of the thousands of pipe joints (from

7,000 to 9,000) in a nuclear submarine consists of either X-ray or ultrasonic examination of the fitting, followed by hydrostatic tests. The whole process is carried out with painstaking care. During the hydrostatic tests, water under pressure is pumped into the piping system. The pressure is increased until it matches the submarine's "test depth" (the lowest depth at which it is designed to operate) and then is increased to assure an even greater margin of safety. Several times thereafter, additional hydrostatic tests are conducted to see if there has been any metal fatigue.

The first nuclear core in the *Nautilus* cost over $4 million and steamed 62,000 miles before it had to be replaced. In testifying before the Joint Committee on Atomic Energy, Admiral Rickover revealed that great progress had been made in increasing core life. The next core of the *Nautilus,* he said,

> cost $3 million and steamed 91,000 miles. The long life cores we will be installing in our submarines cost about $3 million and will run about 400,000 miles . . . which is very important because the ships need not be in shipyards as often as in the past. When we started the nuclear program it was the custom of the Navy to overhaul submarines every 18 months. For the Polaris submarine that period has been extended to about 5 years, to coincide with the life of the nuclear cores. This means that we will get a greater usage factor out of our nuclear ships than we did previously. This is another benefit from nuclear propulsion.

As the nuclear program progressed, the men behind it found ways to make significant improvements. In addition to developing better cores for submarine reactors, they have achieved even greater results with nuclear reactors for surface ships. For example, the original reactor cores for the *Enterprise* steamed for 3 years (over 200,000 miles) before they were renewed; the second set of cores will have about 25 per cent more life, and the third set now under construction will last about 13 years. When the design of the *Enterprise* began in 1950, the Navy had not operated the *Nautilus* or her land prototype, so the planners had to extrapolate from their earlier work on the *Nautilus*. As a result the *Enterprise* was equipped with 8 reactors, each of which would develop more power than the Nautilus reactor. In 1966, the Navy had plans to build another nuclear-powered carrier with only 4 reactors; in 1967, the engineers and designers came up with plans to commit a new carrier to a 2-reactor plant. At the same time they had plans to put nuclear cores that would last 10 years into escort ships.

The more efficient, longer-lived reactor cores are also less expensive than the earlier ones. The first set of 8 cores in the *Enterprise* cost about $64 million. The first replacements ran to a total of $20 million. The newly designed 2-reactor plant for the next carrier to be constructed will be much larger and more difficult to fabricate than those of the *Enterprise,* but the total cost will be only $28 million. The net result is the same propulsion power at less than half the cost of the original power plant, and the new plant will have a life that is about 4 times as long. It has been estimated that the 2-reactor plant will produce power equivalent to 10 million barrels of oil during its lifetime. Therefore, the ship that is delivered with that plant will have a built-in supply of fuel estimated to be worth $25 million—and this estimate does not include the cost of delivering fuel oil to conventionally powered ships. (It is difficult to calculate the possible costs of fuel delivery in war-time situations. If, as combat history has shown, there is some attrition to the fleet oilers from enemy attack, the costs of delivery can increase over the base cost of the fuel by several orders of magnitude.) For any studies based on quantified values, it is difficult to imagine the value that the commander of a nuclear-powered ship would put on the freedom of movement and independence from the supply train he would have in a combat situation.

Nuclear Submarine Hull Design

The nuclear submarine has a newly designed hull that differs considerably from the hull of the conventional World War II submarine. During the immediate postwar period, inquisitive submarine officers who knew the advantage of underwater speed from first-hand experience, began investigating ways to streamline the outer hull. They eventually settled on the present teardrop shape, which is awkward on the surface but very efficient for underwater steaming. The high speeds now attainable created new problems in metal requirements and controls. The new submarine almost flies through the water, and routine turns or maneuvers occur with such rapidity that controls similar to an airplane's are needed. This speed puts unusual stresses on the metal hull, which now is made of steel alloys of greater tensile strength than was required before. Gone is the old deck gun and many other external fittings that offered resistance. So streamlined is the outer shell that even deck fittings and cleats fold flush into the hull.

The first submarine with this new shape was the *Albacore,* which has a conventional diesel plant and improved batteries. She demonstrated conclusively, by setting record after record, that unbelievable speeds beneath the surface were not only attainable, but also brought the submarine into a new era of tactical advantage. Under certain sea conditions, which slowed down surface attackers, the *Albacore* could run away from the fastest destroyer.

The *Nautilus* combined the speed of the *Albacore* with unlimited endurance. She could approach a slow convoy from astern, and could cruise along with the unsuspecting ships while she picked them off one by one. In her first fleet exercises, the *Nautilus* demonstrated conclusively that the U.S. Navy had a weapon that would revolutionize undersea warfare.

Disadvantages and Precautions

One of the few disadvantages of nuclear propulsion turned up soon after the *Nautilus* became operational. Where could it go and in what harbors might it seek haven? Were any special precautions necessary to protect the inhabitants of the seaport?

Since the nuclear reactor of a propulsion plant is designed like a furnace instead of a bomb, there is no danger of a nuclear explosion. The release of energy from the core is controlled by rods of special metal that govern the rate of fission. When the control rods are lowered into the reactor they stop the fission process; when they are raised, fission occurs and the reactor gives off heat. The ultimate fate of a reactor, under certain highly improbable conditions, would be for it to melt. It could not explode. The concern for the health and safety of the general public in areas where nuclear-powered ships operate or are constructed, centers on the amount of radioactive wastes that are discharged by the system.

Early in the history of nuclear propulsion, the Navy developed procedures to control discharges of radioactivity from nuclear-powered ships and their supporting activities. These procedures, which were reviewed and approved by the U.S. Public Health Service and the Atomic Energy Commission, contain discharge limits which are consistent with the standards set by both the United States and the International Commission on Radiological Protection. The Navy has conducted environmental surveys of harbor water and bottom sediment in the areas affected by nuclear ships to ensure that these safety procedures are still effective.

In a report published in January, 1966, the Navy released figures collected during a five-year survey of the primary U.S. harbors, and of Holy Loch, Scotland; Rota, Spain; and Apra Harbor, Guam. These figures included a measure of radioactive liquid wastes, harbor sediment, and an account of the disposal of solid low-level radioactive wastes, such as contaminated rags, paper, and scrap materials. (Solid wastes are shipped to AEC-approved burial sites.)

The report found that: (1) no increase in radioactivity above normal background levels had been detected in the harbor water; (2) there had been no increase of general background radioactivity of the environment; and (3) some low-level cobalt-60 radioactivity had been detected in bottom sediment around a few piers at operating bases and shipyards where maintenance and overhaul of Navy nuclear-powered ships had been conducted for several years. In other words, after twelve years of operating nuclear-powered ships, the U.S. Navy had controlled disposal of radioactive wastes so effectively that its presence was barely noticeable after even the most careful survey. Nonetheless, many ports around the world refuse entry to nuclear-powered ships. Generally speaking, these restrictions stem more from political considerations than from fear of contamination. In some locations, where entry of nuclear ships is forbidden, the crews of nuclear submarines are flown from a remote harbor to a restricted port for rest and recreation.

Living Conditions Aboard

The possession of a true submersible with unlimited endurance beneath the surface brought a new challenge to the Navy—the creation of a healthy environment that would permit a crew of over a hundred men to live and work in a submerged shell for weeks, even months, at a time. A problem of confinement reckoned in hours for conventional submarines brought new dimensions and different considerations in nuclear submarines. Scientists and engineers went to work in three basic areas—atmosphere control, radiation safety, and psychological factors.

Atmosphere control required installation of oxygen generators and air purification equipment capable of working around the clock. The air is monitored at several places around the submarine to determine the concentration of contaminants, and it is treated by a process that oxidizes most organic materials, filters out undesirable particles, cools the air, removes carbon dioxide, and replaces oxygen. The result is a controlled, dust-free, purified atmosphere that is considerably better than that in most cities.

Radioactive levels are checked by a medical team that records the purity of the water and the air and individual exposure to radioactivity. Each man aboard wears a film badge or dosimeter to measure the total dose of nuclear radiation absorbed over a period of time. The film badge is a simple device, consisting of a film packet similar to that used in dental X-ray work. It is worn clipped to the clothing, and it serves as an alarm by absorbing ionizing radiation, which darkens the film in much the same manner as does light. The dose is measured by comparing the unknown film density of a badge to known film density produced by similar radiation under controlled conditions.

Psychological assistance in solving the sealed-space habitability problem begins with the selection of men for submarine training. A battery of tests and interviews screens out potentially unstable applicants. The chosen find that the new submarines are designed with every modern convenience, for a reasonably normal life aboard. There is plenty of fresh water, fresh air, good food, and sufficient space to avoid overcrowding. Living and eating spaces are painted in attractive, subdued colors; there are recreational facilities, music, movies, and organized self-improvement courses. All is designed to increase the limit of the submarine's endurance and to eliminate as far as possible the frustrations of a lonely, monastic life in a sealed shell beneath the sea.

Personnel Training

Another, even more rigid, screening of personnel for nuclear submarines ensures that each man has the mental capacity to acquire the new technology. By 1967, over 15,000 officers and men had been trained for the nuclear naval force in 1 of 2 theoretical schools and in 3 practical schools. The course of instruction features 6 months' theoretical training and 6 months' practical training.

Admiral Rickover, who is as proud of his selection and training system as his technological achievements, has described his program this way:

Those selected undertake a rigorous training program that emphasizes principles and understanding of fundamentals instead of memorization. . . . Nuclear training activities make full use of the time available for training. They operate 24 hours a day, 365 days a year, except leap year. The students have formal classroom work for 8 hours a day and about four hours of homework every night. We provide study cubicles, similar to those used by graduate students at university libraries, so the students can study alone and undisturbed under adequate supervision. Instructors are available at all times, day or night.

He concluded with an expression of his belief that people are the most important ingredient of the program: "You must be your own personnel manager," he said. "Personnel is too important a matter, too vital for the organization, to delegate it to a subordinate. It is the most important function of the man in charge."

The record of success and safety compiled by the growing force of nuclear-powered ships during the past twelve years is evidence that the care and thought given to the selection and training of men has been worth the effort.

POLARIS

Among the German scientists who developed the V-2 rocket during the latter part of World War II, there was a group of young men who believed that rockets could be fired from a submerged submarine. Assisted by an enthusiastic submarine captain, these pioneers bolted mortar tubes to the deck of his U-boat and, in 1942, conducted test firings in the Baltic Sea. The captain took his submarine down to a depth of seventy-three feet and fired the experimental rockets into an adjacent target area several miles away. The report of the experiment met with little success in the German High Command, whose admirals were preoccupied with offensive submarine operations, and who needed every available submarine for war patrols in the Atlantic. The disappointed scientists gave up their submarine experiment and returned to Peenemunde to resume work on the V-2.

The idea of a sea-launched missile lay dormant until after the war, when several U.S. submarine officers revived it. They began a long drawn-out campaign to promote missilery in the U.S. Navy. By 1948, their efforts had led to the development of the 500-mile Regulus missile, which achieved moderate success. The Regulus was an unmanned aircraft fired from a launching track and catapult on the deck of a submarine on the surface. It had only a limited potential: at 600 miles per hour, it was slow; it was vulnerable; and its range was too short. Nevertheless, the Navy regarded Regulus as its primary missile until 1960.

During the winter of that year, President Eisenhower directed the National Security Council to call in a group of the best scientific and technical minds of the country to study the strategic future of the United States. Soviet developments in the missile field posed a dangerous challenge to security of the Free World. The committee, headed by Dr. James R. Killian, President of the Massachusetts Institute of Technology, after a thorough evaluation of Soviet missile progress and the capabilities of the U.S. program, recommended two parallel projects to President Eisenhower: to accelerate the development of the Air Force ICBM (intercontinental ballistic missile); and to develop a 1,500-mile IRBM (intermediate range ballistic missile), which could be launched from either land or sea.

The Special Projects Office

In November, 1955, the Secretary of Defense directed the Army and the Navy to proceed jointly in the development of the Jupiter IRBM; the Army would develop the missile, while the Navy concentrated on the launching system. The Secretary of the Navy established the Special Projects Office to direct the progress of the ship-launched weapons system, and appointed the well-known naval aviator, then Rear Admiral Raborn, to head the office. Under his direction, the Special Projects Office took on the additional task of developing a solid-propellant ballistic missile for use in submarines. Previous tests had convinced Navy leaders that the liquid-fueled missile was too dangerous to take to sea. During the first year of its existence, therefore, the Special Projects Office carried on the two parallel projects, but in 1957 the Secretary of Defense, persuaded by the Navy's imaginative plan to marry its projected Polaris missile to the newly developed and successful nuclear submarine, authorized the Navy to drop the Jupiter program. Instead, it was to pursue a concept officially announced in February, when the chief of Naval Operations issued an operational requirement for a 1,500-mile solid-propellant ballistic missile, capable of being launched from a submerged submarine, to be operational by 1965. The bold plan had great appeal. The proposed FBM submarine would have almost unlimited cruising range, subject to the endurance of the crew. It would be capable of cruising anywhere in the world's international waters, remaining submerged and hidden within range of an enemy's homeland. Its Polaris missile could be fired within minutes after receiving a command, and would not need the long countdown usually associated with liquid-fueled missiles. This mobile, hidden weapon system would increase the United States' deterrent and provide an "assured destruction capability" that would be invulnerable to enemy counterattack.

The Special Projects Office organized the Polaris Submarine Special Steering Group of contractors and military officials to determine the missile and submarine performance requirements. It was important to get this done early in the program, because of the long lead time required for the construction of the submarine. The steering group was divided into a number of committees, each charged with the development of a plan for a particular part of the over-all system: the missile; the launching system; the navigation system; the fire control system; the guidance system; and the submarine. In addition, a separate committee looked into the problems of communications. Another studied the intricacies of recruiting and training the personnel needed for the FBM system.

When the committees finished their individual tasks, they met to merge their plans into one blueprint. The finished product was a masterpiece of industrial planning. Although it contained several "controlling" elements, Admiral Raborn decided to push the whole program at one time. Costly delays would occur if he waited for assurance that one or more of the vital systems would be operational as predicted in the schedule. This decision required a managerial effort of unprecedented challenge, but the Special Projects Office met the demands with imaginative management methods that pioneered a new trend for industrial efficiency and planning.

Polaris Steering Group Duties

A brief description of the major components of the system, each one in different stages of development when the steering group convened, will give an indication of the magnitude of the job:

The Missile. Named "Polaris" after the North Star, and designated A-1 by the Navy, this two-stage ballistic missile was to be powered by solid-fuel rocket motors and guided by a self-contained inertial guidance system. With a weight of 30,000 pounds packed into a compact 28-foot shell, 4½ feet in diameter, it would be launched under water from the submarine's launching tube.

The Submarine. The first Polaris submarines (the George Washington class) would be nuclear-powered ships of 380 foot length, 33 foot beam, and a surface displacement of 5,900 tons. They would carry 16 launch tubes, each containing a Polaris missile that could be launched by an air-ejection system. Air-conditioned throughout, the submarines would have accommodations for 10 officers and 100 enlisted men. (The second-generation Ethan Allan class is about 410 feet long and displaces 6,900 tons; the third-generation Lafayette class is even larger, having a length of 425 feet and a displacement of 7,000 tons. Improvements were incorporated into each succeeding class.)

Missile Guidance. The inertial guidance system would perform two distinct tasks: it would keep the missile on course and maintain its stability; at the proper time, the guidance system would shut off the rocket motors and trigger the separation of the re-entry body from the missile.

Navigation. With a continuously changing position, the Polaris submarine would need a navigation system of greater accuracy than had ever been invented, or else it would not be able to launch its missile with any degree of precision. This need was to be met by a system of gyroscopes and accelerometers that maintained the direction of true north and related all ship movements in such a manner as to produce a continuous, accurate report of the ship's position.

Fire Control. It would be important to have a fire control system capable of firing the Polaris missiles at a rapid rate, or otherwise it might be possible for an alert enemy to calculate the missile trajectory and determine the location of the submerged submarine. The fire control system, therefore, would have to feed into the missile information concerning ship and target coordinates, and the trajectory to be flown, and it would have to prepare and fire the missiles at the rate of about one per minute.

Launching System. The first classes of Polaris submarines would be equipped with air-ejection systems, but the third generation Lafayette class would use a gas/steam generator. There would be a separate launching system for each Polaris tube, capable of propelling the missile from the tube to a position clear of the ocean's surface. There, the solid-propellant fuel would ignite instantaneously. The reliability and stability of the solid propellant would permit the crew to maintain the missiles in constant readiness for use, and its safety features would permit the technicians to have access to vital parts in order to make adjustments while at sea.

Personnel. The crew to man and operate the Polaris submarines would be treated as an important, integral part of the ship. In other words, the "personnel subsystem" would be subject to as careful planning and supervision as the most delicate piece of equipment. Since the training time for some of the guided-missile technicians and nuclear-propulsion specialists would exceed the entire construction period, these men would have to be selected and started on their training program before the keel for their ship was laid. The personnel planners recommended a departure from the Navy's age-old tradition of having one crew to a ship. In order to obtain greatest use of the Polaris force, each submarine would have two crews, each capable of operating the submarine and of firing the missiles. While one crew would have the ship on patrol, the other would be in the ship's home port, taking leave and refresher training in preparation for the patrol at sea.

In addition to the immediate problems of scheduling and monitoring the development of each of the major systems mentioned above, the Special Projects Office had to overcome governmental red tape, obtain funds, compete against programs of the other armed services, and seek the support of the Department of Defense and the Congress. Raborn enlisted the aid of some of the larger airframe and missile contractors, and brought in personnel of special talents from widely scattered posts around the world. His greatest problem was a race with the calendar while he managed a program that required attention to the smallest detail, as well as hundreds of crucial decisions. Thousands of parts had to be designed, produced, assembled, and tested. Shore support facilities had to be built, and the crew selected and trained. As a final graduation exercise in management, the Special Projects Office had to bring all of these miscellaneous elements together and send the entire system to sea.

The Raborn Management Structure

Raborn and a few key assistants designed a management structure for the necessary technical direction, planning, and administration chores that lay ahead. They pinpointed three principal phases required for their management sequence:

definition of *program objectives; program planning and im-plementation;* and *program evaluation.* For guidance in de-termining the program objectives, the Special Projects Office received broad outlines from the general operating require-ments developed by the chief of Naval Operations. With the assistance of the steering group, Raborn and his assistants ex-panded the general guidance with detailed studies to develop the over-all and individual subsystems. Subcommittees of the steering group followed up with monthly meetings to review technical aspects and progress of their assigned areas. Their recommendations were submitted to the steering group at bi-monthly meetings, and approval led to contractual action. Once an industrial contractor won a contract for a part of the Polaris program, he became intimately involved in the plan-ning and evaluation process. His work was constantly moni-tored, and reports on his progress and performance were submitted to the Special Projects Office periodically.

The progress of each critical subsystem was evaluated in the Special Projects Polaris management center, which was the heart of the management structure, and pioneered an effort in concentrated communication display and coordina-tion. In this center, crammed with an impressive display of wall charts, the Polaris leaders evaluated progress and made decisions from information furnished by the following princi-pal reports: fiscal reports on the status of funds committed, expended and remaining; program management planning, progress, and evaluation reports; and technical performance reports on the work in progress. The notable success of the over-all Polaris planning system led to the adoption of many of its planning principles and techniques by industry.

In view of this unique development (usually, industry teaches the government) it should be worth the while to ex-amine the four major Polaris management techniques in more detail: program management; progress evaluation and review technique (PERT); milestone reporting, and line of balance.

The Special Projects "Program Management Plan" was an

official expression of both top level and branch level planning, an indication of achievement against a master schedule, and a basis for decision-making. It was prepared for all major phases of planned effort, updated weekly, and displayed on the wall of the Management Center. Its key feature was the relation of a number of action milestones to key intervening programs of the total task.

The complex task of planning and controlling the entire FBM weapon system effort was accomplished through a statistical technique developed by the Special Projects Office, and today familiarly known in industry and in universities as PERT. With time as a variable, PERT provided a measure of current status against approved plans and schedules; a forecast of future progress and problem areas with the probabilities of meeting schedules; and the effects of proposed changes on established schedules. The technique is based on a flow plan or network of planned events in dependency sequence which lists events and activities and their estimated time for completion. Equations were developed for calculating the mean time and variance for each event in the network. As work progressed, elapsed time estimates were fed into a computer that stored the master plan and all equations in its memory bank. Each new input was run through the system to determine potential slippages, the longest or critical path to completion, and other time-limited paths in the flow plan. The computer calculated the probability of meeting scheduled dates, and, through simulation runs, predicted the effects of alternate courses of action that were under consideration. The PERT technique provided a rapid, two-way flow of information between the Special Projects Office and contractors or subcontractors, and also between different departments and plant management.

Before PERT was developed, the Special Projects Office relied on milestone reporting as its principal management tool for reflecting actual versus planned progress. The milestone method was continued in certain brief work efforts, small lot production of end items, and in other noncomplex areas of production. The technique is simple in that it measures actual progress against established "milestones" (selected points of achievement in meeting the over-all program objective). The contractors telephoned or wired information on milestone progress to the Office, where it was plotted against the master plan for the element under consideration.

The "line-of-balance technique" was based on the "management exception" principle; it provided a graphic portrayal of performance for each controlling element in the FBM system and was used periodically to appraise the procurement and production of end items. FBM planners found it particularly useful in pointing out shortcomings in the production plan and in highlighting the elements that required corrective action.

When the FBM project began, the goal for completion had been set for 1965, but later events conspired to keep the target date moving up. In 1957, when the Soviet "Sputnik" was placed into orbit, Admiral Raborn moved the operational date for the first Polaris submarine ahead to 1963. Later study showed that by accepting a reduced range for the Polaris missile—1,200 miles instead of 1,500—the Navy could move the operational date up to 1960. The increased range would come later in follow-on production. The Department of Defense and the Congress accepted the Navy proposal for accelerating the FBM program, appropriated speed-up funds, and gave Admiral Raborn their blessing. These estimates for acceleration were not guesses; Raborn and his planners had worked out every detail in conjunction with their major contractors, and had simulated the development of each major subsystem in their advanced management system. The computer predicted fair probability of success, and human determination made it come to pass. Where the men in the project had worked hard before, they now attacked the new schedule with inspired energy; the lights in the Special Projects Office burned late into the night and the office force worked seven days a week. Similar work schedules were put into force in the field, at contractor's plants and at the shipyards.

Construction Begins

In January, 1958, construction began on the first three FBM submarines. The first one, the USS *George Washington,* had originally been laid down as the *Scorpion.* It was too small to accommodate the Polaris missile and fire control system, so the FBM engineers decided to cut the *Scorpion* hull in two and to insert a weapon section measuring 130 feet. Calculations showed that the extra weight would not have a serious effect on the submarine's speed or maneuverability. Admiral Rickover personally took the responsibility to deliver the nuclear reactor on time. The workers at the Electric Boat Company's building yard went on three shifts, around the clock. While work proceeded on the *George Washington,* the keel was laid for the next ship of the series, the *Patrick Henry.* More submarines were being built at other yards. The *Theodore Roosevelt* was started at Mare Island, the *Robert E. Lee* at Newport News, Virginia, and the *Abraham Lincoln* at Portsmouth, New Hampshire. Altogether, five submarines began construction in 1958.

Meanwhile, the development of the Polaris missile moved ahead under forced draft. In March, 1958, a dummy Polaris missile made the first successful launching from the submerged launcher off San Clemente Island, California. The launching equipment was moored to the ocean bottom beneath a layer of steel nets directly above it on the surface. The dummy missile, which weighed about fourteen tons, was fired through a hole in the nets to a height of about fifty feet. While the missile was clear of the water, the nets were snapped back in place to cover the launching aperture and to catch the spent missile when it fell back. After weeks of frustrating delay, everything worked smoothly. This success marked the satisfactory completion of a major milestone in the plan.

The key development of the entire system, if any one of the important separate elements could be identified as the pivot on which all of the rest depended, was the solid-propellant fuel for the Polaris missile. As noted, liquid-fueled propellants had been ruled out because of their explosive hazard, size, and complicated readiness procedures. The solid propellant had much more promise—if it could acquire certain characteristics that experts considered almost impossible of attainment. These problems of making the propellant and the rocket motor were solved in time by a trio of European scientists who had emigrated to the United States after World War II. These were the Germans Karl Klager and Willie Fiedler, and Polish Werner Kirchner, who, in the test center of Aerojet General Corporation, worked together to perfect the power system for the Polaris missile.

Test Missile Firings

It was not as simple as it sounds. From September, 1958, to February, 1959, the first five test missiles fired at the Atlantic test range at Cape Canaveral (now Cape Kennedy) were failures. However, the elaborate test equipment gave sufficient indications for the scientists and engineers to develop a "fix" through better quality control of some manufactured items, and through the development of certain metals that could withstand the intense heat generated by the missile motors. Test missiles AX-6, fired in April, 1959, soared out over the Atlantic in a successful test flight.

This firing set the stage for a series of other tests at Cape Canaveral, at San Clemente, and at sea from the weapon system test ship, USS *Observation Island*. By July, 1960, the first nuclear FBM submarine, USS *George Washington*, was able to make two successful firings from a submerged position off the test facilities at Cape Canaveral. In November of that year, the *George Washington* departed from Charleston, South Carolina, for a historic first Polaris submarine patrol. She carried a load of sixteen tactical Polaris A-1, 1,200-mile missiles. When on station, the *George Washington* missiles were zeroed-in on enemy targets, ready in a hidden submerged platform that defied detection. An event that was a dream in the

1950's had become a reality in five years' concentrated effort. Other FBM submarines soon joined the *George Washington* on operational patrols, giving the United States an undeniable world advantage with this new capability in strategic warfare.

Development flight testing of the second generation Polaris A-2 missile began in November, 1960, and met with great success. The A-2 featured many advances over the A-1 missile, including an increased range of 1,500 miles, but it was soon eclipsed by the performance of the third generation missile, A-3. This missile, which was first fired successfully from a submerged submarine in October, 1963, had 60 per cent more range (2,500 nautical miles), but was essentially the same size as its predecessor. The test firing record of the A-3 is remarkable; between July, 1964, and April, 1966, there were thirty successful operational firings of the A-3 from submerged submarines.

Advantages of the FBM Weapon System

Understandably, a great many claims have been made for the FBM weapon system. The principal reasons are clear and simple. First of all, it is a sea-based system, and any enemy action to destroy it would be expended at sea and would not threaten the homeland of the United States (which is not the case with land-based missile sites). The Polaris force does not require bases in foreign countries. Operating from hidden positions at sea, the Polaris system is the least vulnerable to counterattack of all the deterrent systems in the United States' inventory. In the event of the failure of deterrence and the initiation of a general nuclear war, the force of Polaris submarines provides the United States with an assured-destruction capability for retaliation. It can be employed with precision and timing of the government's own choosing. In these days of nuclear proliferation, it has become increasingly important to have the capability of identifying the enemy that attacks. Instant retaliation against the wrong enemy could be disastrous, but certain retaliation against the culprit gives the

United States a freedom of action to permit positive identification, as well as the opportunity to ascertain that the action is correct. Finally, Polaris submarines have a freedom of movement throughout the world's great oceans. They can operate in all the seas that surround Eurasia and force any potential enemies to take very expensive and sophisticated defense measures that, at best, are only partially effective.

The operations of the Polaris missile force today are both ingenious and cost effective. The entire system is designed, supplied, and manned with trained personnel so that it can be maintained with a major portion of the force in a continuous state of effectiveness. Individual submarines are on a three-month cycle of two months' submerged deployment and one month in which they prepare for another patrol. Consequently, two-thirds of the deployed force is on submerged patrol at all times. These submarines are able to receive orders from national headquarters continuously, via low-frequency, high-powered communications networks. Repeated command and control tests have given the nation's leaders confidence in the reliability of the communication system and the viability of the entire FBM weapon system as a nuclear deterrent.

The question of the vulnerability of the Polaris force is often raised. This was recently discussed by Rear Admiral Levering Smith, USN, the present head of the Special Projects Office. The capability of the force cannot be reduced, he said,

> if it is sufficiently difficult to detect, trail, and near-simultaneously destroy the individual submarines. In order that such a submarine be difficult to detect it must remain submerged as much of the time as possible, must be designed and operated to radiate as little acoustic energy as possible, and must have the capability of operating in as large an area as possible, while remaining within range of targets. . . . In order that the submarines be difficult to destroy, they must be equipped with passive and intercept sonar having at least equal detection capability to that of hunting submarines, have adequate speed to evade them when possible, and be equipped with good de-

fensive armament for use when evasion is not possible. . . . When operated so that the opportunities for detection of one submarine by a single attack submarine or surface ship are essentially random, it will be exceedingly costly to destroy almost simultaneously a decisive force of such submarines.

Today, the initial construction program of the FBM submarines is completed. Already, some of the earlier submarines to come off the line have been overhauled, refueled, and modified to carry the A-3 missile. The force in the Pacific became operational in late 1964, when the USS *Daniel Boone* reported to the Pacific Fleet. This force now operates from the advanced anchorage site at Apra Harbor, Guam, where the FBM tender, USS *Proteus* nurses the submarines that return from patrol.

Improvements Scheduled

Efficient as it is, the FBM program is not destined to remain static. More improvements are on the way. In January, 1965, President Johnson announced his intention to authorize the development of a new missile to replace the Polaris A-3. This will be the Poseidon missile, which is described as having "double the payload of the Polaris A-3," and being "twice as accurate." The Poseidon will have a six-foot diameter, as opposed to the four-and-a-half-foot diameter of the Polaris, and will be thirty-one feet long. However, the submarines will be able to accommodate this larger weapon module with only minor modification to the missile tubes.

With this new and improved capability, the FBM submarine force will be a significant deterrent well into the 1980's. By that time, one hopes, parallel advances in human understanding may enable countries the world over to seek more peaceful ways of self-protection and coexistence.

VII

The Navy and Space

Today's U.S. Navy is deeply involved in space programs—not only the explorations of outer space but new penetrations of "inner space," the term used to describe the undersea world now being opened to exploration and exploitation. Similarities between the flashing speed and excitement, and the dangers, associated with the outer space program and the slow, invisible conquest of the murky waters of the undersea world seem few at first glance. Nevertheless, the mysterious ocean depths are almost as challenging as outer space, and promise great benefits to mankind. There are some parallels in the two programs. Perhaps no one knows this better than Commander M. Scott Carpenter, the astronaut-aquanaut who holds the unique distinction of having orbited the earth during May, 1962, in spacecraft "Aurora 7," and having lived beneath the sea during the 1965 test of Sealab II. The most significant common aspect of the man-in-space and the man-in-the-sea programs is simple maintenance of life, well-being, and the incentive of the "spacemen."

Each of these exploratory programs is a national project in which the Navy has definite responsibilities and long-term interests. Already, inventive naval authorities have found many ways to adapt the achievements of the outer space program to customary naval tasks and missions at sea. (Obviously, the design of a satellite that spends two-thirds of its space flight over water offers considerable technological potential for the sea service.) Both the outer and inner space programs may result not only in the development of revolutionary techniques and equipment, but in brand new roles for the U.S. Navy, as well.

OUTER SPACE

The Department of Defense has given the Navy specific responsibility for the development of satellite navigation and, since 1961, has depended upon the Navy for the major portion of the manned-spacecraft-recovery effort. The first is a challenging scientific project, the other a necessary, demanding, but after-the-fact search-and-recovery program. Beyond these specific responsibilities, the Navy's space interests extend to technological offshoots that affect its weapon systems, communications, surveillance, and psychophysiological research. This span of interest includes such subjects as guidance, telemetry, tracking, radiation, weather observations and predictions, instrumentation, space environment, and satellite observations of the ocean's surface.

Although plans for an "earth satellite vehicle" were being studied by the DOD as early as 1947, the United States space program did not get under way until 1958. In 1961, it was accelerated in order to maintain unquestioned U.S. prominence in the science and technology of this new arena and to meet the demands for national security inherent in the exploration and exploitation of space. Project Mercury, which put the first Americans into space, created an unusual demand for Navy support. In the early days, spacecraft recovery was a pleasant, exciting mission that provided the Navy with some of its greatest moments of peacetime pride and an association with a program that excited the imagination of the world.

Despite the fact that man is not the most efficient mechanism for space travel, there was never a doubt that he would eventually pilot a spacecraft. The ability of man to respond to the unexpected, to think, and to perform beyond the capability of a machine increased the chance of success in space flights. In justifying the man-in-space program, the National Aeronautics and Space Administration (NASA) stated that "in spite of his shortcomings, man brings to space exploration certain attributes which no one has ever succeeded in building into a machine. He brings intelligence, judgment, determination, courage and creativity. He can use all of these attributes in case of the unforeseen." Including man in the plans for space flight meant that NASA had to make provisions for an adequate supply of oxygen in the capsule and for maintenance of temperature and barometric pressure at values resembling those of the earth's environment. NASA's scientists had to investigate the problems of sustaining life throughout the strain of high gravity forces associated with launch and re-entry, as well as the weightlessness of orbital flight. They developed squeeze tubes and other sealed containers to hold the supply of food, and found ingenious ways to dispose of waste. Delicate sensors were attached to the astronaut's body to record temperature, pulse, and other indications of his well-being. Small as it was, the Mercury space capsule provided simple means for the pilot's rest, relaxation, sustenance, and safety. The weight of the man and the equipment to support him added several hundred pounds to the satellite and created innumerable problems.

One of the most vexing problems was recovery of the man after re-entry. Unlike a machine, the space pilot was not expendable. The first requisite for assured recovery was the establishment of tracking centers around the world to maintain two-way communications with the spacecraft, to record data, and to provide a continuous, accurate record of the craft's position. The Manned Space Flight Network consists of twelve land-based tracking and data acquisition stations, a central data-processing-and-computer center, and mobile tracking and telemetry ships. These units worked extremely well in all manned space flights, and enabled Space Flight Control to keep a running account of the capsule's location and the activities of the astronaut. However, at the time of re-entry, there was a communications blackout from the capsule, and an alarming period of silence followed as the spacecraft entered its fiery plunge to the ocean. This alarm and excitement has accompanied each manned space attempt from the first sub-orbital, 302-mile flight of Alan Shepard to the spectacular fourteen-day endurance flights of Gemini 6 and Gemini 7. To date, every communication blackout has been broken by the announcement of the successful recovery of the astronaut by the Navy's Manned Spacecraft Recovery Force, Task Force 140. Each time, the Navy Commander has combined scientific advances with such age-old seamanship practices as the use of a small whaleboat and the venerable block and tackle to effect the recovery.

When NASA first approached the Navy for a space recovery force back in 1960, the response was an incredulous gasp of astonishment. As soon as it became apparent that NASA meant business, naval authorities designated the commander of Cruiser Destroyer Flotilla Four at Norfolk, Virginia, as the officer-in-charge of recovery forces. Characteristically, the Navy gave him this assignment as "collateral duty," which meant that he was to remain responsible for "flotilla business" while he took on the additional task of spacecraft recovery. Several years later, as the intensity of manned space flights grew, the commander's space recovery duties became his primary job.

The requisites of the recovery force were: quick location and fast recovery of the astronauts; recovery of the spacecraft; long-range communications; and adequate medical facilities. These requirements later expanded to the provision of space and communications equipment for the news media, a capacity to fly fixed-wing search aircraft, and finally, facilities to support live television. This combination of essential and desirable requirements almost eliminated every class of Navy ship but the aircraft carrier as the prime recovery platform. Consequently, the main recovery force was built around an aircraft carrier, which was supported by destroyers, oilers, land-based patrol aircraft, and helicopters.

Spacecraft orbits have been contained between the latitudes

of approximately 35 degrees North and 35 degrees South, but so far all recoveries have been in northern latitudes, in either the Atlantic or the Pacific oceans. Simply stated, spacecraft recovery is effected by special recovery forces deployed to an expected landing area. However, the job involves a great deal more than just steaming to a designated area on the appointed day and waiting for the capsule to fall nearby. There are many possible areas to cover, and it takes time for surface ships to preposition. In addition, the forces involved spend days in port and at sea practicing with "boilerplate" models of the spacecraft. Essential tasks require placing a flotation collar around the capsule to give it stability and buoyancy, hooking on to the hoisting ring, and bringing the craft safely aboard ship. Smaller ships such as destroyers are equipped with booms of sufficient strength to withstand the load and strain associated with hoisting heavy objects bobbing around in the sea.

Once the preliminary training is over, and the day for launch approaches, the prime recovery ship, backup destroyers, and support ships take position off Cape Kennedy as a precautionary measure in the event that the spacecraft does not obtain orbit. Thereafter, they move from one contingency landing to another, until the actual day of recovery. In some cases, the recovery forces can spend as much as a month at sea on one mission, as happened to the USS *Wasp* when it was prime recovery ship for Gemini 6 and Gemini 7.

In the event of emergencies, contingency recovery areas are established. In the early days of Project Mercury, a contingency recovery capability was established around the world. The earth projection of Mercury's orbit required establishment of recovery forces capable of searching the Atlantic, Indian, and Pacific oceans, as well as the jungles of the African Congo and the wastes of the Australian "Outback." In these earlier efforts, friendly nations assisted by readying search forces to cover their areas of responsibility for each launch. For example, the Australian Air Force prepositioned patrol search planes at Perth and Townsville to cover an ocean area 700 miles from either coast. Australian Navy ships were alerted, as were land forces that might be called upon in the event of the capsule's descent onto the Australian continent. These forces were in constant communication with the Contingency Recovery Center at Pearl Harbor, which was set up by the Commander in Chief, U.S. Pacific Fleet, and was jointly manned by Navy and Air Force personnel. Some of the earlier arrangements were rather primitive. In the case of John Glenn's historic flight, the commercial teletype net between Honolulu and Canberra failed, and the Pacific Contingency Recovery Center maintained first contact with Australian forces by long-distance telephone, which had to be relayed through San Diego, California. Fortunately, none of these remote recovery forces had to be used. However, in 1966 an emergency in the Gemini 8 mission brought the spacecraft down in the Pacific, where a lone destroyer, the USS *Leonard F. Mason,* was standing by to make the pickup.

The problems of spacecraft re-entry are related to dissipation of energy. The capsule receives two kinds of energy when it is placed in orbit—the kinetic energy of motion, and the potential energy due to its altitude in the earth's gravitational field. Before the vehicle can return to earth, this energy has to be dissipated by firing retrograde rockets for deceleration below orbital speed. When the capsule begins re-entry, its predicted impact can be calculated from its speed and re-entry angle with such accuracy that the "miss distance" or error of the point of impact is a small ellipse on the earth's surface, approximately 150-by-50 miles. If recovery forces are prepositioned in the center of this area, it is a relatively simple matter to work backward to determine the exact position in flight when the retro rockets should be fired to bring the capsule down nearby. These rockets can be fired from a signal by a tracking station, by a time mechanism in the capsule, or by the astronaut himself. In some cases, the accuracy has been remarkable. In 1962, astronaut Wally Schirra almost brought his craft, Sigma 7, "down the smokestack" of the waiting carrier, USS *Kearsarge.*

In the first years of the Mercury program, the Navy's recovery requirements were less taxing than they were during the Gemini series, or will be in the Apollo series. The first flights were of much shorter duration, and there were greater time gaps in between missions. In view of the increased tempo of NASA's operations as it pursues its moon exploration project, the Navy's task will increase. Consequently, it has modified the recovery task force to use fewer ships, and has augmented the force with P3V Orion patrol aircraft. Amphibious ships (LPH) have been substituted successfully for the aircraft carrier to relieve the strain on ships of that class, which, during the fighting in Southeast Asia, have had to shoulder additional operating commitments. These changes have not reduced the Navy's capability for recovery; they merely tend to spread the work load. The Manned Spacecraft Recovery Force intends to continue its earthbound support of space flight until some other method of re-entry is found for the American space program.

While the spacecraft recovery task is essential, it gives little impetus to many of the Navy's space interests. More benefits and technological advance for naval affairs are expected from unmanned satellites that can be used for navigation, surveillance, and communication relay.

The Navy's Transit program promises to produce an all-weather navigation system with world-wide coverage. Intended for navigational use by ships and aircraft anywhere in the world, Transit will consist of four satellites placed into orbit in the exosphere (above 425 miles altitude). The satellites' memory systems will permit the reception of data from an injection station and the recovery of data by ships or aircraft for use in computing their locations. The program was initiated in 1960 with Transit I-B, whose performance indicated the feasibility of the navigational system. Since that time there has been a steady succession of Transit satellites into orbit, each representing an advance toward completion of the operational system. Notable among these was Transit III-B, which was placed into eliptical orbit (perigee 117 miles, apogee 511 miles) in February, 1961. It was the first of the series that indicated the feasibility of its memory system receiving orbital path data from a control station. Transit IV-A was the first satellite to carry a nuclear-power system into space. Traveling in a high orbit (perigee 534 miles, apogee 629 miles) Transit IV-A carries a 4½-pound SNAP generator. (SNAP is the abbreviation for "System for Nuclear Auxiliary Propulsion.") The plutonium generator fuel has a "half life" of 89.6 years and is capable of powering a space generator for some time. These earlier efforts have been followed by satellites intended for the operational network, which is expected to be ready for use in the near future. In view of the projected advantages of the Transit system, NASA has made arrangements with the Department of Defense to investigate civilian use of this essentially military navigational system.

The Commander in Chief of the U.S. Atlantic Fleet has estimated that there are approximately 20,000 surface ships at sea in the Atlantic Ocean at any one time. Since this commander has the responsibility for surveillance and knowledge of ship and aircraft operations over a great portion of this area, naval authorities are extremely interested in the use of satellites to augment the Ocean Surveillance System. Satellites equipped with television cameras, infrared, and other kinds of sensors can make invaluable meteorological and surface observations for both military and civilian purposes. In addition to assisting in determining the location of ships on the earth's surface, they can accumulate data on weather, fish migration, icebergs, beach erosion, crop predictions, nuclear explosions —and a number of other nearly unbelievable indices of the activities of nature and man.

While the Navy does not have direct responsibility for developing communication satellites, it looks to this project for vast improvement in the world-wide communications network that is so necessary for the proper operation of its widely spread forces. Satellites Echo, Telstar, and Relay have shown that certain transoceanic communications can be handled at less cost via satellite than by new submarine cables. To date the two primary technical approaches to communications by satellite involve both the passive (Echo) type, and the "active-repeater" type, which stores, amplifies, and retransmits messages.

There are almost unlimited possibilities for scientific advance in this new era of space exploration. For example, past astronomical observations have been hindered by the earth's atmosphere, which bends light rays and distorts electromagnetic radiation. Telescopes on satellite platforms above the stratosphere are discovering quantities of information about the sun's activity, cosmic radiation, and new characteristics of the stars and galaxies. This knowledge has impact for civilian use, and it can also be used in improving the performance of intercontinental ballistic missiles like Polaris. Similarly, satellite observations can be used in determining exact locations and dimensions of specific land and sea areas on earth. Improved accuracy resulting from these measurements can be an aid to navigation, and to the precision of missile trajectories. Concurrently, the study of aerospace medicine, the use of synthetic foods, and the resolution of psychological problems of space environment are expected to have considerable practical translation to nautical applications—especially in the inner space program.

INNER SPACE

The Navy's oceanography and ocean engineering programs are directly responsive to military requirements, but it is quite evident that many of the Navy's needs in this area frequently coincide with similar needs of industry, educational institutions, research foundations, and other federal agencies. This coincidence was explained by Under Secretary of the Navy Robert Baldwin in 1966:

> . . . while pursuing military objectives, the Navy has an obligation to the national interest in ocean technology . . . so many of our defense interests are identical with these other aspects of

the national interest, we will—within the restraints imposed by cost—accept the responsibility for helping develop the national technology needed for mastery of the sea. Mastery in the military, economic, social and political sense.

To date, the major progress and contributions to knowledge of the ocean's secrets and environment have been generated by the Navy's requirements for submarine and antisubmarine warfare. Impetus was added by the *Thresher* tragedy in 1963 and by the recovery of the nuclear weapon lost in deep water off the coast of Spain in 1966; each of these incidents indicated a need for a better capability to conduct recovery and salvage operations at great depths. However, the public's growing interest in the sea may soon parallel the Navy's own, especially as efforts to colonize the ocean floor progress and as man gains more knowledge of the riches that lie at the ocean bottom. A recent report of the President's Scientific Advisory Committee, "Effective Use of the Sea," dealt at length with the role of oceanography in the underwater recovery of oil and minerals, in fish farming, and the conversion of salt water to fresh. Although the Navy seeks principally to increase the operating depths of submarines, to design better weapon systems for depth, and eventually to establish weapon systems and operating bases on the ocean floor, it may well receive added benefits from its cooperation in enlarged civilian pursuit of more peaceful oceanographic programs.

Official naval interest in oceanography began with the establishment, in 1830, of the Depot of Charts and Instruments, which conducted studies in hydrography and astronomy. Matthew Fontaine Maury, whose studies of ocean currents earned world renown, was the first well-known naval oceanographer. During World War I, Thomas Edison became a consultant to the Navy and made many valuable contributions in the development of underwater equipment in the fields of submarine, antisubmarine and mine warfare. Since that time, the needs of the U.S. Navy's growing submarine fleet have spurred many research projects to provide more knowledge of bottom contours, navigation under the polar icecap, submarine photography, wave and current dynamics, and underwater acoustics and sound propagation.

In relation to the unexplored part of the seas now being investigated, the area in which former Navy oceanographic programs were carried out resembles the skin of an orange. As late as World War II, Navy submarines operated very near the surface. Now, with the installation of nuclear power for propulsion, submarines are running deeper with each generation (or class) of ship. To operate submarines more effectively, it is necessary to know more about the continental shelves, sea mounts, trenches, basins, currents, polar ice, and the general contour of the ocean bottom. Similarly, if antisubmarine warfare forces are to hunt enemy submarines in deep water, it is necessary to know more about the properties and characteristics of water at considerable depths, the use of deep sound channels, and the phenomena influencing "bottom bounce" sonar. It is quite possible that the intensified ocean research program of the late 1960's will result in the establishment of naval bases on the ocean bottom to assist in undersea surveillance and to provide logistic support to our own submarine force.

The new Navy effort was described in 1967 by Rear Admiral Odale Waters, Oceanographer of the Navy, as a "crash program." He said:

> We are pushing ahead in all directions with surveys to learn more about the characteristics and behavior of the ocean. In this program we are using every conceivable platform—ships, submarines, airplanes, buoys and, though only experimentally, satellites. . . . This includes the "Man-in-the-Sea" program and the development of a whole family of deep submersibles eventually capable of salvage and rescue as well as scientific work at any depth.

In one program called "Antisubmarine Warfare Environmental Prediction," the Navy has resorted to computer processes to collect data from survey ships, ships of the Fleet, and cooperative ships of other navies and merchant fleets to use in predicting ocean environment. This same data also provides the base for determining optimum ship routing, which predicts the most economical safe shipping route in consideration of sea state, currents, and weather.

Concurrently, in conjunction with activity in the South China Sea, the Navy is updating hydrographic charts and publications, surveying coasts and harbors, exploring rivers and deltas. Where indicated, efforts are under way to collect information in remote areas for possible future amphibious- and mine-warfare operations. These activities are interesting from a purely military point of view, but they do not have the same universal appeal as the deep submergence or man-in-the-sea programs.

By far the best-known Navy deep submersible is the bathyscaph *Trieste,* which in 1960 descended to the floor of the Pacific's Mariana Trench and touched bottom at 35,800 feet. At this depth, nearly seven miles deep, Lieutenant Don Walsh, USN, and Jacques Piccard stayed for twenty minutes, measuring temperature, radioactivity, and exploring the bottom with the *Trieste*'s searchlight. Three years later, off the coast of the United States, when the fate of the nuclear submarine *Thresher* remained a mystery, the bathyscaph *Trieste* doggedly searched the ocean floor until it found the crushed remains of the submarine. In August, 1963, *Trieste* recovered a length of copper tubing and took photographs of other pieces of the hull and some identifiable artifacts of the *Thresher.* By September of that year, the Secretary of the Navy directed that the search for the *Thresher* be terminated, saying that the location of structural parts of the submarine on the ocean floor had been "positively confirmed by the bathyscaph *Trieste.*"

Soon after, spurred by this tragedy, the Navy established the Deep Submergence Systems Project office to develop systems that can perform at great depths. Specific objectives are to procure components and equipment related to the location, identification, and rescue or recovery of submerged bodies in deep water. One of the first accomplishments of that office was the installation of a manipulator arm, an automatic maneuvering system, and a precision navigation system. With the use of sonar transponders as fixed bench marks, the *Trieste* can now determine its own location on the ocean floor with an error of less than ten feet. Another project of promise is the development of a manned, deep-submersible vehicle by the Navy Ordnance Test Station at China Lake, California. This vehicle, called the "Deep Jeep," has performed at a depth of 2,500 feet, and has completed test traverses of the submerged slopes off the island of San Clemente. Sea tests indicate that it may be used in a variety of deep-sea research programs, including geophysical surveys, investigation of sound channel phenomena, and exploration of the "deep scattering layer"—a false bottom for sonar signals caused by concentration of plankton and fish.

The loss of a nuclear weapon off the coast of Spain as a result of a midair collision pinpointed the Navy's need for capabilities in depth operation required for both military and diplomatic reasons. When that bomb sank in 2,500 feet of Mediterranean water, almost all of the existing U.S. capability for operating on ocean depths was assembled hurriedly at the scene. The vehicles included the "CURV" (cable operated unmanned recovery vehicle), the Reynolds Aluminum Company's "Aluminaut," the Woods Hole Oceanographic Institute's "Alvin," and the John Perry "Cubmobile." In the end, the unmanned CURV made the recovery that permitted the world a sigh of relief.

The Navy's shallow water oceanographic program includes the exciting Sealab series of experiments to develop a capability for man to live and work in the oceans. These began in 1963, with an experiment that required three men to live in a chamber at a pressure equivalent to 200 feet of sea water. A year later, Sealab I was anchored off the coast of Bermuda, and four Navy divers conducted experiments to survive and do useful work after prolonged immersion. By far, the most spectacular in this series, Sealab II, off La Jolla, California, in 1965 proved that a large group of men could work with harmony in the hostile environment encountered at a depth of 205 feet. Much more than a mere endurance test of men living in a pressure shell at the bottom of the sea, this project put three teams of ten men successively into underwater habitat for two weeks each (two men spent thirty days below); they not only accumulated over 10,000 man hours under water, but spent 500 hours outside the habitat in swimming and performing specified tasks.

One of the more interesting projects tested in Sealab II was the "saturation diving" concept developed by Captain George Bond, MC, USN. This concept increases tremendously the length of time that a diver can work below the surface. In conventional deep sea diving, the diver wears a "hard hat" suit, is lowered to a prescribed depth for a relatively short period of time, and is brought back to the surface under closely controlled conditions of stage decompression. For every minute the hard-hat diver spends at depth, he has an increasing penalty of decompression to pay back. For example, a deep-sea diver who spends twelve hours at 300 feet, has to spend a minium of sixty hours undergoing stage decompression.

The tissues of a diver's body absorb inert gas while he is submerged. The phenomenon of saturation diving is based on the rate at which both blood and tissues absorb excess inert gas under pressure. Over a period of time, the tissues come to be in equilibrium with the gas content of the blood and the ambient atmosphere. It is estimated that in a twenty-four hour period submerged, the diver's tissues will have absorbed 98.5 per cent of all the inert gas they are capable of absorbing. When his body is saturated, it makes no difference whether the diver stays on the bottom a day or a month before he is brought to the surface. The amount of time required for decompression remains the same. By using constant-rate-of-ascent decompression, he can be brought to the surface in approximately fifty-five hours. When he can live and operate at depth from a habitat that satisfies other requirements of life, the diver can dramatically extend the length of time that he can stay on the bottom.

By using the saturation diving concept, the Sealab aqua-nauts were able to have considerable freedom from surface control. They were able to perform a great amount of useful work under water and made excursion dives from 205 feet to depths of 266 and 300 feet without decompression. When the program was over, they showed no harmful effects after they were safely decompressed and brought to the surface. This was a tremendous step forward in man's ambition to live on the ocean floor, relatively free to explore and work under water with mobility, efficiency, and with endurance akin to what he has on dry land.

In the January, 1966, symposium, Man's Extension Into the Sea, held in Washington, D.C., Commander Scott Carpenter presented a paper on crew selection, training, and daily opera-tions. He pointed out the "tremendous expenditure of time and energy" for routine logistic operations, and made several sug-gestions for improvement in the next of the Sealab tests. Among his recommendations "before we pursue this course much further" were: development of a communication sys-tem among divers, the habitat, and the surface; a durable heated suit that is easy to put on and take off; and develop-ment of a small, light-weight piece of sonar equipment for use by divers in dark water. Commander Carpenter also made some interesting comments on the most unusual member of the Sealab crew—"Tuffy" the porpoise, who was the most popular team member. Tuffy was "a very fine and funny fel-low" and proved that he could not only function as a courier, but could readily locate two separated divers in dark water. According to Commander Carpenter, a porpoise with proper training: "provides a very effective method for locating a dis-oriented diver, and showing him the way home by means of a line trailing from his harness and attached to the lab. When Sealab III is on the bottom at 450 feet, she will be beyond the reach of surface scuba divers and the value of an animal with this training is greatly enhanced."*

Although the Navy's primary interest in this series of programs is oriented toward salvage and maintenance of bottom-mounted equipment, the authorities in charge expect the experiments to contribute much to the general knowledge of the sea. This will hasten the exploration and exploitation of the continental shelves for food, minerals, and recreation.

The rising interest in the sea is reflected in the new impetus of oceanic projects sponsored by the government, industry, and the academic community. Enactment in 1966 of P.L. 89–454, the Marine Resources and Engineering Development Act, had as its purpose to provide for a comprehensive, long-range, and coordinated national program in marine science. It outlined eight broad objectives that dealt with exploration, education, utilization, and improved performance of men in the sea. One of its provisions established, in the Executive Office of the President, a national council with the following membership: the Vice President; the Secretaries of State, Interior, the Navy, the Treasury, Commerce, and Health, Education, and Welfare; the chairman of the Atomic Energy Commission; and the director of the National Science Foundation. The council was charged to submit a report of its findings and recommendations to the President within eighteen months after the enactment of the law. In February, 1967, it completed a preliminary report outlining areas of special emphasis and describing a $462 million program for marine resources and engineering development in fiscal year 1968.

However, this legislation has not served to change the independent nature of the agencies currently having major roles in deep-water study. Senator Claiborne Pell, sponsor of "Sea Grant College" legislation, advocates consolidation of these diverse efforts rather than a piecemeal, program-by-program

* Commander Carpenter was referring to the Sealab III experiment scheduled for 1968, which is to include salvage techniques at depth, oceanographic and marine biological research, and a series of psychophysiological tests of the aquanauts.

advance. One solution proposed is the establishment of a "Wet NASA" to pull together the independent programs of ocean-ology in the same manner that NASA directs the aerospace program. Senator Pell contends that a unified program and an organization to carry it out will produce a "greater thrust" in ocean development. Meanwhile, there is considerable jockey-ing for power and position behind the scenes by the opponents of a super agency. Through all of this administrative turmoil, the Navy continues to press its programs, and remains the dominant agency in the expenditures for ocean science and technology. If the Navy's efforts serve to stimulate ocean de-velopment on a total national front and if a comprehensive, cohesive program emerges, the American inner space program could match the spectacular development and achievements of the outer space program—and, without doubt, provide greater benefits to mankind in a shorter period of time.

In the words of President Johnson, "The frontier of the deep challenges our spirit."

VIII

Grass Roots of the Navy

The earliest colonial settlements in America were beachheads on a new continent. Sea communications supported them. The first ship known to be built in the New World was constructed in 1607 near Bath, Maine. The first thriving business in the colonies along the Atlantic Seaboard was in naval stores—timbers for hulls and masts, resin and pitch for calking, turpentine and oil for paint.

During the Revolution, the American-built merchant fleet formed the backbone of the Continental seagoing forces. Just before the turn of the nineteenth century, when the new Congress of the United States authorized construction of six frigates for the Navy, local shipbuilders were able to send down the ways men-of-war that were to prove superior to similar vessels in the British and French navies. From the beginning, the American people have been builders and users of ships, and as the nation has grown and prospered, they have continued their close relation to the sea and to maritime affairs.

According to Mahan's classic studies of naval history, sea power depends on a number of factors, including naval strength, geographical location, ports and bases, a seafaring people, industrial capacity, and a government that understands the advantages of sea communications. Through the years, these elements have been present in the United States, underwriting the country's expansion and increased interest in world affairs. As naval needs expanded from the comparatively simple requirement of yards to build sailing ships and sailors to sail them, a significant partnership grew, involving the U.S. Navy in many ways with American industry and the community. These are the grass roots of naval strength—the source of ships, submarines, aircraft, and weapons, as well as the men to operate them.

Today, almost every community in the United States has someone in its population who is, or once was, connected with the naval service. The shore establishment has grown to such an extent that there is some kind of naval facility in every state. Very close ties exist between the U.S. Navy and hundreds of businesses, scientific and research laboratories, and educational institutions. To survive, its leaders recognize, the Navy must rely on the productive capacity of industry, the advances of science and technology, and the facilities of educational institutions for the basic education and preparation of naval personnel.

RELATIONS WITH INDUSTRY

In its relations with American industry, the Navy requires assistance in design, development, procurement, and production of hardware, as well as a never-ending effort to seek improvement through scientific advances. Naval procurement procedures are necessarily formalized to conform with certain restrictive legislation, but the Navy's method of handling contracts, specifications, and making payments are admitted administrative obstacles that American businessmen have, unhappily, had to learn to live with. Nevertheless, the record shows that the Navy, industry, and labor can form an effective team. Together, they have made scientific, technical, and industrial advances at first considered impossible. During World War II, the industrial might of the United States produced great quantities of ships, aircraft, and other weapons of war. This successful demonstration of the capacity for expansion and the response of industry during an emergency, created a new working relationship between military leaders and contractors reflected today in the establishment of industrial advisory groups whose specialists serve both the military and industry.

One of the major organizations of this kind is the National Security Industrial Association. When it was founded shortly after the end of World War II, Secretary of Defense James Forrestal viewed it as a channel through which industry could bring to the services its recommendations and views on such matters as contracts, production procedures, specifications, and requirements. Equally important, the NSIA could, he said, "enlist the knowledge and support of industry on mutual problems, especially those involved in scientific research and in technical, industrial, or commercial processes which would be useful." If Forrestal had lived to see the fruition of his hopes in this regard, he would have been grateful, and, as a Navy man, especially interested in certain NSIA accomplishments. As an example, he would note the Antisubmarine Warfare Advisory Committee, which NSIA formed at the request of the Navy to serve in a critical area of defense. In 1967, this committee had almost 900 members from 170 separate industrial organizations, and its members had given generously of their time and talent. During the preparation of the first committee report to the Secretary of the Navy, representatives from industry traveled over 1 million miles and used more than twenty-five man-years of time. The report was so highly considered that the Secretary of the Navy presented the committee with the Navy Certificate of Merit for its members' "outstanding contribution to the antisubmarine capability of the United States Navy."

There are many other examples of military-industrial partnerships, in the form of associations, committees, panels, steering groups, and study groups that range over a variety of interests, including aerospace, oceanography, missiles and rockets, shipbuilding, basic research, applied research, design, and engineering development. In this kind of relationship both Defense and industry groups gain valuable information, as Chief of Naval Operations Admiral McDonald emphasized in

1966 when he told the Navy League (see page 189) that "the contributions of naval operations and research and experience have always been of significant benefit to both science and industry."

The modern Navy is also turning more and more to industry for assistance in its management problems, for expertise in the use of computers, analytical studies, and cost-effectiveness comparisons. In particular, it seeks out "soft ware" firms, which have no vested interest in selling equipment and have earned a reputation for objectivity in their approach to problems. In some of the more ambitious ship and aircraft construction programs, new industry-taught techniques, the use of computer-aided design processes, and new procurement policies promise significant savings as well as superior products.

THE SCIENTIFIC COMMUNITY AND NAVAL RESEARCH

The Navy has had notable success with the scientific community in the management of naval research. This partnership grew out of the total mobilization of scientific endeavor during World War II. As soon as the war ended, the government retrenched and cut back research expenditures, but, in anticipation of this development, Navy leaders had drawn up plans to continue some kind of coordination with nonmilitary research institutions in the conduct of basic research. The Office of Naval Research was established in 1945 for the prime purpose of promoting pure investigation—an approach justified in the statement that "because of its widespread operations on, above, and within the sea and on bordering land (the Navy) must concern itself with virtually every scientific area between the poles, and from the depths of the ocean to outer space."

In creating a climate conducive to basic research, the Navy from the start wrote contracts remarkably nonrestrictive in language, giving the scientist almost complete freedom with his investigation. Through the years, there has been a distinct rapport between the Navy and the research worker, and the Office of Naval Research has sponsored work in some of the most important laboratories of the country, including the research facilities of universities and colleges, private foundations, and nonprofit organizations, as well as those of industrial concerns.

Partly as a result of its creative practices with civilian laboratories, the Navy has had unusual success with its own in-house research program. At present, there are fifteen major Navy laboratories, each promoting an impressive program of either research or engineering development. These naval laboratories have been able to attract capable scientists, whose competence has made possible a continuing research program of surprising sophistication and depth. Some of the results of this program have had a profound influence, not only in military technology, but also in the advancement of general knowledge and in civilian applications of specific discoveries as well. Radar is an example. Credit for the development of this instrument (which was highly classified in its initial stages) goes to the Navy, whose earlier experiments in radio wave propagation led to an examination of radio wave reflection from metallic objects.

The U.S. Navy was the first navy in the world to develop an operational missile that could be fired from a submarine. Navy researchers led the way in perfecting remote radio control of ships and aircraft, and conducted the experiments resulting in the system that guided the Regulus missile in flight. As early as 1923, the Navy was dabbling in radio facsimile transmission of weather maps, and later attempts to adapt this phenomenon to weapon guidance led to the basic research that produced television. Other in-house experiments have produced improved fuels and lubricants, metals of greater tensile strength, and radio homing devices—all of which have found use in civilian application.

Formerly, in-house research was conducted separately by each of the armed services, but now their over-all efforts are supervised and monitored by the Department of Defense, in what is the largest "intramural" R&D program in the government. In 1967, Dr. John Foster, Director, Defense Research and Engineering, announced that about 25 per cent of the work could be conducted in the Defense Department's own laboratories and test facilities and stated that the total Defense R&D budget for fiscal year 1967 would be about $7 billion.* The lion's share of this would go to contracts with domestic industry, universities, colleges, and nonprofit institutions.

Dr. Foster said that industrial interest focused on the two high priority challenges that dominated the program—the maintenance of "the strategic posture based on an assured destruction capability," and "the increasing tempo of a war in Southeast Asia." He predicted continued development of the Navy's Poseidon missile, the F-111B aircraft, and the Air Force Minuteman III missile, and cited the urgency of directing research toward solutions for particular problems identified with the Viet-Nam War. (Some of these problems, as he described them, had a very familiar ring: finding an enemy who uses nature for concealment; seeing enemy targets at night; hitting small targets accurately; detecting tunnels and underground caches, underground and underwater mines, and ambushes; countering mortar attacks; improving means for the defense of aircraft.)

ACADEMIC COOPERATION IN TRAINING PROGRAMS

The Navy's excellent relationships with the country's educational institutions cut across the fields of pure and applied research, business management, and computer theory and application. But they center on something else entirely: naval educational requirements and the many programs that have evolved to train young men (and women) for a complex and demanding profession. Today's Navy needs men who combine

* In an analysis of over-all federal research and development programs for 1967, Dr. V. J. Danilov, executive editor of *Industrial Research,* noted that federal R&D expenditures were leveling off, but that industry was continuing to increase its investment in industrial innovation. He estimated that total government R&D spending in 1967 would reach about $24 billion, of which $15.3 billion would be funded by the government and divided as follows: development, 62 per cent; applied research, 21 per cent; basic research, 12 per cent; and plant, 5 per cent.

engineering and technological skills with those of the political economist, military strategist, and management specialist. In this revolutionary environment, education on a greater scale than ever before is imperative. Moreover, the postwar Navy is of such unexpected size that the U.S. Naval Academy can no longer fulfill its primary mission of producing most of the young naval officers for the fleet. Currently, only about 8 per cent of each year's new naval officers are Annapolis graduates. The rest come from a number of officer programs that are maintained and supported primarily by the nation's general educational facilities, which also are filling a demand for advanced education of senior naval officers.

Some educators estimate that about one-half of what a student learns will be obsolete in another ten years. They urge adoption of the principle that the objective of schools should no longer be to teach facts and statistics, but to prepare a young man to make the best use of his own mental resources. Teaching principles and skills of enduring value that will help the student to meet changes with wisdom and reasoning is one of the aims of the Navy, which is moving away from the expression "education and training" to one of just plain "education."

Naval educators have found that it is not difficult to identify and teach the special professional skills that a young officer will need in his naval environment, but they consider this a short-range task in relation to the more basic one of providing a broad education. Although it is still considered important for an officer to have these peculiarly naval skills, many of which have evolved from age-old practices and experience, it is recognized that alone they are not enough to sustain naval leaders when they acquire greater responsibilities. Continuous technological advance will be a fundamental part of the naval officer's life during his entire career, and officers of the future must have a strong enough foundation in basic scientific and engineering principles to feel at home in the disciplines involved. These young men need to have knowledge, but equally important, they must be able to communicate their ideas accurately with others, to examine alternatives, and to make sound, logical decisions. Accordingly, naval education has subscribed to the theory that an educated man who can solve the unknown problems of the future is more needed than one who has learned certain nautical skills by rote.

The source of new officers is no different from that of their predecessors—high school graduates or college freshmen of better-than-average competence and capability for absorbing an education. Since the source material is much the same, the requirements of this "new education" have to be met by better-quality educational programs and improved teaching techniques. The accomplishment of this first objective is manifest in significant changes in curricula at the U.S. Naval Academy —and in the Reserve Officer Training Corps programs in civilian universities and colleges.

The Academy

At the Naval Academy, certain shop courses have been dropped in favor of more fundamental electives, and the grading system, which formerly emphasized memorized recitations, has been changed to one that gives more credit for an understanding of basic principles. The basic course was studied carefully in order to minimize the teaching of material of a transitory nature and to emphasize material of more lasting value. To make room for the elective courses, much of the old curricula had to be dropped. The heavy emphasis on mechanics and electrical engineering was cut from two years to one, and the language requirement was cut a similar amount, but offset by increasing the number of officers ordered to postgraduate training in the Defense Language School prior to their assignment to a billet that required a language facility.

Other changes are now being instituted at the Naval Academy. After almost a century and a half of experience with a faculty heavily weighted with professional naval officers as instructors, the trend now is toward more civilian instructors and the selection of naval officer instructors who hold advanced degrees. The installation of an academic dean helped to promote more long-range plans for improvement in the course curriculum, and his presence has encouraged more top-flight civilian professors to join the faculty. With all these changes, the Naval Academy remains one of the few institutions in the country that has as its primary mission the development of the midshipman not only intellectually but also spiritually and physically. The Navy admits that any number of schools could teach any separate element better than the Naval Academy, but it also claims, not without justification, that no one school can do a better job of all three at once. Although it remains one of the smaller sources of officers for the naval service, the Naval Academy's crop of talented young men are more highly motivated for a lifetime naval career. Since the end of World War II, the retention of Naval Academy graduates has run close to 80 per cent, as compared to the smaller 35 per cent of officers with NROTC backgrounds, and the even smaller retention records of other officer programs.

Naval ROTC

The Naval Reserve Officer Training Corps (NROTC) furnishes about 10 per cent of each year's new naval officers. The program, which has been active in its present form for over twenty years, is one of the most valued and most copied of military educational systems. Fifty-one colleges and universities participate in the NROTC, which features extremely selective candidate screening and a science-oriented college education, together with naval science courses and training cruises to prepare the candidate for duties with the fleet. In return for a tuition-and-textbook subsidy for four years, the government obtains the services of NROTC graduates for four years as regular officers on active duty. Candidates for the regular NROTC program have to obtain a qualifying score on the college aptitude test, and then must be approved by a state selection board. Each state has an annual quota, and each candidate is interviewed in a personal appearance before his state's selection board. Representatives on the board include members of the educational and business communities of the state. This arrangement not only gives the Navy candidates with a certain degree of motivation toward a naval career, but also helps the Navy to maintain close association with the local communities all over the United States. After twenty years of operations of this kind, the NROTC program is firmly established by reputation and deed and is entrenched as one of the strongest "grass root" connections the Navy has with the public.

Officer Candidate School

The Officer Candidate School at Newport, Rhode Island, is the largest source of junior officers for the Navy. This highly concentrated program of sixteen weeks' intensive study, is provided to college graduates who select the Navy for fulfillment of their obligated service. The student load of the OCS varies with annual officer requirements, and the entire "plant" is geared to this flexibility. Without as much time devoted to naval subjects as at the Naval Academy or the NROTC program, the OCS understandably does not have a correspondingly high retention of its graduates. Nevertheless, the OCS officers have demonstrated over the years that they can keep up with their brother officers from the regular programs, and after about one year with the fleet, are difficult to identify as "different" from the other officers. The OCS graduate has a shorter term of obligated service. Consequently, many young men prefer this route to ensign stripes. Moreover, their value to the country continues long after they are released from active duty. Each then spends a time in the Naval Reserve, and quite often continues this association voluntarily for many years. Special programs, such as the Aviation Officer Candidate (AOC) and the Naval Aviation Cadet (NAVCAD) programs, channel young men from college into flight training.

The Naval Reserve

The Naval Reserve, which numbers approximately three-quarters of a million today had its beginning in the naval militia of several states. In 1887, a bill was introduced in Congress to establish a naval reserve officially, and while it was not enacted into legislation, it gave impetus to the establishment of more units of naval militia. When the War with Spain showed an urgent need for a trained reserve force under federal control, various attempts were made to obtain an authorization for a naval reserve force. Finally, in 1916, the President approved a bill authorizing the establishment of a force that would be composed of former naval officers plus civilian volunteers. The original force was altered in succeeding years by legislation, notably in 1925, 1938, and 1955. After World War II demobilization, when great numbers of trained men returned to civilian life, the Naval Reserve had a wealth of talent, blooded in actual combat. The Navy Department ordered some of its finest officers to Washington to determine the best ways to keep this pool of talent available in the event of future emergencies. As a result of their careful planning, the Naval Reserve has survived many peaceful years without a scandal, frustration, or adverse publicity, and has responded quickly when needed.

Since the end of World War II, naval reservists have been recalled to active duty on two occasions: during the Korean War and the Berlin crisis of 1961–62. In each of these emergencies, they met the challenge promptly, and fulfilled their mission of "meeting the needs of an expanding Navy in times of national emergency." The Naval Reserve goes deep into the grass roots of the United States. Citizen sailors, in either active or passive roles, are important supporters of the Navy, as well as valued counselors. Officially, the Naval Reserve is composed of four categories: Ready Reserve; Standby Reserve, active status; Standby Reserve, inactive status; and Retired Reserve. The category and status determines when each individual reservist is liable for active naval service. All can be called either in time of war or a national emergency declared by the Congress. Additionally, the Ready Reserve is liable for active service in time of a national emergency proclaimed by the President.

The Reserve organization is further divided into Surface, Submarine, Special, and Air programs. The pay units of the Air Program are divided into air wing staffs, squadrons, auxiliary ground units, and auxiliary air units. The pay units of the other programs are known as brigades, battalions, or divisions. During 1967 and 1968, an estimated 125,000 naval reservists participated in pay programs. All nonpay units of the Naval Reserve are called companies or platoons; as the term suggests, these reservists are not paid, but they do obtain retirement credits for participation in the program. In 1958, the Navy adopted, in addition to the four official categories described above, the overlapping Selected Reserve, which provides a capability for immediate expansion of the active forces in the event of an emergency. These reserve forces were given ships and planes, to which their members were ordered, and these operating ships and aircraft are maintained in a ready status by skeleton crews of regular navy personnel. In frequent drill sessions, the reservists who have "orders" to the unit put on their uniforms and report for sea duty, and their commanding officer takes the ship or aircraft out for actual operations.

The Selected Reserve forces are divided into two categories —A and B. The former are the "minutemen" of the Navy and are called the "D-Day augmentation force." These reservists carry mobilization orders effective automatically in the event of an attack on the United States or of full mobilization. Category B "phased augmentation forces" are assigned to units that can be put into active service in a very short time. These personnel are especially selected for designated tasks but do not carry special orders to individual units as do their compatriots in category A. Some are destined to activate ships of the "mothball fleet" in an emergency, while others will report to active-duty units to bring the peacetime allowance up to the war complement.

Regardless of the status or category of the individual reservist, the Navy maintains his file in an automated data bank and often relies on him for advice and information. The skills and wisdom represented in this group of veteran Navy men is enormous, and their patriotic support is valued highly. Reservists of significant stature often serve on naval committees without pay, or report for short periods of active duty to solve a problem that is pertinent to their own expertise. Although the Naval Reserve exists primarily to meet national emergencies, its peacetime contributions are invaluable.

THE NAVY LEAGUE

Many organizations in civilian life have a special interest in the Navy and the sea. The largest of these is the Navy League, an organization founded in 1902, which has steadily but quietly supported the Navy. It is a grass-roots pressure group. The foundation of the Navy League in the United States followed closely the establishment of similar leagues in the lands of the leading naval powers of Europe. The British Navy League led in 1894, and others followed in rapid succession: Italy, 1897; Germany, 1898; France, 1899; Portugal, 1900; Spain, 1901. U.S. Naval Attachés in those countries observed the formation and activities of the leagues with interest and made regular intelligence reports back to Washington. Their reports may have incited naval authorities to give their full support to the Navy League in the United States, but there is no evidence to show that official sanction was the direct cause of its establishment. The American Navy League was born at a meeting of navy veterans of the Spanish-American War in New York City. The birth was not a momentous event; it was scarcely mentioned in the press. But in Navy circles it was hailed as significant. Here, thought naval authorities, was an organization that would unify support for the Navy and make both the public and the Congress aware of the need for a balanced fleet. President Theodore Roosevelt gave the new league his wholehearted support.

The new organization acquired only 166 members in its first year, and its lecturers met little response from an apathetic public. However, membership gradually increased. By 1907, the Navy League was strong enough to lend support to President Roosevelt's bill for naval officer promotion. In this effort, it met opposition from senior naval officers who wished to preserve their rights to promotion as a reward for faithful service, and who resented the idea of promotion by selection. League members voted to petition their congressmen in behalf of the legislation, but their efforts were lost in the face of determined resistance. In 1909, however, under the leadership of Horace Porter, who had represented the United States at the Second Hague Conference and had returned convinced that Europe was heading toward war, the Navy League became the spokesman for preparedness. League members printed pamphlets on the naval program, as well as charts comparing the naval strengths of major powers, and mailed them to prominent individuals throughout the country. League membership soon increased and boasted such distinguished new members as former President Theodore Roosevelt, six former secretaries of the Navy, men who had served in Congress, and many prominent bankers and industrialists. The determined efforts of this era undoubtedly saved the Navy from reduction and promoted congressional support for United States' naval preparedness.

Through the 1920's and early 1930's, the Navy League operated on a meager budget, and its successes on Capitol Hill were more often a reflection of the excitement of the times rather than the result of a determined propaganda campaign. When the American public faced a situation that threatened the security of the United States, that threat inevitably awakened the public interest and caused enactment of remedial legislation. The primary service of the Navy League between World Wars I and II was to serve as a link between the "Navy and the people." In this capacity, it rendered valuable service to the civilian officials of the Navy Department and officers in uniform, neither of whom could promote their policies openly. In time, these officials learned to value the League's ability to tell the Navy story and to print pamphlets and brochures for distribution to legislators. Quite often, the legislators themselves came to depend on the League to supply them with verbal ammunition. One reason why the League has met with reasonable success, and has survived for over sixty years, is that it has steadfastly refrained from attempts to make naval policy. Even when members have occasionally disagreed with Navy policy, they have disseminated information capably. For this loyalty and faithful service, the Navy has consistently defended the Navy League against all detractors.

At a hearing in 1949, veteran Congressman Carl Vinson of Georgia said to the Navy League's president, "You have done a splendid service to your country in advocating that the nation always maintain and keep a strong navy. You aided me in this committee [the House Armed Services Committee] when we were the Naval Affairs Committee during the fight back in 1938 and 1939 when we were trying to build up the Navy." Today, the Navy League continues to preach the doctrine of preparedness, supporting naval strength as one of the best means for preserving international law and order, and aiding naval authorities in their efforts to keep a modern force that reflects the advances of improved technology.

THE NAVY'S IMAGE

Career navy officers and senior petty officers often enter into organized community activities. Navy men join Rotary and other service clubs, chambers of commerce. They assist with the Boy Scouts and participate in local school and church activities. These voluntary acts of individuals reflect to the general credit of the Navy, and help to cement good relations between the Navy and the people of the community. These are invaluable grass-roots connections that produce a two-way flow of good will and understanding.

One of the greatest morale problems that naval authorities face is the welfare and comfort of families while the head of the family is away on extended deployment. Inevitably, there are domestic emergencies, illnesses, or accidents. Some create an urgent need for the return of the serviceman on emergency leave, others can be handled by good neighbors or by organizations such as the Red Cross. It has been found that by bringing representatives of the community into contact with the dependents of servicemen before a large-scale deployment of naval forces, many problems can be avoided. For example, in the cities of San Diego and Long Beach, California, the Navy and community organizations have arranged "dependents' briefings" to spread the word among Navy families of all the services available to them while husbands and fathers are away. These meetings have been highly successful, and have led to a marked reduction of emergency leave cases and improved morale of families, as well as of the men themselves while they are away from home.

The Navy image is the net result of all grass-roots connections, and it is important for many reasons, not the least of which is the willingness of the American people to permit their youth to serve voluntarily in the Navy. The advantages of a volunteer force have been proven over the years, not only in the quality of personnel originally recruited, but also in their retention after their first enlistment. For each serviceman who decides to make the Navy a career, the taxpayers of the country save a considerable amount in government funds that would otherwise be channeled toward training the young man's relief. Particularly in this age of rapid technological advance, the training of men to operate nuclear power plants, guided missile systems, high performance aircraft, and electronic "black boxes" is expensive. In all of its relations with the public—with industry, research organizations, educational institutions, the press, the community, and the church—the Navy stresses the value of mutual support. In the Polaris era, as in the sailing ship days, the naval service depends upon the American people as sources of strength and knowledge, while the people depend upon the Navy for joint action with the other armed services to defend the country and to promote national interests.

IX

The Navy and Congress

With a few exceptions, Congress has traditionally maintained an active interest in the Navy, generally reflecting the policies of each Presidential Administration in naval matters. There have been times when the mood of Congress has caused an alarming naval decline, as in the post–Civil War period, or during the Harding, Coolidge, and Hoover administrations. But conversely, when spurred by an effective Secretary of the Navy, such as Benjamin Tracy in the 1890's, or by Presidential naval enthusiasts Theodore and, later, Franklin Roosevelt, Congress has supported an inspired naval expansion and modernization program.

The broad basis for Congressional responsibility over military affairs is laid down in Article 1, Section 8 of the Constitution. Most significant are the powers to "lay and collect Taxes," to meet defense and other expenditures; to declare war; to "raise and support Armies," and "provide and maintain a Navy;" and "To make Rules for the Government and Regulation of the land and naval Forces."

The distinct difference between "raising" an Army and "maintaining" a Navy has been argued by Army and Navy protagonists to little avail, but naval personnel choose to interpret more permanency in the term "maintain," and point out the fears that the Founding Fathers had of a large standing army. In this age, neither an army nor a navy can be created overnight, but at the close of the eighteenth century, most of the men of America could make the transition from civilian to soldier with ease. The percentage of the male population that was familiar with firearms and outdoor life was much greater than it is now. At the same time, landsmen knew little about the Navy and felt that there was a certain mystery about ships once they disappeared beyond the horizon. They also knew that ship construction was tediously slow and that ships needed care and upkeep for preservation.

Under these circumstances, it is apparent that the first congressmen, many of whom were army veterans, believed that an army, augmented by state militia, could meet an emergency quickly, but that a navy had to be maintained. This fact, together with fresh and bitter memories of British occupation and the forced quartering of troops, led early legislators to adopt a cautious, conservative policy toward the U.S. Army. Although Congress was usually fairly provident in the authorization of funds for the U.S. Navy, through the years it did manage always to appropriate sufficient money to keep a fleet "in being." (Eventually, this led to the soldiers' complaint: "The Marines get the glory, the Navy gets the money, and the Army does the work.")

LEGISLATIVE POWERS

Although the executive power is vested in the President, and Article II, Section 2 of the Constitution provides that he shall be the Commander-in-Chief of the Army and Navy, the vague nature of the boundary between "legislative" and "executive" permits Congress to roam widely in legislating on naval affairs. Thus, it influences the size of the fleets and shore establishment and determines many aspects of Navy Personnel structures. For example, under Section 412 of Public Law 86–149, the armed services must obtain approval of Congress to procure new ships, aircraft, missiles, and research and development funds. Congress also controls and approves the acquisition and disposal of all land for the services, and authorizes all military construction.

Similarly, the Congress determines the nature and composition of the Navy's personnel structure primarily through Title 10 U.S. Code and the Officer Grade Limitation Act. These acts establish rules for promotion, retirement, appointment, and selection of officers, and prescribe officer percentages by rank. The Senate approves all appointments of officers and uses this authority to control the number of flag officers that the Navy may have. As a means to prevent a top-heavy military structure, the Senate Armed Services Committee established in 1955 a ceiling on the total number of flag and general officers permitted in all of the armed forces combined, and set the limits for each service at that time.*

APPROPRIATIONS

It should be kept in mind that the power to appropriate funds carries with it enormous control over naval affairs. By withholding or granting funds, the Congress can influence the composition of the Navy and much of its activity almost as much as it can by direct, substantive legislation. It has used this means to encourage the Department of Defense to increase the number of nuclear-propelled ships in the surface and submarine fleets. By the same method, to some degree, and also by direct legislation, the Congress controls the size and activities of the Naval Reserve, as well as the equipment and facilities in the reserve program.

SUPERVISORY AND INVESTIGATIVE AUTHORITY

As a corollary to its legislative authority, Congress also had a vaguely defined and very extensive power to supervise and investigate the conduct of the executive agencies, either in connection with proposed legislation, or to ascertain the manner in which existing legislation is being carried out. Sometimes this method is used to determine whether addi-

---

* On October 21, 1967, Congress passed legislation to give women officers in the service the same promotion and retirement opportunity as male officers. For the first time in the history of U.S. armed forces, women have the opportunity to become flag or general officers, and the right to permanent promotion to the rank of colonel or captain.

tional legislation may be needed. Investigations may be conducted by the policy-making and appropriations committees and subcommittees or by the House and Senate Government Operations committees, which have wide-ranging responsibilities for oversight of managerial functions. On some occasions, special or select committees are appointed to conduct specific investigations. Some examples of investigations conducted in 1967 are: the investigation of the M-16 rifle by the House Armed Services Committee, and the Senate Preparedness Investigating Subcommittee inquiries into military pilot shortages, and the conduct of the air war in Viet-Nam. These latter investigations, conducted in August, 1967, revealed the sharp differences of opinion between military leaders and the executive branch of the government with regard to the prosecution of the war in Viet-Nam.

RESPONSIBILITY TO CONSTITUENTS

Finally, the influence of day-to-day individual member contacts should not be discounted. Much of this stems from the individual congressman's responsibility to his constituents, which is an extremely important aspect of his ability to stay in office through periodic elections. In this regard, there is a significant difference between a senator, who is elected for six years, and a member of the House of Representatives, who is elected for two years, and is therefore, constantly running for re-election. But all congressmen have a daily work load of cases to take up with either the Department of Defense or one of the individual services. These may range from establishment or closure of a facility in their state, to an appointment to the Naval Academy, to assisting a serviceman in obtaining emergency leave.

The armed services cooperate with members of Congress to the best of their ability on these requests, and have established special offices for maintaining such liaison. It is in this area that motivation for cooperation is more or less on a *quid pro quo* basis. There are unwritten ground rules to cover the actions of both sides. Generally speaking, the armed services "take the heat off" the congressmen in personnel issues, bending the rules slightly in special circumstances. At the same time, there are limits neither side wishes to exceed. There are mutual advantages in this relationship, and one of the unwritten rules that has evolved over time is that a congressman never fails to remember a favor. Sometimes a service's insignificant act of cooperation to help a member of Congress can pay big dividends in a larger issue. However, a failure or oversight can boomerang on the unlucky department.

The work load in this area is terrific. Since servicemen often "write their Congressman" about their personal problems and even military concerns, the work increases as the services are enlarged. The Navy's Office of Legislative Affairs (whose organization will be discussed in detail later) recorded a total of 75,000 written and telephonic requests from the Congress in 1966—almost double the number of inquiries received in 1962. About 70 per cent of these were related to personal requests from individuals in uniform. In addition, the routine work with Congress is increasing. During 1966, there were 922 legislative actions concerning naval affairs, which required 222 committee hearings and 84 investigations on Navy matters.

CHANGES SINCE WORLD WAR II

The present relationship between Congress and the Navy is considerably different from that which existed before World War II. Since then, there have been radical changes in the organization of both Congress and the executive branch affecting the conduct of Navy-Congress relations. On the congressional side, authority and influence are exerted primarily through the committee system. Prior to the post–World War II period, the Navy, as one of the Cabinet departments, appeared on legislative matters before the Naval Affairs committees of the two houses—or before such other committees as might have jurisdiction in limited instances over matters of concern to the Navy—and on appropriations before the Naval Affairs subcommittees of the House and Senate Appropriations committees. The Navy's budget, of course, was transmitted to Congress via the Bureau of the Budget and the President, and, in legislative matters, the Navy's position had to be cleared with the President in accordance with generally established procedures. But the relationship between the Navy and the major congressional instrumentalities was close and direct. On the whole, the Navy fared well under this system, particularly in its relations with the House Naval Affairs Committee under the chairmanship of Representative Carl Vinson in the 1930's and early 1940's.

In the Legislative Reorganization Act of 1946, the Naval Affairs committees in both House and Senate were merged into Armed Services committees having jurisdiction over all the services. Subsequently, the naval affairs appropriations subcommittees were similarly merged into armed services or defense subcommittees.

On the executive side, even more significant changes were initiated by the National Security Act of 1947, which set up the Department of Defense, with the Navy, Army, and Air Force given departmental status, but only the Secretary of Defense having Cabinet rank. Gradually, both in matters of appropriations, and in legislative and other congressional relationships, official, direct access to Congress by the Navy itself was curtailed or closed off altogether. As a first step, the Secretary of Defense ordered that legislation requests be controlled by the Department of Defense. Later, the Secretary agreed to assign to one of the military departments primary cognizance and the responsibility for coordination of over-all effort to see certain legislation through the Congress. The "action department" had to coordinate proposed legislation with each of the other services and the Bureau of the Budget before it was to be introduced on the Hill. Then, in 1954, to promote smoother relations in congressional matters, the Secretary of Defense directed each of the military departments to establish a legislative affairs and liaison office under the immediate direction of each departmental secretary.

After first assigning this responsibility to its judge advocate general, the Navy in 1956 established a separate Office of Legislative Liaison—now called the Office of Legislative Affairs. The general function and responsibility of this office is to advise and assist the Secretary of the Navy and all other principal civilian and military officials of the department on legislative affairs and congressional relations.

Navy Office of Legislative Affairs

The Navy Office of Legislative Affairs (OLA) has a staff of twenty-eight military and thirty-four civilian personnel; it operates on an annual budget (including pay and allowances) of $225,000. With the exception of appropriations which are handled by the Navy comptroller, OLA coordinates and processes Department of the Navy actions and response to proposed legislation, executive orders, and Presidential proclamations that are either sponsored by or officially referred to the Navy. Likewise, it handles Navy participation in congressional investigations and supervises the presentation of statements, testimony, briefings, and reports to members and committees of Congress. OLA also provides members and committees of Congress with information concerning the actions, plans, and programs of the Navy that affect the congressman's home state, Naval District, or his committee business. In order to keep abreast of Capitol Hill concerns, members of OLA (usually WAVES in civilian clothes) monitor the proceedings on the floor of both the Senate and House of Representatives, as well as the more important committee hearings. At the close of working hours, the monitors evaluate their observations and prepare a short memorandum of the day's proceedings for dissemination to appropriate Navy and Department of Defense officials.

The Navy handles an average of about fifty-five to sixty official trips for congressmen each year. These are first cleared and approved by the Department of Defense. The war in Viet-Nam tended to increase the amount and length of congressional travel, and consequently caused more of the OLA personnel (assigned as trip liaison officers) to be absent from their desks. Through hard experience, the Navy has found that it pays to select very carefully the liaison officer for a congressional trip. Officers who are familiar with the intricate workings on the Hill are much more suitable and effective in this role than the general run-of-the-mill officer who would prefer to ignore Congress and handle his routine Navy business in isolation. Through studied care and feeding of congressional members and their staffs for the past eleven years, the Navy OLA has maintained excellent relations with the Congress, and has earned a reputation for effective liaison.

All of the armed services, including the Navy, naturally chafe at times under the restrictions imposed on their conduct of congressional relations, and resort to diverse and sometimes ingenious ways of establishing informal means of access and influence. Somewhat paradoxically, high-ranking naval officers are probably more closely involved today in mending congressional and political fences than they were in pre–World War II days. Then they tended, except for regular appropriations and occasional other special hearings, to let civilian leaders carry the ball. A combination of postwar developments has forced the services and their uniformed as well as civilian leaders to give more and more attention to the cultivation of congressional and public support.

Interservice Rivalries

The changes already noted in executive and congressional organization in defense matters were themselves factors in these developments. The existence of the Department of Defense as an intermediary between the Navy and the Bureau of the Budget, the President, and the Congress, and the merging of specialized (and often more easily persuaded) naval affairs legislative committees and appropriations subcommittees into service-wide committees and subcommittees added many complications to the Navy's congressional relations task. But even more basic were some of the forces that helped to produce these organizational changes. The evolution of air power and the Air Force as an independent service, nuclear warfare, the growing complexity and cost of all elements of war and defense, and postwar trimming of defense expenditures intensified interservice rivalries and differences of viewpoint.

As early as June, 1944, Secretary of the Navy Forrestal foresaw the post–World War II situation and warned Navy leaders:

> The Navy must not be permitted to relapse into one of its periods of neglect. That means that the people must realize that it is an instrument of national policy, an instrument usable and to be used for the purpose of peace rather than war. If that point of view is to obtain and return currency, you will have to do your part in the creation and retention of public confidence in the Navy.

He predicted that postwar economic problems would weaken the Navy to a dangerous point, and he foresaw the coming internecine struggle with the Air Force. A year later, in June, 1945, Forrestal told the midshipmen of the graduating class at the Naval Academy to speak out about the Navy and the "need for its continuance" and warned that "it must have the support of Congress and the people" in order to survive. The accuracy of his prophecies is a matter of historical record.

In the interval between World War II and Korea, the Congress repeatedly voted for smaller military budgets, and the competition between the armed services for funds became more intense. During those lean years, the Navy depended on a few key congressmen in the Armed Services committees to keep the fleets operating. These were the forces that responded quickly and efficiently to emergencies below the threshold of nuclear war. As the executive branch and members of the House and Senate were confronted with situation after situation in which strategic bombing was not appropriate for the military response required, they became more and more attracted to the Navy's arguments for its all-purpose forces.

In the late 1960's, the Navy enjoyed a return to favor. The

experience of the wars in Viet-Nam and Korea, as well as the results of several Cold War crises of less intensity, had vindicated many naval policies. In the interim, dedicated naval supporters in Congress had given Navy leaders the funds and an opportunity to build nuclear-powered ships, Polaris submarines, jet aircraft, guided missiles, and new forces for antisubmarine warfare. This great period of technological advance in the Navy did not just happen. It was the result of a free exchange of information between the Navy and Capitol Hill, and a concentrated effort on the part of the Navy to take an active part in the political process at the seat of the government.

For example, in the post–Korean War period the Navy was almost overwhelmed with support for strike warfare and strategic Polaris forces to the detriment of other important programs. This enthusiasm required delicate handling and continual liaison with important members of the Congress. To avoid "management by crisis" and to seek approval for plans of more enduring value, the Navy had to employ all means at its disposal to convince people in positions of high legislative and executive responsibility that all-purpose forces produced more general strength. This informational campaign employed all of the "grass-roots" connections described in the preceding chapter, as well as some new organizations.

Admiral Burke's Congressional Club

One of the more interesting, unofficial mechanisms that proved very effective in furthering the Navy's views in Congress was instituted by Admiral Arleigh Burke when he was chief of Naval Operations. When the Admiral encountered a senator or representative who clung to obsolete views of warfare, or who was obviously opposed to the Navy without real justification, he marked the legislator for "enlightenment." He would seek out from among his naval officers on duty in Washington, one who came from the home district (home town if possible) of the legislator in question. This officer (preferably young, alert, and clean-cut) was interviewed by

Admiral Burke and enlisted in the cause. His target was the reluctant congressman; his objective, to bring him around to the Navy's views—or, at least, to dilute his opposition to the Navy. The officer would make contact with the congressman through a letter of reference from an important constituent back home and would maintain that contact throughout his tour in Washington. If the congressman was busy when the Navy representative made routine calls at his office, then the officer would chat with members of the legislator's staff. More often than not, the campaign would win the congressman over, and he would find himself taking a "field trip" on board an aircraft carrier or on a nuclear submarine. Generally, one or two demonstrations of the Navy in action at sea would persuade him to a more favorable view of naval budget requests. Burke felt that this unofficial "club" was one of his most important avenues to Capitol Hill; he kept meticulous records of his officer representatives, their calls, and progress reports.

Freshman Briefings

Another Navy technique for "promoting Navy" in the legislative branch that still exists is called the "freshman briefings." Every two years, the influx of new congressmen to Washington for the convening of the legislative body in early January makes the month of December a busy time for the naval officials selected to participate in the freshman briefings. The Navy goes "first class" in these preparations for briefing the new members of Capitol Hill; the agenda for the event is studied by the highest naval officials, and the staff members to participate in the discussions are carefully selected and rehearsed. The briefers are given copies of the biography of each congressman who accepts the invitation of the Secretary of the Navy to meet with him in the Pentagon, and they study the biographies as assiduously as the subject matter they will discuss. From year to year, the method varies. Sometimes, the congressmen are treated with a series of fast-changing, Madison Avenue viewgraph presentations. On other occasions, they participate in panel discussions that are purposely low key. Throughout, the theme of naval policies, naval strengths, and problems of the moment are given a thorough airing, and the series of briefings has proved to be a very effective means for promoting acquaintance, good will, and a mutually valuable exchange of ideas.

TASK FORCES ON THE HILL

Sometimes at the Defense level, and often at the Navy level, special groups of naval officers and civilian officials are formed into task forces to facilitate enactment of important legislation. During the 1950's, the task force system was at its peak in the Pentagon, and those who participated in it were responsible for the successful enactment of important legislation pertaining to pay, Medicare, retirement benefits, promotion, and the Reserve. Since that time, as noted, various offices have been established by the services to replace the temporary task forces with a more permanent staff. However, some of the task force techniques have survived and are used today, and such a legislative liaison assignment in Washington is considered to be both a blessing and a disaster. The naval officer assigned as action officer for promoting legislation works with, or is seen by, some of the most important officials in the Navy. This kind of visibility is considered to be career enhancing. However, the task force member usually works seven days a week, often late into the night, for the duration of the project. Particularly during the hearings by congressional committees, when inquiries by the committee members require research and staff work, he and his associates often work through the night to produce a prompt, accurate reply.

Perhaps the most used task-force or action-officer technique is the backup book. This "book" usually consists of a set of portable locked files suitable for handling classified matter, and crammed with position papers prepared by experts on a wide variety of subjects that might range from the number of Negro officer instructors at the Naval Academy to the latest development of an acoustic homing torpedo. The backup books are used by the Secretary of the Navy, the chief of Naval Operations, and other high officials when they testify before Congress. Although this file is no substitute for brains, it can, in the hands of the alert officer who sits directly behind the witness, be a wonderful source of information when the witness requests a moment to "refresh his memory." Some naval officers who have been unusually adept with the preparation and handling of backup book matters, have been rewarded with promotion for their expertise and dexterity.

The requirements for Navy witnesses before congressional committees vary throughout the session. Some are annual routine appearances in behalf of the budget requests. Other meetings are in support of specific legislation. Since the Congress is the source of all Defense funds and governing legislation, many career officers find it worth while to study the processes involved in obtaining legislation for the armed forces.

Backing a Sample Bill

A theoretical case can perhaps best illustrate these processes. What follows describes the kinds of action that might go into promoting a hypothetical bill to provide educational support for children of Navy personnel on active duty. (Such scholarship legislation is a typical way to provide fringe benefits to help the Navy personnel branch, which has been fighting a losing battle for years to keep its trained and experienced men, and keeps losing both officers and other ranks to the lures of civilian pay.)

The chief of Naval Personnel appoints a small group of officers (a one-service task force) to draft the proposed legislation and prepare arguments for its support. These officers consult educational and legal specialists to determine the ground rules of eligibility and the practical dollar limits for different scholarships. They also develop a means for administering the program, and enlist the aid of the Veterans Administration. To establish documentary evidence in support of the bill, they submit a questionnaire to a sample of career service personnel. When the results of the questionnaire show conclusively that 25 per cent of personnel on active duty would be influenced favorably toward extending their period of service if the bill were enacted, the chief of Naval Personnel directs his team to convert this information into projected savings to the government. An actuary is brought into the group, and he develops charts and tables that show how many millions of dollars in personnel replacement costs would be "saved" if more servicemen extended their period of active service. On paper, it appears that the Navy has a winner.

The legislation is drafted in the form normally used by the Congress; each page and each line on the page is numbered. Now, the proposed bill has to run the gauntlet of service coordination. The Army returns it with a suggestion for inserting clauses on equal opportunity; the Air Force finds a mistake in arithmetic; the Marines want special provisions for children of Medal of Honor winners. The Navy task force irons out all of these suggestions and then coordinates the proposed bill with the Department of Defense. Here, the Navy group meets a Defense analyst who thinks that all service personnel are overpaid, and who suggests that if this bill is approved the services should give up commissaries or other perquisites.

When at last all problems are ironed out, the task group drafts a forwarding letter for signature by the Secretary of the Navy, addressed to the Speaker of the House and the President of the Senate. This letter contains a copy of the bill and explains what it will accomplish, the estimated annual cost, and a statement that the Bureau of the Budget has no objection to the submission of the proposed legislation. The Speaker and the President of the Senate refer the bill to their respective Armed Services committees for staff study. The fate of the bill is in the hands of Congress.

The House committee staff quickly finds a legislative phenomenon in the fine print that will, quite accidentally, permit the children of certain military personnel with long service to draw more scholarship support than GI veterans of the Viet-Nam War. The legislation is returned to the Navy Department for correction, as well as for a few adjustments that will give it a better chance for enactment. The counsel for the Committee on Armed Services also advises certain modifications in the justification for the scholarship bill, pointing out that the Navy questionnaire was submitted to a sample of personnel that included bachelors as well as married men. He suggests that the results be presented to show the views of persons with five, ten, and fifteen years of service, and that the returns from bachelors be culled for separate viewing. The Navy task force, which originally transcribed all questionnaire results to punched cards, sorts the cards with data processing equipment over-night, and finds that the results are indeed strengthened and that they now have a better case. The bachelor servicemen are strongly behind the bill, as are personnel with more than five years' active duty. A legal specialist makes the needed corrections, and the revised bill is returned to the House Armed Services Committee.

The counsel prepares a second analysis of the bill and discusses it with the committee chairman; shortly afterward the bill is introduced in the name of the chairman and is given an H. R. (House of Representatives) number. Representatives from the Navy Office of Legislative Affairs meet with the committee staff to set a day for the hearings. As far as the Navy task force is concerned, the action is reaching its climax. The task force members feverishly prepare backup statements for the key witnesses and write out supporting statements that the witness might or might not read. The officer in charge of the backup books for the Secretary of the Navy and the chief of Naval Operations makes unreasonable demands for position papers, and the task force burns midnight oil again to meet his deadline.

The first day's hearings go well, because the testimony from the more senior officers is generally in terms of broad support.

On the second day, however, the Navy captain who heads the task force is called upon to testify to the details of the bill. From hours of preparation he has at his fingertips statistics and cost figures; he explains not only the necessity for the legislation, but also recounts the history of similar legislation for the U.S. State Department and for the Armed Services of Great Britain. To his considerable relief, he finds that when he does not know the answer to a question, it is perfectly all right to admit it and to promise to "provide the information for the record" at an early date. The hearings close on a hopeful note, and the military witnesses retire, convinced that the exhaustive hearings were businesslike and the Congressmen had reviewed all pertinent facts. Shortly afterward, the scholarship bill is reported out favorably by the Armed Services Committee, and the legislation is passed by the House.

The hearings before the Senate Armed Services Committee follow a similar pattern and are equally successful, resulting in approval by the Congress and quick signature by the President. The task force members are commended by their superiors and go back to their regular assignment.

A Congressman's Expertise

Although the above example describes many of the detailed steps that are requisite for successful enactment of legislation affecting the armed forces, it touches only a remote fringe of congressional interest, and it does not cite the example of legislation that might originate in the legislative branch, which is often the case.

For background in rendering judgments on military legislation, congressmen have to acquire a detailed knowledge on a staggering number of related subjects. As a beginning, they must be thoroughly familiar with the country's national objectives and basic defense policies and have an up-to-date understanding of the threat posed by the military capabilities and probable intentions of potential enemies of the United States. The average layman would be surprised to learn of the number of Congressmen who know in specific and accurate detail the strengths of the Soviet Union's ground and air forces, naval power, rocket and missile capabilities, and military budget insofar as it is disclosed.

Many congressmen, particularly those who serve on the Armed Services and Appropriations committees, have to be familiar with the current status of everything affecting the military establishment of the United States—not only national military policy and the views of the President, who is Commander-in-Chief of all the armed forces, but the force levels of the active and reserve components, and the organization and modernization programs of each military department, as well as major research and development programs. Military strength levels and personnel policies are favorite subjects of study, and veteran members of the Armed Service committees (and the committee staffs) often have a much more detailed knowledge of this area than the majority of military witnesses who testify before them.

The Navy is aware that its continued strength on the seas and its role in the defense of the nation is due, in no small part, to the interest and expertise of the landlocked legislators on Capitol Hill.

X

Influence of the Viet-Nam War

Regardless of the length of the Viet-Nam War, which was continuing as this book neared completion, the action through 1967 was sufficient to determine the major influence that this conflict has had on the U.S. Navy. The military task forced the Navy to adapt to the geography of the region and the nature of the war. In addition to conducting "normal" deep-water operations, naval units had to dust off forgotten capabilities for inshore warfare, and improvise new tactics. Many of these recently acquired or reacquired abilities to operate in shallow or restricted waters have potential use in other areas of the world where the geographic configuration is similar and the people are dependent on water for their major lines of communication.

ON INSHORE WARFARE

Not since the days of the Civil War has the Navy become so enmeshed with river warfare, coastal surveillance and patrol, boarding and search, combat and logistic support of forces ashore, hit-and-run amphibious raids, and shallow-water mine fields. Though one hundred years' span separates these two wars, there are many parallels between the naval operations. The primary task of the Navy in each, to cut off the infiltration of arms, ammunition, and supplies from the sea, and to interdict similar traffic on the inland waterways, stems from the striking likenesses of the bayous of the Gulf Coast, the treacherous Florida Keys, and the stretch of the South

Atlantic coastline of the United States, to the Mekong Delta and the South Vietnamese coastline below the 17th Parallel.

The Union Navy had the tougher job. During the Civil War, the Navy blockaded 3,500 miles of hostile shores dotted with innumerable bays, inlets, and rivers. Every pound of logistic support and every personnel replacement had to come by sea from bases in the North. Inshore warfare was conducted on 3,600 miles of rivers that were valiantly defended from many almost impregnably fortified positions. Yet near the end of the war, the Union Navy had such tight control of the Mississippi River, an unarmed merchant steamer could make the eight-day voyage from St. Louis to New Orleans without incident.

American naval forces in Viet-Nam patrol 1,100 miles of coast, on which they have several suitably located operational bases for small craft, and they receive considerable assistance from indigenous forces. Friendly inhabitants watch the coastline and communicate with naval control points by radio. U.S. aircraft fly daily surveillance patrols, covering in one hour the distance that Union ships might travel in weeks. Underway replenishment ships supply fresh food, mail, ammunition, and vital spare parts, and helicopters evacuate the wounded and provide rapid delivery of small logistics items.

The above contrast is not meant to imply that inshore warfare in Viet-Nam is an easy task. The problems of river warfare, for example, require special craft and tactics today just as they did during the Civil War. The Viet Cong guerrilla who lurks in the lush banks of the Mekong River is as deadly an enemy as the Confederate "Swamp Johnny" who haunted the Mississippi Delta. But there are many lessons to be learned from a study of Secretary of the Navy Gideon Welles' Civil War annals and the detailed, handwritten reports of Union commanders. Perhaps the most significant is to see the value of retaining for future use the skills learned at first hand through bitter experience. The United States may, some day, be asked to oppose counterinsurgency in other areas where rivers, canals, and coastal waters are the primary means of communication.

During World War II, there was little need for an inshore war capability. That was an entirely different kind of war, in which major naval forces opposed each other primarily in blue-water action. However, for the foreseeable future, repetition of that kind of naval warfare appears remote. There is more chance of lower-keyed naval operations, and these could parallel the coastal and river operations in Viet-Nam in terms of the following major naval tasks: coastal and river patrol; logistic transport; gunfire support; land raids; minesweeping; special forces; personnel evacuation (or pilot recovery). In most of these tasks, the performance of U.S. naval forces was improved with the introduction of new types of craft and equipment. In some cases, the old but proven small amphibious craft of World War II were adapted to meet local conditions. The great bulk of American naval strength in the South China Sea could not be brought to bear in the shallow-water war.

The Vietnamese coast south of the Demilitarized Zone is like a sieve. It has been estimated that on any given day, about 50,000 small junks work this 1,100 miles of coastline in fishing and freighting activities, presenting the Viet Cong with a great opportunity to infiltrate arms, ammunition, and supplies to small pockets of guerrilla forces. It is impossible for coast watchers to spot the junks that have rifles or grenades buried under a load of fish. This requires boarding and search at sea, or careful inspection by loyal authorities ashore. In most instances, there are neither facilities nor inspectors available for land inspection, so the great share of the patrol task falls to seaborne units.

As evidence mounted that the amount of infiltrated supplies had reached the danger point, the Republic of Viet-Nam requested the U.S. Navy to assist in policing their coastline and declared territorial waters inside the three-mile limit a defensive sea area. Within this area, any ships, boats, and small craft engaged in suspicious activity were stopped and searched, and violaters severely punished. The Republic of Viet-Nam also declared that it would exercise control of the sea in the "contiguous zone" between three and twelve miles from the coast. In order to avoid international complications, the Vietnamese phrased this declaration carefully; they invoked measures necessary to prevent infringement of their "customs, fiscal, immigration, and sanitary regulations." Beyond the twelve-mile limit, the Vietnamese Government declared that it would take necessary steps to prevent infringement of its laws by any ships "presumed to be South Vietnamese." In effect, this gave patrol forces in the area a hunting license to stop and search any suspicious vessel from the shore break to the high seas. This last defense provision was aimed at the larger craft that sailed from a Communist port well out to sea to avoid inshore patrolling forces, and then set course directly for the shore and a rendezvous with the Viet Cong. In February, 1965, the destruction of a coastal freighter using this tactic netted about eighty tons of contraband supplies. The encounter brought home to the South Vietnamese the realization that armed seagoing freighters outgunned their small ships and presented a threat beyond the capacity of their navy.

Operation Market Time

In response to the Vietnamese request for assistance, the U.S. Navy sent a force of mixed surface vessels to form the nucleus of "Operation Market Time." By plunging headlong into this low-key surveillance task, the Navy was caught off balance. Used to only blue-water operations or the requirements of amphibious landings in shallow waters, the destroyers, coastal mine sweepers, and support craft had no established doctrine or procedures applicable to their responsibilities. During the first month, the ships merely observed the passing action and reported any suspicious vessels to units of the South Vietnamese Navy, who stopped and searched them. When this proved to be an inefficient use of American forces, Vietnamese liaison personnel were placed aboard the U.S. ships to facilitate search operations. Under this arrangement, both the U.S. and South Vietnamese elements of Operation

Market Time actively participated in establishing a *cordon sanitaire* along the Vietnamese coastline. During the period from August, 1965, to October, 1966, this joint force closely observed approximately 650,000 ships and junks, stopping and searching 110,000 of them. It has been difficult to assess the results of Market Time, but the record should not rest on the amount of contraband discovered. After the Civil War ended, it was found that the Union blockade of the Confederacy had had a profound effect on the sources of contraband shipment. Thousands of tons of goods rotted on the wharves of Bermuda and Caribbean harbors because of the hazards imposed by the blockade force. In Southeast Asia, the amount of contraband discovered at sea might well be only a small portion of goods originally available for shipment, but withheld because of the stringency of the surveillance operations.

Among the lessons learned by U.S. forces engaged in Operation Market Time, the primary ones were the need for organization, communications, and a *modus operandi* that did not antagonize innocent Vietnamese. In addition, there was a clear requirement for small ships, swift enough to overhaul suspicious vessels but of shallow draft and long endurance. Modern destroyers and larger ships represent considerable "overkill" in this kind of work, and their large personnel complements made for inefficient use of resources. The organization that finally evolved featured coastal surveillance centers at intervals along the South Vietnamese coast for coordination of communications, intelligence, and control of operations. The positions of friendly surveillance craft were kept current, and suspect ships, either discovered by air patrol, reported by coastwatchers, or spotted by surface patrol ships, were tracked until intercepted and searched. The techniques resembled those of a modern police control office in a large metropolis.

Through long months of experience, American visiting parties from U.S. Navy ships established an effective, but inoffensive, tactic for boarding and search. Inspection teams usually consisted of an American naval officer, a Vietnamese officer, a gunner's mate, a damage controlman, and a signalman. The junks were hailed with the "loud hailer"—an electric megaphone—and ordered alongside for inspection. More often than not, the crews of ships inspected responded with good humor, and they were usually given a token amount of food or cigarettes for their trouble. Many veterans of coastal traffic carried signs printed in English, bearing instructions for the best method of boarding their craft and listing the nature of their cargo. The record to date reveals that approximately 5 per cent of the persons detained proved to be Viet Cong, and another 10 per cent turned out to be South Vietnamese deserters, draft dodgers, or smugglers.

Operation Game Warden

Closer inland, the surveillance operations on the rivers, canals, and the mangrove swamps of the Mekong Delta and the Rung Sat Special Zone had to be handled by smaller craft and helicopters. This operation, called "Game Warden," is a definite throwback to the Civil War and a much more dangerous mission than the Market Time patrol, because the river forces are often close to, or between, enemy-held shores. The Game Warden force uses fast patrol boats (the newer ones are called PBR's—patrol boat river), river mine sweepers, and a version of the Army UH-1B helicopter. During early operations, in the spring and summer of 1966, U.S. Army pilots flew the helicopter support patrols. Later, Navy pilots took over. The purpose of Game Warden has been extended beyond surveillance of inland waters and denial of their use by the Viet Cong for the movement of men, supplies, and food into a combat operation in which river assault groups of the South Vietnamese Navy support small amphibious operations. The over-all effect of the combined American and South Vietnamese effort on the inland waterways has been encouraging. During the first six months, Game Warden forces boarded and searched 42,000 river craft, captured junks carrying contraband, interdicted troop movements on the river banks, enforced a stringent curfew, and destroyed many food and arms caches of the enemy. In some areas, Game Warden shut off the Viet Cong river canal communications entirely; in others, the patrol activity and harassment have denied guerrilla forces the mobility that they need for survival.

ON NAVAL GUNFIRE SUPPORT

Naval gunfire support, which was mentioned briefly in an earlier chapter, was thought to be a "lost art" of the modern Navy only a few years ago. As a matter of fact, some of the newer, double-ended guided-missile ships delivered to the fleet in the early 1960's had no gunfire-support capability, and were barely equipped to defend themselves against an armed junk. This class of ship was a good example of overoptimistic dependency on guided missiles, and the dangers of short memory. When the requirement for gunfire support was levied on the Seventh Fleet, the task fell to the ancient cruisers, World War II destroyers, and the few newer destroyers that were equipped with five-inch fifty-four-caliber guns. If naval authorities were now asked to define the primary influences of the Viet-Nam war on the Navy, many would undoubtedly choose this "return of the naval gun."

The requirement for gunnery excellence burst suddenly in August, 1964, when North Vietnamese torpedo boats attacked destroyers USS *Maddox* and USS *C. Turner Joy* in the Gulf of Tonkin. After that battle, all destroyers in the Pacific Fleet were required to undergo rather strenuous training in the use of their gun batteries against small, swift targets. In addition, greater emphasis was placed on shore bombardment, particularly the "call fire" phase, which linked the firing ship with a spotter located ashore. This training paid significant dividends; gunfire support ships were in great demand along the South Vietnamese coast, and some destroyers responded to as many as fifteen calls for support in one day. The accuracy of fire, quick response, and reliability of these ships now equal or exceed the performance of gunfire support ships during World War II.

Complete control of the sea has given the United States

many opportunities to exploit waterborne amphibious raids and landings south of the 17th Parallel. None of these approached the scale of the huge landing operations of World War II, but they did constitute a large part of the effort in Viet-Nam. All of the forces required for successful amphibious operations have been available: attack carriers for air cover; cruisers and destroyers for air defense and gunfire support; mine sweepers, amphibious assault ships, landing craft and troop-carrying helicopters for the landing assault; and cargo and auxiliary ships for logistic support. Landing operations have ranged from the Cam Lo River near the Demilitarized Zone to the Mekong Delta south of Saigon.

ON THE SEABEES

The activity in Viet-Nam also brought the Seabees back to their own again, and more or less assured their future for many years to come. The construction tasks they have undertaken in the Vietnamese ports and countryside have direct application to other underdeveloped countries of the world that may, some day, require U.S. influence to restore stability. The SeaBees have built roads, airfields, constructed port facilities near Saigon and Cam Ranh Bay, and undertaken a number of projects that have direct civilian application and lasting utility. These include warehouses, barracks, field hospitals, river and harbor improvements, cargo-handling facilities, schools, and fresh water wells. The United States' intention to release these assets after the war was evidenced by negotiation in 1967 of a contract with an American management and research firm for development of plans to integrate the SeaBee works into the civilian economy. This transfer should produce long-lasting benefits. The SeaBees' construction program, at its height in 1967, was the largest of its kind in the world. A force of 6,000 SeaBees, 37,000 Vietnamese, 4,000 U.S. civilian workmen, and an additional 5,500 journeymen from other Free World countries, worked around the clock on emergency construction. Despite combat zone restrictions and changing priorities to meet the needs of the war, the workmen achieved significant success, for example, laying 3,500 feet of concrete in one day and exceeding their monthly goal of $40 million worth of work in place. In other programs that are part of the over-all development campaign—the "other war" in Viet-Nam, directed against poverty and disease—Army and Marine units have set the stage, with naval participants including Sea-Bees, medical and dental personnel, technicians, advisers, and thousands of sailors joining together to help make the programs work.

On Operations in General

It can be said that the Navy had most of the ships, aircraft, and weapons needed when the conflict erupted in Viet-Nam. However, the juxtaposition and redeployment necessary to obtain the desired concentration of forces in the South China Sea and to establish logistic lines of support placed heavy strains on naval operations. To meet the unusual logistic demands alone, the Navy's Military Sea Transportation Service in 1967 used a force of over 300 ships. About one-third of these were MSTS-chartered ships, and another third were activated from the Reserve Fleet. The entire war effort drew heavily on personnel and reserve stocks of equipment and material, and forced the Navy to operate at an exceptionally high pace. It was, nevertheless, ready to meet the tasks of the conflict—all but one. Chief of Naval Operations Admiral McDonald called this "small patrol boat operations."

The Small Patrol Boat Inventory

In a speech at Los Angeles in January, 1967, McDonald admitted that the Navy had been "caught short" when it was asked to organize an effort against infiltration from the sea. He pointed out that stopping illegal entry into the United States itself had always been the job of the Coast Guard. In that regard, he noted:

the South China Sea coastline of South Viet-Nam—from the DMZ to the southern tip—is just about the same length as the U.S. coastline between Cape Cod and Cape Kennedy. Realizing that our U.S. Coast Guard had the task of preventing rum runners from entering this area during the days of Prohibition and then keeping spies out during World War II, I called a friend in the Coast Guard and asked if he could tell me what forces had been required—just to give me some sort of realistic starting point. In a little while, he called back and said, "Admiral we used 25 destroyers, sixteen 200-foot cutters, 225 patrol boats, 16,991 men, 1,350 dogs, and 2,400 horses."

The Navy moved quickly to build up its patrol craft inventory. Many versions of amphibious craft (LST, LSM, LSI, LCU, PGM, LCM) were adapted, and Coast Guard cutters, conventional PT boats, motorized junks, and mine sweepers joined the force. Industry was asked to investigate the manufacture of various aluminum-hulled, fiberglass, or plastic patrol boats. Tests showed that water jet propulsion was highly efficient and suitable in shallow-water operations; a water-jet-engine, fiberglass-hull craft proved to be one of the most effective boats on the river. The jet principle was adopted in a new hydrofoil gunboat scheduled for delivery to the fleet in late 1967. Designated the PGH (patrol gunboat-hydrofoil), it is powered by water drawn through rear struts into a centrifugal pump and jetted through nozzles near the stern. The 60-ton PGH, armed with a 40-mm gun, an 81-mm mortar and twin 50-caliber machine guns, will be capable of speeds over 40 knots in waters too shallow for conventional craft. Hydrofoils such as these, plus "hover" craft, skimmers, new patrol boats (Swifts), and armed helicopters will probably make up the bulk of the Navy's river patrol force in the future.

Return of the Battleship

As the number of aircraft lost over North Viet-Nam increased, Navy analysts looked for a more efficient way of destroying military targets north of the DMZ. A survey of the area showed that almost half of the targets lay within range of the sixteen-inch gun—the main battery of most of the battle-ships of World War II. Since several of these venerable ships lay in good state of preservation with the "mothball fleet," the analysts set out to see if the activation, manning, and opera-tion of a battleship would be practical. The studies showed conclusively that if the battleship were manned with a reduced crew, it would more than pay for itself in the South China Sea. The manpower cut included a reduced engineering force and acceptance of less than full speed as an operational constraint. In 1967, the battleship proposal made such a good case that the Department of Defense authorized the Navy to activate the USS *New Jersey,* and prepare it for operations with the Sev-enth Fleet. Although the resurrection of a battleship is signifi-cant, it does not herald the return of that class of ship to regular operating forces. It does, however, indicate a need for the sixteen-inch gun, or its equivalent.

Other Functional Capabilities

In generating new naval requirements and demonstrating the logic of retention of other Navy capabilities that were be-ing considered for reduction or elimination before the war started, the conflict in Southeast Asia can be expected to have other significant long-range influences on the Navy.

The first and most obvious influence embraces blue-water operations. Units of the Seventh Fleet were patrolling the waters of Southeast Asia before the Tonkin Gulf incident of 1964. They were on the spot when they were needed, and they remained there until presence was no longer required. If the Seventh Fleet force had been withdrawn or driven away, the ground war in Viet-Nam would have come to a precipitous halt—a fact so apparent to the Congress and appointed officials responsible for Defense planning that it served to under-write the Navy's general purpose forces and to forestall im-pending reductions.

The ability of the attack carrier, particularly in comparison of its performance with that of land-based tactical air, has been forcefully demonstrated. Similarly, the air action has shown that there is a definite requirement for a variety of aircraft. The twenty-year-old A-1 Spad, a propeller-driven, slow workhorse, performed more effectively in many types of missions than faster, newer aircraft. The eleven-year-old A-4 has flown more combat air missions over North Viet-Nam than any other single type of airplane. The S-2 Tracker, an antisubmarine warfare plane, has proved more cost-effective for medium-range surveillance missions than any other aircraft in the South China Sea. However, the patrol squadrons have conducted most of the air patrols. The F-4 Navy fighter has been the finest fighter aircraft on the scene, its performance so universally excellent that it has been adopted by all of the armed services as the first-line fighter. The A-6 all-weather attack aircraft, introduced into the action by the Navy, was the first all-weather attack aircraft ever used in combat. The weapons used by these aircraft—Sidewinder and Sparrow missiles in air-to-air combat, and air-to-ground ammunition such as Zuni and Bullpup—were all developed by the Navy before the war started, and were available in quantity when they were needed. As a matter of fact, the Navy supply of "iron bombs" sustained certain kinds of air strikes by both Navy and Air Force planes until industrial production could meet the increased demand. Summing up, the case for the attack carrier, its aircraft, and air weapons was proven by actual experiment, and the Navy showed commendable foresight in peacetime preparation for a "shooting" war.

On the other hand very little justification has emerged in the Viet-Nam experience for the antisubmarine carrier (CVS). The absence of any submarine opposition relegated that force to routine patrols and exercises. Its mere presence may have discouraged hostile submarine action, but it is more likely that submarines were withheld because of fear of escalation, and the ease with which the submarine might be identified. Perhaps the most significant result of this experience was the

Navy's realization that the possession of two different kinds of carriers might be a luxury. The CVS normally carried a mixture of A-4 aircraft and ASW aircraft and, when the need became paramount, one CVS was converted into an attack carrier (CVA). Conversely, it was apparent that the aircraft complement of the CVA might be modified to give it an antisubmarine warfare capability. Insofar as the conduct of the war was concerned, there was no hard-and-fast requirement that dictated a mandatory number of carrier-based air strikes against North Vietnamese land targets. If the attack carrier air wing were modified to include ASW aircraft, its potential for air strikes would be reduced, but the amount of reduction might not be critical. The proper mix of a carrier wing of that kind could be determined by careful study, and the result might well prove to be justification for a more modern, jet-powered antisubmarine aircraft, to operate from CVA's and CVS's alike.

SOME CONCLUSIONS

In its early stages, the trouble in Viet-Nam elicited random Navy response with conventional air strike, amphibious, logistic, and special force operations. This tied down conventional Navy forces that might well have been better employed elsewhere. As the war grew bigger, the use of these forces was more appropriate, but this fact does not camouflage the inadequacy of naval forces for inshore warfare and for support of counterinsurgency forces in earlier phases of low-keyed operations. The lesson in this regard is very clear—the task of inshore warfare and counterinsurgency should be separated from the conventional organization and identified as an element of naval warfare in its own right.

Some of the kinds of forces needed for shallow water operations have already been identified, but the Navy role in early counterinsurgency operations has not been fully explored. It is too late to determine much about this task in the Viet-Nam theater; the time for that was in the early 1960's before the torpedo boat attacks in the Gulf of Tonkin. It is never too late, however, to examine a problem such as this by careful staff studies and analysis. This effort might produce the naval counterinsurgency force that is now only a gleam in the eyes of a few far-sighted naval officers. Such a force could function as a mobile staging and air base, a communications center, and a reconnaissance base—invulnerable to terrorist attack in the early stages of insurgency or revolution.

The evidence of recent naval preparedness for the majority of operations in Viet-Nam and elsewhere indicates that the lessons of Southeast Asia will not be ignored. In future years, the Navy will probably be as adaptable to the wearisome and difficult but necessary tasks of counterinsurgency and inshore warfare as it is to the more exciting operations of the jet age.

XI

Continuing Problems and Issues

It is difficult to sift significant problems out of the many issues that demand the attention of top Navy management. Quite often, problems of the moment appear paramount. For example, when the tempo of the operations peaks, as in the Viet-Nam War, the major problems appear to be operational. But although these problems often pose grave and serious questions, they are usually transient in nature, and experienced naval officers take them in their stride. Beneath them and the sometimes frantic flow of dispatches and telephone calls they inspire, there are several long-range, complex problems that must be considered. These are the more durable issues, of profound significance to the Navy, whose solution often seems unattainable. Three are discussed here: the high cost of weapon systems; ship construction and nuclear propulsion; and manpower.

COST OF WEAPON SYSTEMS

The high cost of defense in a rapidly changing technological environment has often been singled out for discussion with technical audiences. In late 1966, Paul H. Nitze, then Secretary of the Navy, told a convention of aerospace and electronic systems representatives that the technological advances achieved in the two decades since World War II had produced "tremendously improved capabilities in our weapon systems." However, he pointed out that time had also afforded the same opportunities to opponents, who had not been idle. In some instances, he said, they had "equaled or surpassed us," although the United States still maintained a slight lead in the ability to produce complex systems. In a hostile environment, the outcome of a technological race for weapon superiority has always been a matter of gravest importance. History is filled with examples of military invention that gave one country a temporary advantage on the battlefield or at sea. But until World War II, none of these advantages had the potential for rapid world conquest or a capability for destruction beyond imagination. Nor did they produce problems that called for so much brilliance in solutions, such efficient use of material and trained technical resources. Nitze told his audience the key is effective management of the extensive technological capability he called "one of our nation's most priceless resources."

The main problem of Defense management is to direct scientific advance at a price the nation can afford. Costs have increased so much that, Secretary of Defense McNamara has said, we are "in danger of pricing ourselves out of business in terms of real resources." The Navy fighter aircraft is a good example of the change, growth, and expense associated with advance in weapon systems. In 1945, this aircraft weighed 15,000 pounds, flew at 400 miles per hour and cost about $65,000. The fighter aircraft of today fly four times as fast, weigh three times as much, and cost about $2 million each. The experience is the same across the entire span of weapons and their components—ships, missiles, tanks, electronics, sensors, communications, ammunition, etc. This growth has almost reached the limits of complexity, the constraints of space, weight, and maintainability, as well as the upper limit of the amount of gross national product that can be allocated to defense in peacetime. Inevitably, this situation leads military management to select weapons and force structures that are best suited for national security within available resources.

In this selection, modern managers have come increasingly to rely on "systems analysis" and "cost effectiveness" in Department of Defense decision-making. These techniques have been adopted by the military services as the best means to present and support their requirements for a share of the Defense budget. The disciplines exploit areas in which mathematics and economics can provide solutions and uncover those in which judgments have to be made. For decision-makers who clearly realize that the new disciplines reduce the number of judgments required, but do not eliminate them altogether, systems analysis and cost effectiveness are excellent management tools.

When these approaches were first used in the Pentagon, they were resisted as an incursion of the analyst into military planning. In recent years, however, each of the armed services has developed, through formal education and crash training courses, a cadre of younger officers who are well versed in the techniques. Those not fortunate enough to receive special training have managed to get by with a little self-study, and an understanding of the major principles, particularly "quantification" and "optimization."

The quantification of military capabilities has been a major contribution of systems analysis to defense planning, and has produced such measures as "total kill probability" of alternative forces, the "number of U.S. fatalities" in a nuclear war, or the "days to deliver" a specified military force overseas. In quantifying military capability, the systems analysts use a "scenario" to describe a situation or range of situations in which the military capabilities under study can be used against an enemy. Military judgment has a significant influence in the development of a scenario, and each model is reviewed and evaluated by military specialists in the light of their training and experience. Given a scenario and the ability to quantify major military capabilities, the analysts need only to add costs to the problem and they are ready to proceed with the comparison of alternatives. Generally speaking, the costs considered include initial procurement costs, operating costs, and indirect costs. These have been studied in such depth in recent years that they are fairly well standardized. The three basic steps of systems analysis of alternative weapons systems then devolve to (1) "costing" each system, (2) "playing" these systems within situations or scenarios which reflect military judgment, and (3) "quantifying the output" in terms of military capability.

The difficulty of quantifying many capabilities led the analysts to adopt a system of arranging successive alternatives in "rank order," or priority. In many cases, particularly when the outcome of the study depends on varied enemy response, this optimization can become a massive computation that requires computerized methods. Even so, it is often difficult to compute a clearly defined answer, and one in which all concerned have high confidence. This desired end requires the computation of a series of values from which the decision-maker can exercise his judgment. For example, the kill probability of a torpedo may have a "best value" of 30 per cent. The analyst may well introduce a wider span of consideration by adding an optimistic estimate of 40 per cent and a pessimistic estimate of 20 per cent, and optimize each case. Or, he may vary different parts of the study scenario (such as elimination of certain overseas bases from U.S. use) to test the "sensitivity" of this elimination on the mathematical results. The results of this kind of analysis can become series of solutions—and the final judgment might be to "hedge" or to buy enough of the system to handle the pessimistic case. If the system is unusually expensive, the limitation of resources might sway the decision maker to select the most optimistic case. At the very least, he has a foundation on which to base his decision, and he can make a more reasoned approach to the problem than he could if the techniques of systems analysis were not utilized.

The opponents of systems analysis—and there are many within Congress—are quick to point out that analysts with no military experience are often prone to ignore military judgment and to have unsubstantiated confidence in their analytic approach. Their doubts and reservations emerged clearly in a new round of disagreement between Defense and the Congress on the subject of nuclear propulsion (a debate in which Representative Chet Holifield, Vice Chairman of the Joint Atomic Energy Committee, on May 29, 1967, said that the new aircraft carrier USS *John F. Kennedy,* "was obsolete when it was launched" a few days before).

Some people are also concerned that proponents of systems analysis have gone overboard in using the study approach to promote service ambitions. A situation that finds the Air Force producing studies to show that their bomber and interceptor forces are more cost effective for national security than the Navy's antisubmarine forces, or the Navy disclosing a study that compares the Air Force "tactical air" unfavorably with carrier-based systems, is, they feel, unhealthy. Spurred by the competition for the defense dollar, it might, as one Congressman suggested, soon find most of the personnel in the Pentagon "studying other studies."

The Navy's several years' experience using the analytical approach to decisions (coupled with the Defense program-planning-budget system for striking a balance between defense needs and fiscal resources) has stimulated its leadership toward a better understanding of modern management techniques. When the initial resistance to the new methods was replaced by an objective response to the challenge, naval officials were rewarded by the discovery of new ways to utilize the natural advantages of sea power. At the same time, this intellectual awakening gave Navy decision-makers an awareness of and an ability to combat the weaknesses and limitations of the new disciplines. Conversely, they found many areas in which their own house should be put in order. As a result, there are important new study efforts under way to support new ship designs, to obtain valid data on fleet performance and readiness, to develop better command and control systems, to combine and automate surveillance systems, and to improve world-wide logistics. As costs of defense systems continue to rise, the competition for funding these systems in a peacetime environment will remain keen. Some of the most important decisions on

future security will have to be made within the next ten years
and—in the absence of anything better—will, in all probability, be made on the basis of systems analysis, tempered by
objective military and scientific judgment.

SHIP CONSTRUCTION AND NUCLEAR POWER

Among other naval problems and issues of importance, few
can exceed the import of the construction of new ships. The
terms that most often crop up in discussions of this problem are "block obsolescence" and "nuclear propulsion." Since
World War II, many types of naval ships have not been supported by an adequate replacement program. Instead, Navy
requests for new construction have been deferred or reduced,
time and again, on the grounds of economy. The result is a
long line of ships approaching retirement at the same time,
with no replacements planned. For example, expected reductions of multipurpose destroyers and cruisers during the next
eight years (1967–75) will not be offset in kind by construction. Further, the types of replacements that are scheduled
reflect a significant loss of fleet capability in certain mission
areas.

Figures released by the Navy in early 1967 showed the loss
of a total of 156 destroyer types and 8 cruisers by inactivation
during this 8-year period. At the same time, the new construction program provided for only 66 new ships or conversions,
which means a net reduction of 98 ships of this important category. The cruisers, which will not be replaced, represent a 43
per cent reduction in the fleet's ability to provide air defense
in the 40-to-100 mile range, and over 50 per cent loss of naval
gunfire support with heavy guns. The multipurpose destroyer
will be replaced, in the main, by the new class DE (antisubmarine warfare) escort, which has a top speed of 27 knots and
considerably less firepower. Although adequate for certain
missions, the new DE cannot match the general-purpose destroyer in support of amphibious assault or land forces, destruction of shore targets, air defense, or the destruction of surface
targets, and is too slow a ship to operate with fast carrier

attack forces. Of the 66 new ships authorized during the period of this projection, 56 will be DE's—and only 1 ship of the total program is scheduled for nuclear propulsion.

The reluctance of the Defense Department to support nuclear propulsion in major surface ships is notable. In fact, the application of nuclear power to surface ships has been almost at a stalemate for several years because of the higher initial cost of the nuclear-powered model. The Navy has pressed for nuclear-powered carrier strike forces (aircraft carriers and destroyers) through new construction, and has demonstrated that this force is superior in many ways over the conventional force. Analysis shows that if the costs of nuclear propulsion were spread over the 25-year life cycle of the ships, it would represent only a 3 per cent increase over the total cost of building and operating the force, including its aircraft and logistic support.

Remembering that it took the Navy forty years to change from sail to steam, and that it will take much longer than that to shift to nuclear-powered surface ships at the present rate, naval leaders have stubbornly continued to promote an acceleration in the nuclear-propulsion building program. In this effort, they have had the support of several congressmen who take pride in their initiative in nuclear matters. Congressman L. Mendel Rivers of the House Armed Services Committee recently said, "I am convinced, and I think it is fair to say that the Congress as a body is convinced, that the Navy of the future must be nuclear powered." Mr. Rivers went on to castigate the Department of Defense for its reluctance to support nuclear power, saying, "The Committee feels that the Department of Defense has been extremely dilatory in pushing nuclear power for surface ships." He added that approval of a nuclear-powered guided-missile frigate would serve to "express the will of the Congress that greater and more rapid progress be made in the field of nuclear-powered surface ships" and that this action would "help to break the logjam of disinterest . . . in the Pentagon with respect to nuclear power."

The Defense record in this regard shows provision for the

first nuclear frigate, USS *Bainbridge* in the fiscal year 1959 building program, and none thereafter. It was the Congress that changed the 1962 building program to authorize nuclear power for the frigate USS *Truxton*. In the 1963 program, the Congress authorized nuclear power for a frigate that was to have the Typhon missile system, but this ship was canceled because the missile system proved impractical. During the next three years, the Department of Defense did not request any major fleet escorts. On its own initiative, the Congress authorized $150.5 million in the 1966 program for a new nuclear-powered frigate, and urged the Department of Defense to ask for funds for a nuclear frigate in the 1967 program. The Department not only declined to ask for the additional funds, but it also refused to use the funds appropriated for the nuclear frigate. This led to a joint Senate-House authorization bill of June 30, 1966, that provided for the construction of the nuclear frigate previously authorized and contained the following statement: "The contract for the construction of the nuclear powered guided missile frigate for which funds were authorized under Public Law 89–37, and for which funds are authorized to be appropriated during Fiscal Year 1967, shall be entered into as soon as practicable unless the President fully advises the Congress that its construction is not in the national interest."

When the Secretary of Defense presented the 1968 budget request to the Congress, he did announce an intention to build two more nuclear carriers, one in fiscal year 1969, and "one in a later year." With regard to nuclear-powered major escorts, he acknowledged the additional funds provided by the Congress the year before, and reported that "we have decided to proceed with construction this year, building it ahead of the time it will actually be needed to support the plan for one high speed nuclear-powered escort for each of the four planned nuclear-powered carriers."

This statement made explicit Defense plans to limit nuclear propulsion for major escorts to four carriers, although the

Navy and many congressmen look forward to a program of building all major combatant surface ships with nuclear power. The Navy, after detailed study of military effectiveness and a comparison of present and past experience of naval forces in combat, holds strongly that, in the words of the chief of Naval Operations,

> The endurance, tactical flexibility, and greater freedom from logistic support of nuclear warships will give the United States an unequaled naval striking force. Our new warships, which the Navy will be operating into the twenty-first century, should be provided with the most modern propulsion plants available. To do less is to degrade effectiveness with grave implications for national security.

As the argument over nuclear power dragged on, the fleet escort problem grew more acute. In 1967, the Navy established a special project office to stimulate studies and produce workable plans for a destroyer replacement program beginning in fiscal year 1968. In this regard, there was welcome encouragement from the Department of Defense. In his posture statement to the Congress, 1967, the Secretary of Defense said that he was considering the adoption of the "total package" procurement concept of a large purchase over several years of newly designed fleet escorts. His budget request for fiscal year 1968 included $30 million to initiate concept formulation and contract definition of destroyers and destroyer escorts. This approach is promising, but there are many obstacles between a declaration of intent and the delivery of new ships. The Congress has not embraced the "package procurement" of ships built by one contractor as wholeheartedly as the Department of Defense has—and the question of how many vessels will use nuclear propulsion remains unsettled.

MANPOWER

Historically, the military has had a continuing manpower problem. In the days of sail, the Navy record was one of forced service, physical hardship, and brutal discipline. This was the period of the press gang, of "Shanghaiing," of the cat-o'-nine-tails. In the U.S. Navy, discipline was never as harsh as in some foreign navies, but flogging and other severe punishments existed until abolished by Congress in 1850. Since that time, punishments have grown progressively more moderate, and the emphasis on maintenance of discipline has shifted in favor of constructive leadership. With this change, and the advances of technology, the general manpower needs of the Navy also switched from brawn toward brains. The illiterate, muscular coal heaver and barefooted deck hand were replaced by trained engineers or bright high school graduates who could be trained in any number of skills. The meager wages and drab living conditions of the past have given way to a salary scale that is competitive with organized labor. Relatively spacious quarters feature stainless steel lockers, foam rubber mattresses, and bunks with individual reading lamps. Food served rivals that on the menus of the best restaurants. Almost all ships have laundries, a barber, and well-ventilated or air-conditioned living spaces. With this new environment, one might well wonder why the Navy should have continuing personnel problems, which include a high rate of personnel turnover, low retention, shortages of skilled personnel, and excessive training costs. Unfortunately, it does.

In 1966, it was reported that an annual average of 10,000 new officers and 100,000 recruits had been needed over the preceding six years in order to maintain strength levels. And these gross numbers do not show the critical need for men of superior intelligence and ability to operate highly complex weapon systems, to man nuclear power plants, or to service high-performance jet aircraft. Approximately sixty skilled areas are available for enlisted personnel, and an even wider range of choice for officer specialists, but there are similar manpower needs in civilian life, where wages and salaries are more attractive, and where life is less arduous. Exit interviews with departing personnel give some insight into their reasons for leaving the naval service. Probably the greatest single cause is simply that the Navy today is different from the "old" days before World War II. During the past two decades, U.S. Navy commitments overseas have kept a great portion of the fleet away from the ships' home ports. It is not unusual for a young man with a new family to spend 50 per cent of his time away from home. As his length of service increases, this period of separation diminishes, but the pressures produced annually take a toll in discharges.

The large and unexpected size of the Navy is an important factor in the problem. If the United States had only a dozen ships instead of almost 1,000, there would be little difficulty in obtaining the number and kind of people needed to operate them. A percentage of the American population has always liked to go to sea. When the Navy was relatively small, there used to be waiting lists at every recruiting station. A recent study showed that in 1890 the military and naval services needed only .02 per cent of the U.S. labor force. Today, this requirement represents 3.60 per cent of that force. Judging from the number of persons who go into and out of the armed services each year, the nation has exceeded by an order of magnitude the percentage of the population that prefers a military career. The Navy seldom resorts to the draft for its new personnel, but naval recruiters candidly admit that the existence of the draft for other services guides many a young man to the Navy recruiter's door. Presently, Navy personnel problems include an imbalance in retention, which sees cooks and barbers staying on active duty in large numbers while more highly skilled specialists and officers with advanced degrees leave.

The Navy is still an exciting life. There is no surfeit of adventure, but it is principally a young man's service, with attractions, opportunities, and operations that appeal to those with few personal responsibilities.

In the nature of things, it appears that a lifelong Navy career is only for a few. Those who choose this path find it rewarding and satisfying. But there are many young men who would like to spend some years in naval service before settling down in civilian life. The Navy could make substantial gains in solving its manpower problems if it were to come up with some attractive contracts making it possible for its men to serve for reasonable, well-rewarded periods short of a full working life.

XII

Tomorrow's Navy:
What New Harbors?

In the 1966 edition of the U.S. Navy's official *Naval Review,*
Sir Peter Gretton raised the question of a limited war at sea
between the United States and the Soviet Union. He argued
that since the United States and Great Britain depended so
much on the sea and shipping for their existence, Communist
leaders might instigate a war against shipping on the high seas
to upset the balance of Free World economy. He believes that
such a war could begin with the detention of ships in Russian
and in Soviet satellite harbors, the closing off of areas of the sea
to commerce and fishing, harassment on the high seas, blockade, perhaps, the actual sinking of ships by "unknown" submarines. Sir Peter admits that the navies of the United States
and Great Britain could also exercise the same option against
Communist shipping, and that a full-scale war at sea would
result. Such a war would quickly become one in which
submarines played a decisive offensive role, and in which antisubmarine warfare and convoying in the World War II tradition would come to the fore.

Similarly, former Secretary of the Navy Paul Nitze made
frequent references to a limited war at sea, which he, too, considered to be an option for the United States as well as for the
Soviet Union. In his 1966 Navy Day speech at Charleston,
South Carolina, he said, "We envisage the possibility of a war
confined to the sea with little or no associated land action.

. . . a contest of attrition which we must be able to sustain and to win." On another occasion, he pointed out that a war at sea could be bitter and grim, but "seldom results in lasting harm to real estate." To him, one of the primary tasks for the Navy is to keep the capability "to defeat any enemy at sea and to confine any war that starts at sea to the sea"—with balanced antisubmarine warfare forces.

The U.S. Navy that might be called on to engage in this or any other type of war—the Navy of the 1960's and 1970's—is already afloat or fairly well defined, and has been described in the pages of this book. But what of the fleets of 1980 or 1990?

Admiral Horacio Rivero, USN, and other Navy leaders predict a mixture of "the commonplace and the exotic," featuring recognizable versions of carriers, cruisers, submarines, and destroyers, "plus a host of amphibious and auxiliary types." Admiral J. S. McCain writes that the application of technological achievement to naval purposes is "limited only by our imagination." None of the experts give precise descriptions, but there is enough evidence in current naval documentation to make reasonable forecasts.

FORECAST OF FLEET REQUIREMENTS

As indicated in the preceding chapters, estimates of future military requirements must be made in terms of a scenario depicting the environment in which the forces will be used. This forecast will be confined to a description of likely naval forces fifteen or twenty-five years hence, in a world of continued challenge and tension. In this scenario, there is still overwhelming need for military forces. The Soviet Union has continued her drive for sea power, achieving pre-eminence in merchant shipping and ranking second only to the United States in naval power. United States access to foreign bases is severely restricted by political restraints, forcing the nation to put more of its striking power at sea. Man's exploitation of outer space will have progressed beyond expectations, but there is no "ultimate weapon" in the sky eliminating requirements for conventional military forces. Naval forces are more valuable than ever. Fleets continue their world-wide development. Man's extension into the deep ocean and continental sea beds has opened new vistas—naval, commercial, and political.

In the latter regard, it is important to note what former Chief of Naval Operations Admiral David McDonald pointed out to a group of industrialists in 1967: that the United States had acquired, in 1964, with ratification of the 1958 Geneva Convention of the Continental Shelf, more territory where its sovereign rights of exploitation are unquestioned than in any other single action in its history. The right to exploit the natural resources of the Continental Shelf opened an area larger than the original thirteen colonies, the Louisiana Purchase, or the purchase of Alaska. Noting the existing pressures of population and the depletion of land resources, Admiral McDonald said that he did not expect such pressures to diminish and that, as science and technology expand, mankind may face the question of sovereignty in waters above a sea bed. "Will," he asked, "a nation which has sovereign rights over a particular portion of the sea bed control the waters above, just as a nation now controls the airspace above its sovereign land mass? If so, will the sea continue to be free?"

Against these background considerations, most naval experts foresee a need for fleets that will be a combination of the old and the new. The Polaris force, armed with missiles of increased penetrative capability, accuracy, and destructive power will remain critically important. Some of the forty-one fleet ballistic missile submarines now in commission may still be operating in the 1990's, but the majority will have been replaced by quieter, deeper-diving versions. The Polaris force may be augmented by surface ships with launching platforms that are well camouflaged, fixed missile stations in watertight capsules on the ocean floor, or free-floating, unmanned missile platforms beneath the surface, whose positions will be calculated instantaneously by computerized systems as they drift in undersea currents. All of these systems, and, in fact, any others the United States may adopt to base more of its strategic forces at sea, will serve as prime general war deterrents.

In almost every projection of the international situation, diplomats warn of a reduction of access to foreign bases. The United States is well aware of the vulnerability of foreign bases and overflight rights, and experience with France and Libya may well influence Defense Department authorities to place more reliance on seaborne systems for other naval tasks. These will include the provision of mobile tactical air support in remote areas of the world, as well as stationing airborne anti-submarine warfare systems in midocean areas. Both requirements can be met with the carrier force, equipped with nuclear propulsion and new generation multimission aircraft with all-weather capability. In all probability, the strike aircraft will be designed primarily for attack missions. Task force defense will be taken over by advanced surface-to-air missile systems that range from completely automatic stand-off weapons to one-man shoulder weapons, or by the point defense rapid-response missile. The antisubmarine-war aircraft will be a Turbofan Tracker of high speed and endurance, equipped with updated sensors and automatic data-processing equipment.

Submarines

Since the U.S. Navy places so much emphasis on antisubmarine warfare, and history is full of instances of what submarines can accomplish, the development of the United States' own submarine-warfare capability will, doubtless, continue. The attack submarines of the future will be faster, deeper diving, and quieter than those now in the Navy's inventory. They will be nuclear-powered and equipped with sophisticated weapons capable of destroying surface ships or other submarines. In their own defense, they will have improved deceptive measures, decoys, and false contact generators. These true submersibles will pose a viable threat to the merchant marine and naval forces of any potential enemy and will require the allocation of a considerable portion of its defense budget to the maintenance of antisubmarine-warfare systems.

Aircraft

Rounding out the forces for antisubmarine warfare, in all probability, will be more advanced, land-based aircraft. Through the 1970's, the present P-3, which has the speed and endurance to cover large areas, will operate from bases in the continental United States and from island bases under U.S. control. The loss of any foreign bases will be compensated for by retention of aircraft carriers and by exploitation of their flexibility and concentration of power in remote ocean areas. It is quite possible that miniaturization of electronic systems will permit a reduction in the size of the present patrol aircraft and lead toward the development of a common antisubmarine-warfare fixed-wing airplane capable of operating from aircraft carriers and island bases alike. In that event, the VP, or patrol aircraft (now represented so well by the Lockheed P-3), and the VSX, or follow-on, carrier-based aircraft, may be merged into a common design.

A new aircraft capable of vertical or short take-off and landing (VSTOL) may revolutionize naval air power. The true VSTOL will have an ability to hover, land, or take off from small areas, and then change to a high-speed attitude for supersonic flight. Although the VSTOL program has been in limbo for over fifteen years, recent progress is promising. Some believe that, if these aircraft come into their own, they could eliminate the need for large carrier decks, catapults, and arresting gear and could operate from small platforms carried on almost any sizable ship, although, from the practical viewpoint of maintenance requirements, it appears that an established central platform would be preferable.

New Surface Ships

Prospective development of high-speed surface ships in the next decade has excited naval planners. Vice Admiral John P. Colwell recently unveiled a model of a seagoing high-speed "surface-effect" ship and said, "It is quite possible that we are on the threshold of an advancement in sea lift capability so significant that it could revolutionize the character of the Navy."

Admiral Colwell was speaking of the general research effort to design high-speed ships that have reduced "water drag." For centuries, marine engineers have known that the beautiful, but power-consuming bow waves of conventional displacement ships create formidable drag on the ship's hull and require tremendous increases in power for a small increase in speed. The most promising approach to elimination or reduction of drag is simply to devise a means of getting the hull out of the water. The most successful schemes tested to date are the hydrofoil and two "surface-effect" craft—one an air-cushion, flexible-skirt design, and the other the captured-air-bubble type.

The hydrofoil, shaped like an aircraft wing and extended beneath a ship, lifts it clear of the water as long as a minimum speed is maintained. Tests of hydrofoil ships to date have been limited to small craft, but their performance, especially in rough water, is very good. The Navy has sponsored the construction of larger hydrofoil ships for test and development, and, in the spring of 1967, it took delivery of a 320-ton hydrofoil and began a series of advanced tests. The results of this program may lead to development of high-speed amphibious ships, but many engineers believe that the upper limit of foil supporting structures and power transmission difficulties have already established a practical limit to the size of the hydrofoil ship. This size is considerably smaller than the high-speed, ocean-going ship envisioned by naval planners.

Either the air-cushion, flexible-skirt, or the captured-air-bubble ship may be the answer. Both ride on a cushion of air maintained by high-speed fans independent of forward speed. In the flexible-skirt design, the air escapes from under the hull through jets in the sides. This craft operates about six inches above the surface and can attain speeds ranging from fifty to eighty knots. Its sea-keeping ability and stability in surf are far superior to those of conventional craft, which suggests adaptation to amphibious landing tasks. The captured-air-bubble design actually touches the water's surface at the forward and after ends of the hull and has longer, rigid side walls in lieu of a flexible skirt—giving it the advantage of reducing the amount of power lost through escaping air, but at the expense of additional drag. Only the parts that touch the water are made flexible, so that they rise and fall as they encounter waves. Of the two surface-effect ships considered, the captured-air-bubble design appears to be more feasible for construction of large ocean-going ships. Because the flexible-skirt craft loses too much power through the skirt, it is limited to air-propulsion systems. The greater speeds attainable with both types suggest serious consideration for their use in a number of naval tasks. Naval forces capable of speeds of up to eighty knots would be immune to most submarine attacks, could make high-speed transits without escort, could accomplish amphibious landings rapidly and with fewer casualties, and could respond to distant emergencies much faster. Their full capabilities will be reached only through a long and careful program of research, test, and development, but current estimates indicate that a multithousand-ton, eighty-knot ship is definitely in the future.

MEN FOR TOMORROW'S NAVY

Many of the manpower problems cited in the preceding chapter will have been solved or changed within the next twenty-five years.

Pay differentials, which now exist in the form of proficiency or hazardous-duty pay will, in all probability, be formalized into separate pay scales for different skills—much as in civilian life now. There is a precedent. The Navy of 1900 had a similar system, in which masters-at-arms and boatswain's mates were the best-paid ranks because they had greater responsibility. Balance in the enlisted rating structure will be maintained by selective re-enlistment, and screening boards will trim off excesses in the so-called soft skills at the twentieth year of service, if not before.

The Navy officer structure will continue to emphasize youth, and officers may be promoted to flag rank while they are in their early forties. The Navy will retain the flag officer statutory retirement at sixty-two. (The Army and Air Force, which now have mandatory retirement in the thirty-fifth year of service, will probably drop their practice in favor of the Navy retirement system.) The officer structure will tend to become more and more specialized, perhaps leading to a division into "Wet" and "Dry" categories, much like those in the British Navy. In other words, two major career patterns will be available to young officers when they start their careers: one will lead toward fleet operations and ship or squadron commands; the other will lead to technical specialization and material management primarily in shore billets. Those following the command option will get advanced training in strategy, tactics, logistics, economics, politics, and diplomacy in service schools and colleges. The value of the analyst in uniform will have been amply demonstrated, and a greater proportion of officers will receive training in operations and systems analysis, and in economics and resource management.

The training of enlisted specialists will decrease in intensity and depth, according to predictions by the Personnel Research Division, with advances in miniaturization and the development of microelectronics circuitry and functional devices simplifying many of the Navy's maintenance problems. Standardized material management procedures and preventive maintenance, supervised by a computer data bank, will result in greater mean time between failures of equipment. Complex circuitry will give way to simpler "black boxes," and there will be fewer requirements for technicians in uniform or factory representatives afloat to keep the systems operating. Automation, particularly in engineering spaces and in ship control functions, will reduce the personnel manning requirements; in 1967, the Navy sought contractual assistance for an investigation of automation in new destroyers.

As a greater proportion of ships become nuclear-powered (and, consequently, long-legged), it may prove to be more cost effective to keep these ships on distant stations for longer periods of time, and to rotate crews. The Blue and Gold crew rotation of the Polaris submarines has worked out extremely well and has kept morale high in this important force, which stays on undersea patrol for sixty days at a time. Similar systems could be developed for ships that are deployed for unusually long periods, and for small ships, such as mine sweepers, that require up to six or seven weeks' transit time across the Pacific. Whole crews need not be rotated at once. It might be preferable to adopt a "level manning" principle, which calls for percentage rotation periodically while on station and staggered reliefs for key officers such as the commanding officer, the executive officer, and heads of departments. If relief personnel are flown from their home port to the ship, and those who are relieved are flown back home, the long transit time to a place like the South China Sea becomes inconsequential.

Finally, it can be assumed that both the officers and the enlisted men of the U.S. Navy in the future will be made even more aware than they are at present or have been in the past of their individual, sometimes frightening, responsibility for the peace of the world. In periods of tension, U.S. naval units today are in constant touch with authorities in Washington, who monitor their every action in close detail. Reliable radio communications have tied all farflung units to central control. Since any ship or aircraft carrying nuclear weapons— even tactical nuclear weapons with limited power—could, through ill-considered or hasty action, set off World War III, or at least involve the United States in tense, potentially explosive, foreign-policy negotiations, the concept of centralized control has been accepted reluctantly by leaders in the field.

At present, such supervision can cause problems. For example, during the Tonkin Gulf incident of 1964, the naval commander was "overcontrolled" from Washington. While his ship was under attack, he was so besieged with questions that he was almost unable to fight. This brought forth the famous "Fight, don't write" order from his local superior officer, who believed that the situation was reasonably limited and that reports could be made after the action ended.

In future years, such overt, direct observance may be less necessary. Satellites and other sensors will detect important movements and will feed information into automated surveillance centers. Opposing nations will have rather complete pictures of military dispositions and actions around the world. However, as long as military units carry weapons of such power that their use threatens every nation, the responsibility for their control must be shared jointly by service leaders and heads of state, each of whom must have confidence that the men at the other end of the line are absolutely capable of exercising judgment and restraint.

The requisite knowledge and personal qualities of those who might some day be participants in a military moment of truth for the world were expressed by the late President Kennedy when he addressed the graduating class at the Naval Academy in 1961. He said:

> Fifty years ago the graduates of the Naval Academy were expected to be seamen and leaders of men. . . . Today all of you must, of necessity, be prepared not only to handle a ship in a storm, or a landing party on the beach, but to make great determinations which affect the survival of this country. . . . You must understand not only this country but other countries. You must know something not only about strategy, tactics, logic and logistics, but also economics, and politics and diplomacy and history. You must know everything you can about military power and you must also understand the limits of military power.

His words, true for 1961, may be expected to hold for the sailor, the aviator, the submariner, the astronaut, and the systems analyst of tomorrow's Navy.

Appendix I
U.S. Naval Districts

District	States, Counties, and Territories	Headquarters
1	Maine, New Hampshire, Vermont, Massachusetts, and Rhode Island	Boston, Massachusetts
3	Connecticut, New York, and the northern part of New Jersey	New York, New York
4	Pennsylvania, southern New Jersey, Delaware, and Ohio	Philadelphia, Pennsylvania
5	Maryland and Virginia (less certain counties bordering Naval District, Washington, D.C.), West Virginia, Kentucky, and northeastern section of North Carolina	Norfolk, Virginia
6	Remaining portion of North Carolina, South Carolina, Georgia, Florida, Alabama, Tennessee, and Mississippi	Charleston, South Carolina
8	Louisiana, Arkansas, Oklahoma, Texas, and New Mexico	New Orleans, Louisiana
9	Michigan, Indiana, Illinois, Wisconsin, Minnesota, Iowa, Missouri, North Dakota, South Dakota, Nebraska, Kansas, Colorado, and Wyoming	Great Lakes, Illinois

District	States, Counties, and Territories	Headquarters
10	United States territories, possessions, naval reservations, and naval activities in the geographical area of the Caribbean Sea	San Juan, Puerto Rico
11	Arizona; Clark County, Nevada; southern part of California including counties of Santa Barbara, Kern, San Bernardino, and all counties south	San Diego, California
12	Utah, Nevada (except Clark County), and northern part of California	San Francisco, California
13	Washington, Oregon, Idaho, and Montana	Seattle, Washington
14	The Hawaiian Islands and islands to the west and south, including Midway, Kure, Wake, Johnston, and Palmyra Islands, Kingman Reef, and Kwajelein	Pearl Harbor, Hawaii
15*	Panama Canal Zone	Balboa, Canal Zone
17*	Alaska including the Aleutians	Kodiak, Alaska
Naval District Washington, D.C.	The District of Columbia; the counties of Anne Arundel, Prince Georges, Montgomery, St. Marys, Calvert and Charles in Maryland; and the counties of Arlington, Fairfax, Stafford, King George, Prince William, and Westmoreland in Virginia	Washington, District of Columbia

* To be placed under a sea frontier or area command.

Appendix II
Navy Career Opportunities

The programs available for entry into the naval service in either an officer or enlisted category are subject to frequent minor changes, but the basic information is shown below. Anyone interested in these programs should check with the nearest recruiting station for current details.

PROGRAMS FOR ENLISTED MEN'S TRAINING AND EDUCATION

For	Program	Requirements	Comments
Non-high school graduate (male)	On-the-job training	Age 17 through 30	Training in over 60 technical job fields, and specialists' schools for those who can qualify.
Vocational school graduates	Vocational school graduate training	Age 17 through 30	Training in 36 major career fields, including electronics, precision equipment, administrative and clerical, printing and drafting, engineering and hull construction, and aircraft.
High school graduate (male)	High school graduate training programs	Age 17 through 30	More than 50 specialists' schools available in aviation, electronics, nucleonics, medical-dental, and general subjects.
High school graduate (female)	Waves	Age 18 through 25	Most specialists schools open to male candidates are also open to Waves with the exception of sea-going ratings.
Junior college graduates (males) or men with at least 1 year of college	Junior college training programs	Age 17 through 30	Same as High School Graduate Training programs except that candidates with 1 or 2 years of college work may qualify for enlistment in pay grades E-2 or E-3 respectively.

PROGRAMS FOR OFFICER TRAINING AND EDUCATION

For	Program	Requirements	Comments
High school graduate (male)	Naval academy	Age 17 through 21; unmarried.	Four years of intensive education. Graduate with BS degree and USN commission.
High school graduate (male)	Regular Naval Reserve Officers Training Corps (NROTC)	Age 17 through 21; unmarried.	Receives educational expenses, monthly subsistence allowance to defray living expenses. Program available in over 50 colleges and universities. Bachelor's degree and USN commission upon completion.
In attendance at NROTC college (male)	Contract Naval Reserve Officers Training Corps Program (NROTC)	Age 17 through 21; unmarried.	$40 monthly subsistence allowance in junior and senior years. Commissioned USNR after graduation.
In attendance at college (male)	Reserve Officer Candidate (ROC)	Age 17 but not more than 27½ when commissioned. Must enlist in USNR prior to enrollment.	Two 8-week summer courses. Pay for rate held in Naval Reserve. Transportation paid home to home, and textbooks, quarters, and food provided during summer training.
In attendance at college (male)	Aviation Reserve Officer Candidate (AVROC)	Not less than 17 when making application, nor more than 26½ for Naval Aviators and 27½ for Naval Flight Officers at time of commissioning. Must have obtained sophomore status.	Pilot or flight officer training. Must attend two summer flight training sessions, each following sophomore and junior years. Commissioned in USNR after graduation.
In attendance at college (female)	Officer candidate (women) college junior program	Must be in junior year. Must have reached age 20 prior to graduation and commissioning the following summer.	Eight-week basic indoctrination course following junior year. Eight-week officer training after senior year. Commissioned USNR. Two-year tour of duty.
In attendance at college (male and female) (jr. and sr. nurse students)	Navy nurse corps candidate	Second semester sophomore; women must be unmarried; working for BS degree in nursing or toward a graduate degree; age under 34 at time appointed.	Enlisted E-3 with active duty pay and allowances, tuition and books; commissioned ensign 6 months before graduation.

Category	Program	Requirements	Details
In attendance at college (female)	Women students and intern program	Age 18 through 31½.	Appointment as ENS Medical Service Corps, active duty pay, allowances during final year, training as dietitian, physical or occupational therapist.
College graduate (male)	Aviation officer candidate	Age 19 through 25.	Eighteen months' flight training. Commissioned in USNR on completion of first 11 weeks.
College graduate (male)	Naval aviation officer candidate	Age 19 through 27½.	Approximately 11 months' naval flight training. Commissioned in USNR on completion of first 11 weeks.
College graduate (male & female)	Officer candidate school	Bachelor's degree. Males 19 to 27½, Females 20 to 27½ at time of commissioning.	Sixteen weeks (men or women) Officer Candidate training. Assignment to general line or specialists' duty. Men 3 years or women 2 years tour of duty.
Professional (male)	Theological students	Applicant must be accepted by accredited school.	Inactive commissioned officer status in USNR. Active duty after graduation.
Professional (male & female)	Medical-dental students	Applicant must be accepted by accredited school.	Inactive commissioned officer status in USNR. May apply for active duty after graduation.
Professional (male & female)	Senior medical students	Applicant must be in junior year in an accredited school.	Appointment as ensign, USNR, active duty status in senior year with pay. Complete work on degree at own medical school.
Professional (male & female)	Navy intern-medical	Medical college senior or graduate; participant National Intern Matching Program.	One-year rotating internship in approved Navy hospital as lieutenant, full pay and allowances. Serve military obligation upon internship completion.
Professional (male & female)	Navy intern-dental	Applicant must be a senior in an approved dental college.	One-year rotating internship in Navy teaching hospital as lieutenant, full pay and allowances. Serve military obligation upon completion.
Professional (male & female)	Direct commission (healing arts)	Graduate of approved medical or dental school; licensed to practice in United States.	Opportunities in all branches of medicine.
Professional (male & female)	Direct appointment, nurse corps, USNR	Age 19½ to 34½ at time of application; registered nurse when appointed.	Appointment as ensign, lieutenant junior grade or lieutenant, depending on age, education, and experience; serve in various fields and expansion of professional experience.

Bibliography

Books and Periodicals

BALDWIN, HANSON W. *The New Navy*. New York: E. P. Dutton & Co., 1964.

BARNES, WILLIAM R. (ed.). *The Constitution of the United States and the Declaration of Independence*. New York: Barnes & Noble, Inc., 1965.

BARR, JAMES, and HOWARD, WILLIAM E. *Polaris!* New York: Harcourt, Brace & World Co., 1960.

BRODIE, BERNARD. *A Guide to Naval Strategy*. New York: Frederick A. Praeger, 1965.

CALVERT, JAMES. *The Naval Profession*. New York: McGraw Hill Book Company, 1965.

CARRISON, DANIEL J. *The Navy from Wood to Steel. 1860–1890*. New York: Franklin Watts, Inc., 1965.

CASTILO, EDMUND L. *All About the U.S. Navy*. New York: Random House, 1961.

COLBY, CARROLL B. *Our Space Age Navy*. New York: Coward-McCann, Inc., 1962.

COONEY, DAVID M. *A Chronology of the U.S. Navy: 1775–1965*. New York: Franklin Watts, Inc., 1965.

DAVIS, VINCENT. *Postwar Defense Policy and the United States Navy, 1943–1946*. Chapel Hill: The University of North Carolina Press, 1962.

FALL, BERNARD B. *The Two Vietnams*. New York: Frederick A. Praeger, 1964.

FREUCHEN, PETER, and LOTH, DAVID. *Peter Freuchen's Book of the Seven Seas*. New York: Julian Messner, Inc., 1957.

GIMPEL, HERBERT J. *The United States Nuclear Navy*. New York: Franklin Watts, Inc., 1965.

HITCH, CHARLES J., and McKEAN, ROLAND N. *The Economics of Defense in the Nuclear Age*. New York: Atheneum, 1965.

HOWARD, JOSEPH L. *Our Modern Navy*. New York: D. Van Nostrand Co., Inc., 1961.

HUNTINGTON, SAMUEL P. *The Common Defense: Strategic Programs in National Politics.* New York: Columbia University Press, 1961.

KAKIN, GEORGE M., and LEWIS, JOHN W. *The United States and Vietnam.* New York: The Dial Press, 1967.

KAUFMANN, WILLIAM W. *The McNamara Strategy.* New York: Harper and Row, 1964.

KNOX, DUDLEY W. *A History of the United States Navy.* New York: G. P. Putnam's Sons, 1948.

LIVEZEY, WILLIAM E. *Mahan on Seapower.* Norman, Oklahoma: University of Oklahoma Press, 1954.

MAHAN, ALFRED T. *The Influence of Sea-Power upon History, 1660–1783.* Boston: Little, Brown & Co., 1890.

MITCHELL, DONALD W. *History of the Modern American Navy.* New York: Alfred A. Knopf, 1946.

MORISON, SAMUEL E. *The Two Ocean War.* Boston: Little, Brown, 1963.

PAOLUCCI, DOMINIC, "Factors Affecting the U.S. Choice of the Mix of Land-based and Sea-based Missiles in the 1970's." (*The National War College Review,* 1966.)

POTTER, E. B. *The United States and World Sea Power.* Englewood Cliffs, N.J.: Prentice-Hall, Inc., 1955.

PRATT, FLETCHER. *The Compact History of the United States Navy,* rev. ed. New York: Hawthorn Books, Inc., 1962.

RAPPAPORT, ARMIN. *The Navy League of the United States.* Detroit: Wayne State University Press, 1962.

ROSCOE, THEODORE. *This is Your Navy.* Annapolis, Maryland: United States Naval Institute, 1950.

SCHILLING, WARNER R., HAMMOND, PAUL Y., and SNYDER, GLENN H. *Strategy, Politics, and Defense Budgets.* New York: Columbia University Press, 1962.

STEVENS, WILLIAM O. *The Story of Our Navy.* New York: Harper and Bros., 1918.

TURNBULL, ARCHIBALD D., and LORD, CLIFFORD L., *History of United States Naval Aviation.* New Haven: Yale University Press, 1949.

UHLIG, FRANK, JR. (ed.). *1966 Naval Review.* Annapolis, Maryland: United States Naval Institute, 1966.

———— *1967 Naval Review.* Annapolis, Maryland: United States Naval Institute, 1966.

VILLIERS, ALAN. *Men, Ships and the Sea.* Washington, D.C.: National Geographic Society, 1963.

Government Publications

Aviation in the United States Navy. Washington, D.C.: U.S. Government Printing Office (0–763–050), 1965.

15th Annual Report, National Science Foundation. Washington, D.C.: U.S. Government Printing Office (NSF 66–1), 1966.

Hearing Before the Joint Committee on Atomic Energy. Naval Nuclear Propulsion Program. 89th Congress, 2d Sess. Washington, D.C.: U.S. Government Printing Office, 1966.

Naval Orientation. Washington, D.C.: U.S. Government Printing Office (0–617350), 1962.

1966 Armed Forces Report. Washington, D.C.: U.S. Government Printing Office (0–211–310), 1966.

1966 Shipbuilding and Conversion Program. Washington, D.C.: U.S. Government Printing Office (0–781–312), 1965.

Polaris Management. Washington, D.C.: U.S. Government Printing Office (0–584–983), 1961.

Report of the Committee on Organization of the Department of the Navy. Washington, D.C.: U.S. Government Printing Office (0–501–626), 1959.

Report on United States Defense Policies in 1961. 87th Congress, 2d Sess. Washington, D.C.: U.S. Government Printing Office, 1966.

The Department of the Navy. Washington, D.C.: U.S. Government Printing Office (0–639–527), 1962.

The New Four Ocean Challenge. Washington, D.C.: U.S. Government Printing Office (0–731–349), 1964.

Index

A-4 Skyhawk aircraft, 128, 133, 222, 223
A-1 Spad aircraft, 222
A-7 Corsair II aircraft, 133
A-6 Intruder aircraft, 128, 133, 222
ABM; *see* Anti-ballistic-missile defense system
Academic cooperation in training programs, 182–89
Adams, John, 4, 8
AEC; *see* Atomic Energy Commission
AEF; *see* Airborne-early-warning aircraft
Aeronautics, Bureau of, 76, 121, 123
AGC; *see* Amphibious command ship
Air Force, United States: and Congress, 202; and interservice rivalry with Navy, 202; and Minuteman missile, 90, 182; missiles of, 147; in Suez crisis, 39; in Viet-Nam, 34, 46; after World War I, 119
Air-ground cooperation, 46–47, 66
Air spotter aircraft, 49–50
Air-submarine team, 100
Air transport, 37, 44
Airborne-early-warning aircraft (AEF), 127
Aircraft: A-4 Skyhawk, 128, 133, 222, 223; A-1 Spad, 222; A-7 Corsair II, 133; A-6 Intruder, 128, 133, 222; air spotter, 49–50; Airborne-early-warning (AEF), 127; carrier on-board delivery (COD), 128; drones, 110–11; E-2A Hawkeye, 128; F-8 Crusader, 132, 133; F-4 Phantom, 127, 132, 133, 222; F-111B, 132–33, 182; P-3 Orion, 133–34, 166, 241; Patrol (VP), 241; Picket, 113; RA-5c Vigilante, 128; S-2F Tracker, 240; SP-5 seaplane, 134; VSTOL, 241; VSX, 134, 241
Aircraft carrier: anti-aircraft defense, 110–14; antisubmarine warfare carrier (CVS), 65, 133, 134, 135, 222–23; attack carrier (CVA), 66, 87–91, 106, 123–24, 134, 221–22, 223; development of, 119 ff., 132; escort carrier, 94; in Korean War, 46, 47, 87, 90; and manned spacecraft recovery, 163, 166; nuclear-powered, 90, 123–29, 136,

140, 141, 232; in nuclear war, 51, 54, 90; in strike forces, 86–91; in Tachen islands evacuation, 39; in Viet-Nam War, 34, 36, 46, 47, 87, 90; before World War II, 27, 120–21; in World War II, 29–30, 32, 33, 87–91, 92 ff., 119
Aircraft procurement, 132–34
Albacore, USS, 142
Alliance, USS, 6
Allies: in World War I, 24–26, 31; in World War II, 93, 94, 102
"Aluminaut," 172
"Alvin," 172
Amphibious assault craft, 104–6
Amphibious command ship (AGC), 104
Amphibious Force (Task Force 76), 64, 66
Amphibious operations: assault craft in, 104–6; assault landings, 101 ff.; in Civil War, 48, 101–2; defined, 101; gunfire support in, 114; in Korean War, 48–49; in Napoleonic Wars, 101; Navy–Marine Corps team in, 103–4; nonassault landings, 103; planning of, 103, 106; "surface-effect" ships in, 242–43; in Tachen islands evacuation, 39; in Viet-Nam War, 34, 49, 213, 218; in World War II, 31–33, 48, 102, 218
Amphibious Ready Group, 66
Amphibious transport, dock (LPD), 104
Annapolis; *see* Naval Academy, United States
Anti-aircraft defense, 110–14
Anti-ballistic-missile defense system (ABM), 53, 54
Antisubmarine warfare (ASW), 24–25, 27–28, 31, 46, 68–69, 92 ff., 98 ff., 100, 106, 122, 133–34, 169, 170–71, 230–31, 240; *see also* Submarine
Antisubmarine Warfare Advisory Committee, 179
Antisubmarine warfare carrier (CVS), 65, 133, 134, 135, 222–23
Antisubmarine Warfare Environmental Prediction, 170–71

255

Maddox, USS, 217
Madison, James, 75
Mahan, Alfred T., 21, 24, 177
Maine, USS, 21–22
Man-in-space programs, 40, 160 ff.
Man-in-the-sea program, 170, 171
Management Information, Office of, 83–84
Manila Bay, Battle of, 22–23
Manned Space Flight Network, 162
Manned Spacecraft Recovery Force (Task Force 140), 161, 163, 166
Manpower problems, 233–36, 243–46
Maria Teresa, 23
Marine expeditionary brigade (MEB), 105
Marine expeditionary force (MEF), 105
Marine expeditionary unit (MEU), 105
Marines, United States: and Barbary pirates, 11; Commandant of, 77, 78, 80, 83; in Dominican Republic crisis, 41; Fleet Marine Force, 66, 69, 79, 80, 81; headquarters of, 73; in Korean War, 48; in Lebanon crisis, 39; Navy–Marine Corps team, 103–4; in Seventh Fleet, 65; troop-carrying helicopters for, 134; units of, 105; in Viet-Nam War, 47, 219; in World War II, 31
Maritime Resources and Engineering Development Act of 1966, 175
Martell, Charles B., 92, 95
Maury, Matthew Fontaine, 169
MEB; *see* Marine expeditionary brigade
Medicine and Surgery, Bureau of, 73, 79, 83
Medium landing ship, rocket (LSMR), 106
MEF; *see* Marine expeditionary force
Merchant marine: and Barbary pirates, 6–7, 11; in colonial times, 4 ff.; and impression of seamen by British, 12; in Korean War, 44; after Revolutionary War, 6; in Revolutionary War, 177; as supply ships, 109–10; in World War I, 25; in World War II, 28, 32, 93
Mercury Project, 161 ff.
Merrimac, 19–20
MEU; *see* Marine expeditionary unit
Mexican War, 17
Midway, Battle of, 30, 88, 127
Milestone reporting, 152, 153–54
Military capability; *see* Systems analysis
Military Sea Transportation Service (MSTS), 69, 79, 219
Miller, H. L., 128
Mills, Earle, 137
Mine Force, 64
Mines: in Civil War, 18–19, 20; in World War II, 25–26
Minesweeping, 106, 216
Minuteman missile, 90, 182
"MIRV"; *see* Multiple individually-targeted re-entry vehicle
Missiles: air-to-air, 113, 127, 133; air-to-surface, 133; in anti-aircraft defense, 113; anti-ballistic (ABM), 53, 54; Bullpup, 133, 222; Fleet ballistic missile

(FBM), 52–53, 136, 148; ICBM, 147; IRBM, 147; Jupiter, 147, 148, Minuteman, 90, 182; "MIRV," 53; Poseidon, 53, 159, 182; Regulus, 99, 147, 181; Sidewinder, 113–14, 127, 222; Sparrow, 113, 114, 127, 222; in submarine warfare, 98 ff., surface-to-air, 113; Talos, 113; Tartar, 113; Terrier, 113; Typhon, 232; Zuni rocket, 133, 222; *see also* Polaris missile
Mitchell, "Billy," 110
MLF; *see* Multilateral force
Mobile logistic support, 107–10
Mobile Logistic Support Force (Task Force 73), 66
Moffett, W. A., 120, 121, 122, 123
Monitor, 19–20
Morris, Robert, 4
Morrow Board, 122
MSTS; *see* Military Sea Transportation Service
Multilateral force (MLF), 51
Multiple individually-targeted re-entry missile ("MIRV"), 53
Multipurpose amphibious ship, 104

Napoleon, 8, 11, 12, 101, 102
Napoleonic Wars, 8, 11, 12
NASA; *see* National Aeronautics and Space Administration
National Aeronautics and Space Administration (NASA), 161–62, 163, 167, 176
National Defense Reserve Fleet, 109, 219
National Security Act of 1947, 76, 77, 199
National Security Act of 1958, 77
National Security Council, 147
National War College Forum, 53n
Nationalist China, 39, 40
Nautilus, USS, 99, 138, 140 ff.
Naval Academy, United States, 102, 117, 183, 184–85, 186, 197, 202
Naval Affairs Committee, 198, 199
Naval Air Bases Command, 72
Naval Air Force; *see* Aircraft carrier, Naval aviation
Naval Air Systems Command, 129
Naval Air Technical Training Centers, 130–31
Naval Air Training Command, 73, 129–31
Naval aviation: and air defense, 111 ff.; and aircraft procurement, 132–34; and aviation support, 129–34; beginnings of, 116 ff.; Bureau of Aeronautics, 76; and dirigibles, 121–22; and first trans-Atlantic flight, 118–19; Fleet aviation commands, 131–32; flying boats, 118; in Korean War, 33, 46, 47, 123, 131; Naval Air Bases Command, 72; Naval Air Systems Command, 129; Naval Air Technical Training Centers, 130–31; Naval Air Training Command, 73, 129–31; Naval Aviation Reserve, 129, 131; support by, 36, 46–47, 92 ff.; in Viet-Nam War, 34, 46, 47, 123; in World